W9-BVX-479

The Natural Wealth of Nations

OTHER NORTON/WORLDWATCH BOOKS

Lester R. Brown et al.

State of the World 1984	*State of the World 1995*
State of the World 1985	*State of the World 1996*
State of the World 1986	*State of the World 1997*
State of the World 1987	*State of the World 1998*
State of the World 1988	*Vital Signs 1992*
State of the World 1989	*Vital Signs 1993*
State of the World 1990	*Vital Signs 1994*
State of the World 1991	*Vital Signs 1995*
State of the World 1992	*Vital Signs 1996*
State of the World 1993	*Vital Signs 1997*
State of the World 1994	*Vital Signs 1998*

ENVIRONMENTAL ALERT SERIES

Lester R. Brown et al.
Saving the Planet

Alan Thein Durning
How Much Is Enough?

Sandra Postel
Last Oasis

Lester R. Brown
Hal Kane
Full House

Christopher Flavin
Nicholas Lessen
Power Surge

Lester R. Brown
Who Will Feed China?

Lester R. Brown
Tough Choices

Michael Renner
Fighting for Survival

THE NATURAL WEALTH OF NATIONS

Harnessing the Market for
the Environment

David Malin Roodman

The Worldwatch Environmental Alert Series
Linda Starke, Series Editor

W. W. NORTON & COMPANY
New York   London

Worldwatch Database Disk

The data from all graphs and tables contained in this book, as well as from those in all other Worldwatch publications of the past two years, are available on disk for use with IBM-compatible or Macintosh computers. This includes data from the State of the World *and* Vital Signs *series of books,* Worldwatch Papers, World Watch *magazine, and the* Environmental Alert *series of books. The data are formatted for use with spreadsheet software compatible with Lotus 1-2-3 version 2, including all Lotus spreadsheets, Quattro Pro, Excel, SuperCalc, and many others. To order, send check or money order for $89 plus $4 shipping and handling, or credit card number and expiration date (Mastercard, Visa, or American Express), to Worldwatch Institute, 1776 Massachusetts Ave., NW, Washington DC 20036. Or you may call 1-800-555-2028, fax us at 1-202-296-7365, or reach us by e-mail at wwpub@worldwatch.org.*

Contents

Acknowledgments

The seeds of this book were sown in early 1991, when I found a well-thumbed copy of E.F. Schumacher's *Small is Beautiful* on a friend's bookshelf. At the time, I was studying the dry mathematical language that physicists use to articulate the laws of nature, and was struggling hard to stay interested. His book introduced to me to a field known as ecological economics, an experience that changed my life. The excitement I felt as I paged through that book was a sign of Schumacher's power as a writer and my readiness for something new.

I spent the rest of that academic year guiltily skipping math lectures and reading books by Herman Daly, Amory Lovins, Kenneth Boulding, and other important thinkers on environmental policy and economics. It was an impulsive move, but seven years later, I remain on the course I chose then. So I modestly echo Isaac Newton when I say that I stand on the shoulders of giants. This book develops one of the most important messages of their work, which is that reforms of the way governments raise and spend money are central to making industrial economies environmentally sustainable.

The Natural Wealth of Nations also draws ideas from many other writers and colleagues in the rapidly expanding field of environmental fiscal policy, including some who were kind enough to review drafts of the two Worldwatch Papers on which the book is based. These include Nils Axel Braathen, Clifford Cobb, André de Moor, Douglas Koplow, Norman Myers, Stefan Speck, and Ronald Steenblik. I also owe intellectual debts to people "in the field," who have directly affected or have been directly affected by the policies others only write about—from an Alaskan fisher to a former Swedish finance minister. I name some of these thinkers and doers in the text, and list many more in the notes. I thank all for their work and the time they gave me.

I am grateful to Lester Brown for creating a unique institution, the Worldwatch Institute, that has not only made possible the writing of this book but has fostered my development as an analyst and writer. My work on environmental taxes over the last few years has been supported by a grant from the Wallace Genetic Foundation, and the particular interest of Robert Wallace in these issues is gratefully acknowledged.

Overall, research at Worldwatch is supported by the following: the Nathan Cummings Foundation, the Geraldine R. Dodge Foundation, the Ford Foundation, the Foundation for Ecology and Development, the

William and Flora Hewlett Foundation, the W. Alton Jones Foundation, the John D. and Catherine T. MacArthur Foundation, the Charles Stewart Mott Foundation, the Curtis and Edith Munson Foundation, the David and Lucille Packard Foundation, The Pew Charitable Trusts, the Rasmussen Foundation, the Rockefeller Brothers Fund, Rockefeller Financial Services, the Summit Foundation, the Surdna Foundation, the Turner Foundation, the U.N. Population Fund, the Wallace Global Foundation, the Weeden Foundation, and the Winslow Foundation. In addition, the support of numerous individuals through the Friends of Worldwatch campaign is deeply appreciated. Special thanks also go to the newly established Council of Sponsors: Toshishige Kurosawa, Kazuhiko Nishi, Roger and Vicki Sant, Robert Wallace, and Eckart Wintzen.

One secret of Worldwatch's success is the extensive internal reviews that all our publications undergo before they reach the public. For reviewing drafts of this book, I thank Seth Dunn, Hilary French, Gary Gardner, Molly O'Meara, and Michael Renner. Heartfelt thanks also go to Richard Bell for a valuable unsolicited last-minute review of Chapter 7, and to Christopher Flavin for gentle but penetrating feedback on the entire work. My colleagues' reviews have made *The Natural Wealth of Nations* twice the book it would have been.

In addition, I thank two other reviewers. Jane Peterson provided detailed comments on several chapters and edited the two earlier Papers, thus exercising subtle and salutary influence over the entire work. And Dorothy Bukantz reviewed one of the Papers, a fact that I inexcusably omitted from its acknowledgments.

As my teacher from ages 8 to 14, Dorothy helped me find my writing voice and taught me to think politically. Indeed, perhaps it was she who sowed the seeds of this book, and Schumacher who only awoke them from high school–induced dormancy.

A series of invaluable assistants at Worldwatch also helped me prepare this book and the earlier Papers. They include interns April Bowling, Giovanna Dore, Matthew St. Clair, and Michael Strauss, as well as former Staff Researcher Jennifer Mitchell. All were flexible, good-humored, and indefatigable in their pursuit of elusive facts.

Finally, I am indebted to Hoangmai Pham for her support, and offer this book in joyous celebration of our first 10 years together. She has helped me become who I am.

David Malin Roodman

Worldwatch Institute
1776 Massachusetts Ave., N.W.
Washington, D.C. 20036

April 1998

Foreword

Wealth. For most of us, the word conjures up piles of gold coins, stacks of $100 bills, or a bank vault full of jewels. Even the dictionary gives this as one definition of wealth: "all property that has a money value or an exchangeable value." The fact that this book title has to describe its topic by modifying the word "wealth" with "natural" indicates how rarely we join the concepts of value and natural resources in our minds.

In *The Natural Wealth of Nations*, David Roodman explores how society's fiscal policies have long reflected this narrow view of wealth. And how that has now gotten us into trouble when it comes to establishing sustainable economies. All societies today are enmeshed in complex systems of subsidies and tax supports that affect the health of our basic life-support systems, but that do so thoughtlessly. They have developed piecemeal during this century in response to short-term needs, such as supporting jobs in a threatened sector, but have carried on well past the time they provided help.

The Natural Wealth of Nations unravels these systems, highlights those that are doing the most harm to the environment as well as the economy, and suggests solutions. These include charging appropriately for nature's services, making polluters pay for the damage they cause, and sometimes paying people—and business—not to pollute. As the world settles into the post–cold war era, it is increasingly clear that market economies will remain the dominant economic system for the foreseeable future. David discusses how to harness the market's strengths, and also compensate for its weaknesses through regulations where appropriate. One important step along the road to sustainability is reform of today's complex tax systems.

This book is the ninth in the Worldwatch Environmental Alert Series, which includes volumes on food security in China, redefining national security, and water scarcity. (See page 2 for a list of all the titles in the series.) Soon on its heels will be *Life Out of Bounds* by Chris Bright, on the threats posed by bioinvasions. We hope these help you along your own road to a more sustainable world.

Linda Starke, Series Editor

The Natural Wealth of Nations

1

Harnessing the Market

A little girl in Stuttgart, in southern Germany, stands on tiptoe to reach a switch on a wall. Pressing it with the tip of her finger, she is instantly rewarded with the warm glow of electric light, and she settles down to play.

When she flips the switch, the little girl sends a tiny wave through the global economy. In order to meet the need she has expressed, the economy adjusts—finely, imperceptibly. When the copper contacts meet, a signal flashes through wires in the walls to power lines outside, spirals through a transformer down the street, and races overland on high-voltage lines to the regional power company's control center, which in turn sends out electronic orders to lumbering coal plants and natural gas turbines that can throttle up or down with the

agility of airplane engines. Around Stuttgart, the cumu-
lation of millions of trivial acts—turning on lights,
opening refrigerators, watching the evening news—
shapes electricity demand over the hours, days, and
years. In response, power company executives issue a
steady flow of directives to buy coal from kilometer-
deep mines in the Ruhr valley to the north, or natural
gas piped across 10 time zones from Siberia. They also
make decisions about hiring and firing workers, about
building and scrapping power plants—and, in effect,
about how much pollution to pump into the air.

The economic wave spreads from there. When a
power company increases its monthly coal order, prices
in the world's electronically integrated coal markets rise
slightly. Other coal buyers cut back in response, or producers raise output, until supply and demand rebalance. If the company expands its payroll, the local job
market tightens and wages rise, enticing workers in
other regions to relocate there. Freight companies that
deliver more coal buy more barges, perhaps fashioned
in Norway with electronics made in South Korean
plants built with American money.

Then some of the ripples sent round the world by
the flip of switch flow back to their source, through fees
for services rendered and goods delivered. The
American banks charge interest, a cost that the Korean
manufacturers pass on to the barge makers. The coal
miners must be paid too. As these goods and services
flow through the power company to the girl and her
family, they are accompanied by a bill—more precisely,
by a slightly higher bill for electricity.

It is the way the girl gets light so effortlessly that
inspires envy in those less fortunate—thanks not so
much to what Thomas Edison invented in the nine-

teenth century as to what Adam Smith discovered in the eighteenth. As a perceptive witness to the birth of the industrial revolution, Smith saw that one source of the rising "wealth of nations" was the operation of competitive markets for goods such as wheat and cloth. Today, markets allow a global economy with a billion or more participants in roles from actuary to zinc miner to operate relatively smoothly and efficiently, all without requiring what is beyond human ability: conscious planning of these complex interactions.[1]

The power company, for example, need not decide how a family should use electricity, nor how coal companies should extract coal. That would be an unmanageably complex task, as Soviet planners discovered. The company needs to know only how much of these energy forms are required and at what price—information that markets supply with ease. And the company is just one node in a vast economic network, each bound to its neighbors by markets for coal, barges, steel, or capital.

What is remarkable about the market system is that, unlike the light bulb, no one invented it. Markets just happen, and have been happening since prehistoric people traded obsidian for pelts. As Friedrich A. von Hayek, an Austrian-American economist and ardent defender of the market, wrote: "I have deliberately used the word 'marvel' to shock the reader out of the complacency with which we often take the working of this mechanism for granted ... if it were the result of deliberate human design, and if the people guided by the price changes understood that their decisions have significance far beyond their immediate aim, this mechanism would have been acclaimed as one of the greatest triumphs of the human mind." Perhaps because no one invented the market, its usefulness as a tool of economic management often went underappreciated in the twentieth century, as governments from Poland to North Korea attempted to banish it altogether.[2]

But if the market's spontaneous origin has led many to underestimate its value, the market's power has dazzled others into overlooking its shortcomings. As the new century dawns, one structural flaw is becoming increasingly dangerous and increasingly apparent. Many costs of industrial activity are *not* incorporated into markets. Emissions of microscopic dust from a coal plant near Stuttgart, for example, trigger sometimes-fatal asthma attacks among local residents. Sulfur dioxide emitted by the plant causes acid rain, which damages buildings downwind, lakes and streams with commercial fisheries, and forests that already sustained so much acid damage during the 1980s that Germans coined a term for it—*waldsterben*, or "forest death." The plant's carbon emissions, meanwhile, speed global warming. And radon and coal dust swirling in mine shafts afflict miners with debilitating lung disease. Then there are the toxic chemicals leaching into underground aquifers from mountains of waste piled at minemouth.[3]

These events, too, are part of the ripples set in motion when the girl touches the switch. But they do not reflect back to their source. They do not show up in the electricity bill. If they did—if environmental costs were passed back to consumers the way other costs are—the price of power from coal plants would jump roughly 50 percent, according to an exhaustive study produced by the European Commission. But since the costs are not passed back, coal power remains cheap, and clean alternatives such as wind power struggle to compete.[4]

As this story suggests, a key problem behind today's environmental problems is that prices do not "tell the ecological truth," in the words of Ernst Ulrich von Weizsäcker, founder of the Wuppertal Institute in Germany. Though the market is a powerful tool for economic progress, where its edges meet the planet it is mainly as a saw, shovel, or smokestack—as an instrument of destruction rather than protection. Environmental costs are hidden from those who impose them, so industrial economies tend to foul air and water as if pollution were harmless and to consume resources as if they were inexhaustible. That is why urban smog and forest death are often treated as necessary, if regrettable, steps on the path of economic development, while public health and environmental security for future generations are treated as costly luxuries.[5]

Prices that lie are also why making ends meet for the individual has become a budget-buster for the planet. Many Americans, for example, have difficulty finding an affordable home in a neighborhood where they do not have to drive a kilometer to buy milk. Nor can they yet acquire Toyota's new, high-efficiency, ultra-low-polluting car, the Prius. Toyota has put off selling it in the United States because it is pricier than regular models, and so cannot compete in a country where gasoline costs less than bottled water. And most U.S. residents cannot purchase electricity made from the sun or the wind, though surveys suggest that many would pay a premium for it.[6]

Thus people who wonder why it is so hard to do what is environmentally so vital are partly right if they yield to the urge to blame "the system." The price system that guides economic activity is itself flawed. The question is how to fix it. Regulations have played the dominant role to date in protecting the environment. But for precisely the reason that central planning has run aground almost everywhere it has been tried, regulations—or really, regulators—are not up to the task of reengineering industrial society on their own. Other tools will be needed as well.

Creating an environmentally sustainable economy will take nothing less than an eco-industrial revolution—a sweeping and complex event that defies government planning. A few industries will fall, others will rise, and many will evolve radically. Unlike today's essentially throwaway economy, a sustainable economy will recycle materials the way a healthy ecosystem does, draw energy from renewable sources, and use all its resources much more efficiently. Bringing resource use down to environmentally sustainable levels and sharing the quota among a global community of 10 billion affluent people calls for major per capita reductions in energy, wood, minerals, and water use. Averting climate change, for example, will require that industrial countries cut carbon emissions—caused mainly by burning fossil fuels—90 percent. These changes will affect where people live, how they move about, and how they make everything from bottles to buildings.[7]

Some of these changes are already practical but are not occurring. Engineers and architects know how to make paper from crops other than trees and how to plan neighborhoods where biking and walking are convenient. They can even design cars with three times the fuel economy of today's models and build affordable homes from earth instead of wood.

Environmental progress also depends on accelerating the development of new, clean technologies, a process of discovery that is intrinsically unpredictable.

No agency can plan it.[8]

Markets, on the other hand, excel at engineering systemic change. Markets made the industrial and digital revolutions possible. Properly harnessed, they can also guide the next industrial revolution, toward environmental sustainability. The key is for governments to enforce the "polluter pays principle," which says that when people act in ways that hurt the environment, they should be held accountable for the damage they do. This commonsense idea was first cloaked in the authority of economics 80 years ago by Cambridge don Arthur Cecil Pigou, and has become a textbook staple since. "Polluter pays" has been practiced much less than preached, however.[9]

The most direct way for governments to enforce "polluter pays" is to *tax* activities that hurt the environment. Germany, for example, could tax each kilowatt-hour of electricity generated from coal at a level roughly reflecting its hidden environmental costs. The tax would make cleaner energy forms, such as wind power, more competitive. Higher electricity prices would also encourage families to unscrew their Edison-vintage light bulbs and replace them with modern compact fluorescent lamps (fluorescent tubes twisted into bulb-sized packages), which are four times as efficient.[10]

An alternative to environmental taxes is for governments to *auction off permits for pollution and resource depletion*, then allow businesses to trade the permits among themselves. Climate change treaty negotiators in Kyoto, Japan, in 1997 opened the door to this possibility for greenhouse gas emissions. Pollution rights would join pork bellies as tradable commodities.[11]

The signature similarity between the two methods is that both put a price on pollution and resource depletion, turning environmental protection into a profit opportunity: the more companies and consumers reduce the environmental harm they cause, the more they save. Unlike most regulations, which set minimum standards, market-based techniques can create an ongoing prod for improvement without restricting people's flexibility in responding. Experiences in many countries show that businesses leap at such opportunities, creating technologies that conserve resources and slash pollution rates, often at surprisingly low cost. Tax and permit systems both exploit humanity's greatest resource: its creativity in problem solving.

Tax increases sound like the bad news in "polluter pays." But the good news, ironically, is that tax burdens are already substantial in most countries. So there are plenty of taxes to cut with the dollars raised from new environmental taxes or permit auctions. A tax *shift* would result—not a tax increase. Today, nearly 95 percent of the $7.5 trillion in tax revenues raised each year worldwide comes from levies on payrolls, personal income, corporate profits, capital gains, retail sales, trade, and built property—all essentially penalties for work and investment. Applying taxes of 20–50 percent to wages and profits and none to pollution is neither fair nor economically sensible. Governments are undertaxing destructive activities and overtaxing constructive ones.[12]

One reason the environmental tax idea has caught on slowly despite its 80-year pedigree is that environmentalists and government planners historically have preferred the surety of regulation over the more hands-off tax approach. To be sure, regulations have done much good. They have clamped down on emissions from smokestacks, tailpipes, and factory drain pipes and have banned DDT and other chemicals outright. Market-oriented approaches, meanwhile, have their own limitations. For example, it is impractical to measure—and thus tax—the pollutants pouring from a city's million cars. What is becoming clear to many environmentalists and policymakers is the virtue of integrating the two approaches, giving freer rein where possible to industry's own problem-solving ability. And they are not alone. Polls in the European Union and the United States have found that 70 percent of respondents support the idea of "green tax reform," once it is explained. Many political parties in Northern Europe have endorsed it, as have the European Trade Union Confederation and the Union of Industrial and Employers' Confederation of Europe.[13]

Preliminary experience with market-oriented environmental policies also offers hope. Countries from Canada to China have levied thousands of environmental taxes, on everything from gasoline and pesticides to sulfur and carbon emissions. Only a few dozen standouts have been implemented with tax rates high enough or permit caps tight enough to do much environmental good, but these few have provided evidence of the effectiveness of the approach when properly pursued. The Netherlands has used taxes to reduce industrial emissions of various water pollutants 72–99 percent. The United States has used taxes to phase out ozone-depleting chemicals. New Zealand regulates most of its fisheries with tradable permit systems. And since 1991, six European countries have taken the seminal step of directly linking tax hikes on environmental harm to cuts in conventional taxes—mostly wage taxes, which contribute to unemployment by making workers more expensive for firms. (See Chapter 9.)[14]

Yet for all the sense that "polluter pays" makes, "paying the polluter" still prevails in most countries today. Germany, for example, spends $7.3 billion each year (in 1997 dollars) to keep its old, expensive coal mines competitive. Were electricity buyers forced to pay for that subsidy, the cost of coal power in Stuttgart would rise another 60 percent relative to today's prices. Worldwide, myriad government policies shunt at least $650 billion a year toward activities that harm the environment, from mining and logging to driving—a circumstance that is especially absurd with governments spending billions more to fight the side effects of these activities.[15]

Another environmental revenue reservoir, now only partly tapped, lies in windfall profits earned from natural resource extraction and use. The U.S. government, for example, currently charges hardly a penny for gold, platinum, and other minerals taken from public land. Fair royalty charges could raise billions of dollars per year and eliminate the windfalls currently bestowed on mining conglomerates. In similar fashion, many developing nations sell rainforest logging rights for a small fraction of what they are worth. Significant revenue potential also lies in auctioning or leasing a seldom considered natural resource—the airwaves—to cellular phone companies and television networks and, most of all, in capturing more of the windfalls that occur when land values rise thanks to resource scarcity or public spending on nearby infrastructure.[16]

Altogether, phasing out most subsidies for pollution and resource use and phasing in taxes on them could give governments trillions of dollars with which to cut conventional taxes on work and investment. The scale of the potential shift will vary over time and from region to region and household to household. But as a rough estimate, eliminating 90 percent of the subsidies and phasing in full taxes on the use and abuse of nature could raise $2.4 trillion annually, enough to cut conventional taxes by a third—enough, in other words, to eliminate the income tax in many countries, or the sales tax, or the payroll tax. In industrial countries, tax hikes and subsidy cuts would cost each person perhaps $2,000–2,500 a year, while the simultaneous tax cuts would save as much. In developing and former Eastern bloc nations, where incomes are lower, the change would be $40–500 a year per person. From the long perspective of fiscal history, then, the changes would be neither particularly huge nor overly rapid. The levies that now dominate tax codes hardly existed in 1900.[17]

As a package, environmental fiscal reform would curtail environmental harm by making it seem as expensive as it is. And when pollution and resource depletion did occur, it would ensure that more of the profits would flow into the public treasury, where they would substitute for other taxes. In sum, reform would *replace private profit from unsustainable abuse of our natural inheritance with collective profit from sustainable use*. Massachusetts Institute of Technology economist Paul Krugman hinted at the potential scale of the shift in a fictitious retrospective from the year 2096 that he wrote for the *New York Times Magazine*: "In the early 1990's, the Government began to allow electric utilities to buy and sell rights to emit certain kinds of pollution; the principle was extended in 1995 when the Government began auctioning rights to the electromagnetic spectrum. License fees ... have [now] become the main source of Government revenue; after repeated reductions, the Federal income tax was finally abolished in 2043."[18]

As with any proposal for a policy sea change, significant objections usually leap to mind among thoughtful people first encountering these ideas. Don't subsidies for mining protect jobs? Won't new energy taxes hurt the poor and constrain domestic companies in international competition? Isn't it wrong to buy and sell the right to pollute?

This book explores these and other concerns. Most of them contain important grains of truth, but can be addressed in practical and straightforward ways. As Part I details, for example, the harmful subsidies that today primarily define governments' fiscal stance vis-à-vis the environment largely fail on their own terms even as they consume taxpayer and environmental resources. They do little to stimulate growth, save jobs, or protect consumers, and some do the opposite. Part II lays out the elements of an alternative vision—of fiscal policy that would involve almost no environmentally harmful spending, make judicious use of subsidies for environmental protection, rely heavily on taxes on resource windfalls and environmental damage, and make major cuts in conventional taxes.

Part III examines the practicality, fairness, and economic effects of the new approach, drawing examples from pioneers in the field. Chapter 11, for instance, suggests that when legislators apply environmental taxes to domestic companies, they should levy comparable taxes on imports in order to prevent foreign firms from gaining an unfair advantage. Special steps are also needed to shield the poor from the effects of price hikes.

The final chapter confronts what is often the major sticking point when pressing for change: politics. The trillion-dollar fiscal changes proposed here are inherently, fiercely political. Indeed, the persistence of environmentally harmful subsidies today is a tribute less to sound policy rationales than to the political clout of the recipients. And what slows progress toward environmental tax reform is that those who would be on the losing side almost always fight harder to prevent change than the potential winners do to advance it. The political arena is itself a sort of market, where the currencies are votes, campaign contributions, and even bribes. The realities of this political market must be factored into any effective proposal for harnessing the economic market to protect the environment.

Adam Smith was right in perceiving that the market is a key to the wealth of nations. But the modern era demands that we revise his insight. The market system today threatens environmental, thus economic, disaster. One of humanity's greatest challenges now is to contain the industrial dynamism that exploded out of the European Enlightenment without extinguishing it. If the market is to begin protecting the natural wealth of nations, without which no other wealth is possible, then governments must overhaul how they raise and spend money. Thoroughgoing, careful environmental tax and spending reform would make global society healthier, more secure, and more prosperous. Air would be safer to breathe and water safer to drink. Natural resource use would slow to environmentally supportable rates. Taxes on work and entrepreneurship would fall. Environmental protection, more than exploitation, would become the watchword of economic development. In short, environmental reform of fiscal policy would create a world most people recognize as the one they hope their grandchildren will inherit—whether they grow up in Stuttgart or Santiago.

I

The Price of
Paying the Polluter

2

Subsidy Anatomy

Few public policies are as unpopular in theory and popular in practice as subsidies. The very word can make economists shudder and taxpayers fume, turn the poor into cynics, and enrage environmentalists. Yet to judge by government budgets and natural resource policies around the world, subsidies are in permanent fashion.

One source of the apparent hypocrisy is that no one can agree on what constitutes a subsidy: one person's special interest pay-off is another's wise investment in the public good. Every year, statisticians tell us, the global economy produces some $30 trillion in goods and services. Roughly a quarter of that—more than $7.5 trillion—flows into government coffers through taxes and then out again to pay for everything from social security to supersonic fighters to fruit fly research. Some of it, such as a superfluous highway in a powerful legislator's home district, is transparently "pork barrel." Much more of it, from welfare to defense spending, is subsidy in someone's eye but is nonetheless sincerely justified in the name of good causes, including stimulating economic growth, protecting jobs, enhancing national security, eliminating poverty, and fostering technological advance.[1]

Although the concept is admittedly fuzzy, the term "subsidy" is used here to describe a policy that marshals public resources to alter risks, rewards, and costs in order to favor relatively specific groups or activities—such as consumption of energy rather than consumption in general.

Some conservatives attack all subsidies as market manipulations destined to do more harm than good. Giving free play to Adam Smith's "invisible hand," they argue, is the best way to make the economy work for society. But real economies never perform as perfectly as the unfettered ones in economics textbooks, which is why governments regulate slaughterhouses, stock traders, and monopolists. Moreover, all but the market's most ardent defenders acknowledge that what economists term "efficient" outcomes—those that maximize material wealth—can end up working against collective visions of how society should be shaped. Among other things, unregulated markets can allow abject poverty and extinguish the last wild places.[2]

Thus there can be good reasons to subsidize. It is hard to imagine, for example, how the American railroad network could have been built so quickly in the nineteenth century without major subsidies and land grants from Congress, or how India could have fed itself since the 1960s without a concerted government effort to support—and subsidize—the use of high-yielding crop varieties and farming methods, or how the Internet could have taken the world by storm in the 1990s without U.S. R&D support in the 1960s. Of course, even if these economy-transforming subsidy programs performed well on their own terms, many also did serious harm. Westward railroad expansion hastened the demise of Native American civilizations. And the agricultural Green Revolution disrupted traditional farming societies and led to overreliance on pesticides and unsustainable groundwater "mining." But these examples do show how government can use subsidies to reshape society according to given definitions of the common good.[3]

Unfortunately, subsidies that are effective even in this qualified sense are more the exception than the rule. In practice, every subsidy is an untidy confluence of idealism, historical inertia, and politics. Many are never as useful as their supporters want to believe; others outlive their usefulness. Thus it is important to scrutinize existing and proposed subsidies for effectiveness and worth. To the extent that they serve obsolete ends, reach undeserving beneficiaries, create perverse incentives, or generate exorbitant costs to achieve reasonable benefits, they waste money and hurt economies.

Of course, judging subsidies is a highly political act. Nevertheless, there are several commonsense principles of subsidy design that are hard to dispute in the abstract. (See Table 2–1.) The public's money should be used sparingly, only to attack serious problems such as poverty and environmental deterioration. When used, subsidies need to be sharply targeted. They

Table 2–1. Commonsense Principles of Good Subsidy Policy

- Subsidies may be warranted if they make markets work more efficiently—for example, by tilting the market against technologies whose environmental costs are not reflected in their prices.

- Subsidies may be warranted if they serve causes other than economic efficiency, such as slowing the disintegration of company towns or feeding the poor.

- Subsidies should advance the goals ascribed to them.

- Subsidies should be efficient: they should target intended beneficiaries directly and exclusively.

- Subsidies should be the cheapest way to do what they are supposed to do.

- All costs, including environmental costs, should be counted when weighing the worth of subsidies. This entails difficult comparisons between different kinds of harms and benefits.

- Subsidies should be fair. They should not aid some people while forcing up taxes on or ignoring the needs of those at least as deserving.

SOURCE: Worldwatch Institute.

should reach only those meant to be helped. They should not aid some people while ignoring the needs of those at least as deserving, such as by lowering the price of clean water to people who receive it rather than extending access to people dying from the lack of it. And subsidies should cease when they are no longer needed. Most fundamentally, their benefits should justify their full costs—fiscal, environmental, or otherwise. Such principles are straightforward. Yet few environmentally harmful subsidies obey them, as Part I will illustrate.

Worldwide, subsidies worth at least $650 billion—the equivalent of 9 percent of government revenue—specifically support natural-resource-intensive industries and activities, including logging, mining, oil drilling, livestock grazing, farming, fishing, energy use, and driving. (See Chapters 3–5.) This amount far exceeds what is spent on environmentally protective subsidies, such as for soil-conserving farming practices, and what is raised from environmentally protective taxes, such as on energy use. Overall, fiscal policies are decidedly anti-environmental.[4]

Not surprisingly, since most government spending takes place in industrial countries, particularly western capitalist ones, that is also where most of these subsidies are found. Western countries spend hundreds of billions subsidizing agriculture, and also hide many road building costs from drivers. Formerly communist countries also offer hefty subsidies: they sell energy to consumers far below cost. And the world's cheapest electricity can be found in Punjab state in India, where it is free for farmers.[5]

What is distinctive about these subsidies is that they cost the public twice: in the pocketbook, and by harming the environment—which is to say, harming the public health and the economic security of future generations. Almost all the activities supported deserve some role in even the most environmentally sound global economy. But giving them an extra boost pushes the economy toward resource exhaustion rather than husbandry. Since environmental limits are nonnegotiable, pushing the economy against them is ultimately counterproductive.

Of course, governments rarely set out to degrade the environment when they create these subsidies. Rather, as with subsidies in general, they offer most in the name of such causes as stimulating economic development, protecting communities dependent on resource-intensive industries, enhancing national security by reducing oil import dependence, and helping the poor by lowering electricity prices.

Thus it is conceivable that many of these subsidies are justifiable, despite their environmental and financial costs. Unfortunately, however, it is hard to find a subsidy for environmentally destructive activities that does much good at reasonable cost. Some strive for obsolete or questionable goals. Mining and grazing subsidies that some governments long ago instituted to encourage European settlement of territories taken from indigenous peoples are one example. Other subsidies are largely ineffective—for instance, nuclear power technology is foundering despite the tens of billions of dollars that taxpayers have poured into it. Still others have been undone by the very environmental destruction they encouraged. Subsidies designed to support the fishing industry, for instance, have only accelerated overfishing and fishery collapses. Most others, like those for heating fuel in Russia, reach their intended beneficiaries to some extent, but only inefficiently. Much of the money leaks into the hands of people who need it less.

In sum, subsidies that support resource-intensive activities and industries invite a four-pronged indictment: they increase the cost of government; the higher taxes they necessitate discourage work and investment; they fail on their own terms; and they hurt the environment.

As noted, the total for environmentally harmful subsidies probably exceeds $650 billion. Few governments have even tried to assess the magnitude of the subsidies they give, and of those that have tried, none has fully succeeded. In addition, some of the subsidies, such as free liability insurance for the nuclear power industry, nearly defy evaluation, being as hard to estimate as the probability and costs of a nuclear meltdown.

An enumeration of the side effects of these subsidies virtually catalogs today's environmental problems. Subsidies for logging and mining accelerate deforestation and water pollution. Those for coal production directly add to local problems like land disturbance and global ones like atmospheric buildup of greenhouse gases. Crop production subsidies in industrial countries have been found to correlate with higher rates of pesticide and fertilizer use, thus increasing water pollution. The list of adverse effects goes on, from smog to nuclear waste generation. Of course, dollar for dollar, some subsidies do much more harm than others. For the amount of money spent, pesticide subsidies are probably among the most damaging to the environment (and to farm workers' health). Across-the-board crop production subsidies, though a hundred times larger on a global scale, do conceivably the same amount of harm, since their impact on spraying decisions is more indirect.

Environmentally harmful subsidies can be roughly broken into three categories. (See Table 2–2.) The granddaddy of them all is the resource subsidy—the giveaway or below-cost sale of access to publicly controlled resources. When authorities dedicate public land to, say, logging or ranching, they may prevent other uses of the land that are more economically beneficial, such as letting mountain forests stand to prevent flash flooding below. Or they may prevent uses that are

*Table 2–2. Overview of Environmentally
Harmful Subsidies*

Activity	Examples, Annual Cost	Side Effects
Resource Subsidies: Giveaways or Below-Cost Pricing of Publicly Controlled Resources		
Mining	Zoning in many countries of publicly controlled lands, sometimes inhabited by indigenous peoples, for mining.	Fragment habitats and homelands; poison waterways, killing fish and birds.
Logging	Zoning of publicly controlled controlled lands for logging; spending on logging roads and other assistance exceeding timber sale proceeds in North America and Australia.	Destroy homelands and habitats; accelerate deforestation, leading to flooding and stream siltation.
Grazing	Zoning of publicly controlled lands for grazing; spending on fence maintenance and other assistance exceeding grazing fees in North America and Australia.	Contribute to desertification and destrution of stream habitats.
Cash Subsidies: Payments, Tax Breaks, and Market Interventions		
Mining	$9.4 billion in aid for uncompetitive coal mines in Germany, Japan, Spain United Kingdom. More in China, India, Russia, Ukraine.	Contribute to water pollution, acid rain, and global warming.
Fishing	$14.0–20.5 billion in tax breaks and payments for fuel, boats, and so on for fishers worldwide.	Promote overfishing, which reduces catch, employment, and ecosystem health.
Agriculture	Payments and price supports worth $288 billion in western industrial countries; billions more in subsidies for pesticide and fertilizers in developing countries.	Generally encourage environmentally destructive farming and overgrazing.

Activity	Examples, Annual Cost	Side Effects
Infrastructure Subsidies: Charging Users Less than Full Costs of Infrastructure		
Water Use	$14 billion more spent on drinking water projects than earned, and $23 billion more on irrigation water projects in developing countries; $2.5 billion lost in the United States. Similar losses in Australia, former Soviet Union.	Lead to water waste and soil salinization, undermining world's ability to feed a growing population; harm river and lake ecosystems.
Energy Use	55 billion in fossil fuel and electricity subsidies for consumers in developing countries; $68 billion in former communist nations.	Contribute to problems from smog to global warming.
Driving	Excess of $111 billion in United States in tax breaks and road spending over what drivers pay in fuel taxes and other fees.	Encourage low-density, car-based land use patterns, contributing to oil import dependence, smog, and traffic jams.

SOURCE: Worldwatch Institute, based on sources cited in Chapters 3–5 and 8.

simply beyond valuation, such as the life-sustaining activities of indigenous peoples, whose activities may be less lucrative than commercial extraction but not necessarily less worthwhile.

Indeed, the idea of economic value begins to stretch thin when extended to such forced transfers of indigenous peoples' land. Assessments of economic value are based on the assumption of voluntary exchange: to say that something is worth a thousand dollars is to say that people would freely surrender it for that. But how does one calculate the cost to the indigenous Dayak people in the Malaysian state of Sarawak of the loss of forests on their homelands, which the government has brought about by sanctioning large-scale logging by outsiders? What is lost is a way of life.[6]

In some cases, governments actively assist companies extracting resources from the public domain, and even spend more than they earn selling the resources. Like its counterparts in several industrial countries, for example, the U.S. Forest Service spends more facilitating the sales of public timber in many of its forests, particularly by funding logging road construction, than it earns. If it passed the full costs back to industry, logging in most public forests would turn from a moneymaker to a money loser, and would cease.[7]

Just as frequently, however, governments sell resources at prices high enough to cover their costs—but still far lower than they could. Developing countries such as Malaysia, Indonesia, and Ghana have spent little out-of-pocket to support logging on lands they control. But they have sold hardwood concessions there for a song, earning only a modest profit. Meanwhile, logging companies have obtained timber worth $100 for typically $33 or less, capturing billion-dollar windfalls. The U.S. and Canadian governments take the same laissez-faire approach to mining on their lands, offering little assistance but charging almost nothing for access.[8]

In such cases, governments sell resources above the cost of providing them but below their value. The distinction between these two benchmarks is crucial. If sale prices are below cost, the only way to end the subsidies is to halt the sales. But if companies deem the resources worth buying even when they are sold above cost, further raising the prices to market rates—that is, selling public resources for what they are worth—will not save trees or gold-laden hills. Defining "market value" as the highest price at which the resources will sell still ends up with the resources being sold. If Brazil raises the price it charges for $100 worth of mahogany from $33 to $100, for instance, loggers would probably still take most of the trees. Turning that around, leaving the prices low sometimes does not in itself hurt the environment.

This observation leads to a surprising conclusion. Some subsidies for environmentally harmful activities are not environmentally harmful. Such subsidies, therefore, will be treated separately, in Chapter 7. Even these subsidies, however, make activities like logging inordinately profitable and force up government dependence on other taxes. And the ability to grant them can prove irresistible to those in power. Had huge windfalls not been obtainable from liquidating Philippine forests, for example, more trees would remain standing today. President Ferdinand Marcos would not have been able to use cheap logging rights to buy support from his political and military allies.[9]

The second major subsidy family consists of cash handouts, tax breaks, subsidized credit, favorable exchange rates, and other market manipulations designed to tilt the market in favor of certain industries or activities. They are here called cash subsidies. Sometimes these are meant to foster change through the development and use of new technologies, such as solar energy and pesticides. More often, though, they attempt to protect workers or investors in established industries from powerful forces of change, such as automation, foreign competition, and a dwindling resource base. In the United States and Canada, for instance, multibillion-dollar production incentives for domestic oil and gas producers that originated in the crisis years of World War I remain woven into tax codes.[10]

Many subsidies in this family arise indirectly when governments set out to guarantee industries certain prices or sales volumes and discover that distorting the economic fabric creates tears and wrinkles that only money can patch up and smooth over. To protect domestic hard coal mines and the politically powerful workers who depend on them, for example, Germany requires its utilities to buy 35 million tons of coal from the mines each year. But with that coal costing three times as much as imports, the government would find it nearly impossible to enforce its edict if it did not offer power companies generous grants to narrow the price gap. Similarly, governments in many Indian states have decreed that their utilities will sell electricity for next to nothing to farmers who use it to pump groundwater. What keeps the utilities viable is a lifeline to the public purse.[11]

Even more subtly, some subsidies resulting from market manipulations do not cost the public treasury a cent, flowing instead straight from consumers to producers. For example, by restricting food supply—by taxing food imports, subsidizing exports, and paying some farmers not to farm—governments in western industrial countries raise food prices enough to transfer $140 billion a year from buyers to sellers, according to the Organisation for Economic Co-operation and Development. For consumers, such hidden "cross-subsidies" are taxes by another name. In the United States, sugar producers receive $1.4 billion a year extra from consumers thanks to policies that keep domestic sugar prices at twice the world level. Historically, high sugar prices have also stimulated cane growing in Florida, contributing to phosphorus pollution in the Florida Everglades wetlands.[12]

Important but tough-to-evaluate subsidies in this second family also result when governments shoulder private risks. Early in the history of civilian nuclear power, to cite one example, the U.S. government capped utilities' liability for damage from nuclear accidents and assumed the rest of the risk itself, free of charge. Since the likelihood and costs of a nuclear meltdown are impossible to evaluate reliably and are potentially huge, no private insurance company will take on the risk. Without this ongoing subsidy, there probably would be no nuclear industry. It is thus, in a sense, invaluable.[13]

Subsidies in the third major group, infrastructure subsidies, arise when governments do not just aid certain industries, they run them—mainly by building pipelines, power lines, roads, and other infrastructure. It is a rare government that passes the full costs of these giant investments back to the users. Moreover, government-run businesses, such as publicly owned electric companies, usually do not have to pay taxes the way private companies, such as manufacturers of energy-efficient lights, do. As a result, driving and using water and energy seem much cheaper than they are. That elevates demand, leading to resource waste, pollution, and traffic jams. The full costs of road building and maintenance in the United States, for instance, where they have been most extensively studied, are roughly $111 billion a year above what drivers pay in fuel taxes and tolls there—equivalent to some $400 per person.[14]

The rest of Part I devotes a chapter to each major

subsidy family: resource subsidies, which are usually justified in the name of stimulating economic development; cash subsidies, which are generally seen as protecting industries besieged by hostile economic forces; and infrastructure subsidies, which are sometimes defended as holding down the cost of living for low-income households. Since few of these subsidies work well on their own terms, almost all are ripe for reform through better targeting toward intended recipients, shifts to new ones, or complete phaseouts. (Another important type of subsidy, for R&D into environmentally relevant technologies, will be dealt with in Chapter 8.) What keeps subsidies in place ultimately has more to do with politics than policy, but taking them at face value provides a starting point for analysis.

3

Resource Subsidies

Visit Dubois, Wyoming, on a bright day and the colors will dazzle you: the deep green of conifer forests, the golden-brown of dry brush, the azure and ivory of snow-capped mountains against a cloud-filled sky. If you stroll around the town, you might also catch signs of what makes it an attractive social environment for the 2,000 people who live in the area year-round. The post office is the center of social life, as locals arrive throughout the day to collect mail, cross paths, and check up on one another.[1]

But if you head for the eastern edge of town, you will find a less appealing sight: the remains of one of the largest stud mills in the United States. Until 1987, the U.S. Forest Service had fed this Louisiana-Pacific mill a steady diet of timber from nearby Shoshone and

Bridger-Teton National Forests at public expense. In order to extract the timber, it had steadily expanded the road network running into forests, which became pockmarked with clearcuts. In total, the Forest Service spent $1.2 million more each year supplying the wood than it earned selling it to Louisiana-Pacific.[2]

In 1987, the Forest Service officially announced that it would drastically curtail logging near Dubois. The forests were giving out, the taxpayer cost was high, and the pockmarked landscape may have threatened property values in the nearby hotspot of Jackson Hole. Almost immediately, Louisiana-Pacific said it would close its mill, which many saw as a death sentence for the town. "A lot of people were concerned that the town was just going to dry up and blow away," says John Murdock, a local retired economist. Timbering and milling had been part of the town's economy for nearly a century. The work paid well by national standards, and, counting jobs in the grocery stores and repair shops where workers spent their money, the mill supported a third of the town's employment. After the closure, many former mill workers left their families in homes half-paid-for and became truckers. Some families left altogether. The population dropped by hundreds.[3]

But John Murdock, the man who understood the economy's dependence on the mill, also foresaw the benefits of independence. Murdock had done surveys that showed the local economy was already more diverse than most residents realized in 1987. It was a strengthening magnet for hikers, fishers, hunters, horseback riders, and snowmobilers. More important, its natural beauty and strong community were drawing permanent settlers, the sort who—freed by modern technologies—could work any place with a telephone jack and a Federal Express drop box. The quality of the natural environment was thus an economic asset. Feeding local forests to the mill, Murdock suggested, was constraining the local economy more than supporting it, by repelling potential settlers.[4]

By the early 1990s, events had turned Murdock into a modest prophet. Average income in Dubois grew 8.5 percent a year after the shutdown, while that for Wyoming remained unchanged. The population rebounded, lifting real estate prices. Self-employed people—from writers to one of the world's top Porsche repairers—arrived by the dozen. Small businesses materialized, catering to the needs of new residents and tourists. And the town's Chamber of Commerce prevailed upon the Forest Service to revoke an oil exploration permit it had granted Conoco nearby. It argued that exploration would disturb the environment and so hurt the town's economy more than help it.[5]

Dubois is not exceptional in its economic dependence on a healthy environment—nor in its slowness in recognizing its dependence. In many parts of the world, the economic value of the unscathed mountain and the untouched forest—as a tourist draw, a food source, shelter, preventer of floods—has always surpassed that of clearcut timber and strip-mined ore. In others, extraction once had the economic upper hand, but has since lost it.

Yet worldwide, many governments use their control over natural resources to subsidize one economic approach—liquidation—much more than the other—preservation. They are treating publicly owned forests, minerals, and oil deposits as assets that are worthless unless converted to salable commodities. Left over from another era, these resource subsidies are perpetuating what Kenneth Boulding, one of the first ecological economists, called "the cowboy economy," one that eagerly depletes the resources at hand in the apparent belief that there will always be more just beyond the illimitable frontier. Usually these forms of support are, or were, meant to stimulate regional economic development. But they often turn out to do the opposite.[6]

*   *   *   *

In North America and Australia, giveaways and low-priced sales of government-held resources date to the second half of the nineteenth century and the early twentieth century. The resources and space in newly acquired territories once seemed inexhaustible and underpopulated, and from this perspective the natural response was for governments to offer minerals, timber, water rights, and land as inducements to would-be colonists, usually for nothing. In the United States, these policies also resonated with the Jeffersonian ideal of the yeoman farmer—or small-time miner or rancher—come to conquer the wilderness, improve the land, and build a better life and a great nation. Settlers scattered eagerly across the land, staking and defending claims to gold deposits, cattle range, and waterways. First come, first served.

As governments gradually caught up with the settlers, formalizing resource law, they generally ratified existing arrangements as a political expediency, locking into place enormous and ongoing transfers of wealth. Many of these supports—although they involve governments giving away resources or selling them for less than they are worth, which would be folly for any private business—are so embedded in the cultural landscape that recipients no longer see the supports for what they are. The recipients defend them in the halls of legislatures as entitlements. In the words of historian and legal scholar Charles Wilkinson, the resource subsidies are the "lords of yesterday," born of one era and exercising sway in another, far different one.[7]

The U.S. government alone has given away 400 million hectares (a billion acres) over the last century or so—half the country's continental expanse—and today offers cheap access to millions more. Miners of gold, silver, platinum, and other hardrock minerals are free to stake claims on a large fraction of public land in Canada as well as the United States, claims that take precedence over other land uses. And in the United States, mining companies are legally entitled to stake claims on an additional 24 million hectares (60 million acres) of land the government long ago sold into private hands—though they cannot touch any buildings on the land. In 1991, residents of a subdivision in Silver City, New Mexico, discovered the mining company Phelps Dodge staking claims in their backyards. The company later withdrew the claims, however, deciding that they were not worth the bad publicity.[8]

In addition to zoning a great deal of land for extractive industry, governments often cover operating and cleanup costs. Modern cyanide heap leach mining, a technique invented by the U.S. government and given to industry for free, consists of grinding chunks of terrain into powder and then percolating billions of liters of cyanide solution through it to extract trace metals, creating huge poisonous ponds. At a gold mine complex in South Dakota's Black Hills, at least a thousand birds died after drinking from cyanide-laced ponds between 1983 and 1992. A small toll perhaps—until it is multiplied several thousandfold. In the United States alone, mines have contaminated 19,000 kilometers of rivers and streams. The U.S. government has accepted liability for environmental cleanup at thousands of abandoned mines, a liability estimated at $33–72 billion by the Mineral Policy Center in Washington, D.C.[9]

Likewise, some governments help cover operating costs for ranchers and loggers on the public domain, for example by repairing fences or building logging roads. Often the governments spend more on maintenance than they earn in timber royalties or grazing fees. Passing these costs back to beneficiaries would make logging and grazing on much public land unprofitable and lead to curtailments. The U.S. and British Columbian governments, for example, lose hundreds of millions of dollars administering public rangelands, partly because of what they spend and partly because they lease the lands at roughly a third of private rates. Hundreds of U.S. ranchers then go on to sublease their public grazing permits at market rates and pocket the difference.[10]

In the United States, forests losses are driven by a process as centrally planned as any found in China. Every year, as part of the budgeting process, congressional committees filled mostly with representatives who hail from timber states—and who appear at the top of timber companies' campaign contribution lists—set a production quota for public forests. This target then percolates down through the pyramid-like Forest Service bureaucracy until it reaches local foresters, who must then do whatever it takes to meet their quota, from building roads in once-roadless wilderness to requiring loggers to clearcut.[11]

Annual losses on forest administration hovered in the $300–400 million range in the United States in the first half of the 1990s, according to Randal O'Toole, an economist and director of the Thoreau Institute in Oak Grove, Oregon. The Forest Service, he points out, would rank among the top five U.S. corporations in terms of assets. Going by revenues, it would at least make the Fortune 500. But based on net income, it can only be classified as bankrupt. In effect, the general taxpayer is paying timber companies to raze public forests. Similar losses, at least $170 million a year, have been documented in the Australian state of Victoria. Losses like these lead to the perverse conclusion that taxpayers would be better off banning such resource-intensive activities on many public lands and splitting the savings with industry—in other words, paying loggers not to log and ranchers not to ranch.[12]

The biggest U.S. money-loser is the Tongass National Forest in Alaska, which is both one of the world's largest temperate rainforests and a "vast pulping colony," where 500-year-old trees are turned into cellulose used to make throwaway nylon stockings. The government spent $389 million between 1982 and 1988 on roads and other services for private clearcutting operations there, yet earned only $32 million—not surprising, since it was selling towering Sitka spruces for $2 each. The Tongass timber concession has come under increasingly vociferous attack from environmentalists and deficit hawks in recent years, leading to the closure of both pulp mills that once depended on it. (But like Dubois, Wyoming, the former mill town of Sitka, Alaska, has bounced back from the initial economic trauma, buoyed by patronage from cruise ship tourists.) The powerful Alaska congressional delegation has so far kept Tongass open for logging trucks, however, and kept the profits flowing toward their campaign contributors. Now the raw logs, still sold at a loss, supply pulp mills in Japan.[13]

There is little doubt that these giveaways of land, minerals, and timber have met their historical purpose of spurring settlement and economic exploitation of the New World. Indeed, by the standards of the nineteenth century, they have succeeded to the point of superfluousness. By the standards of the twenty-first, they are counterproductive. Thousands of indigenous communities have been eliminated or squeezed onto small reservations. The ranges of many native species, such as the buffalo, have also shrunk to fragments. In the continental United States, 95 percent of the forests, including most public ones, have been logged at least once. In Australia and the arid American West, overgrazing of cattle has robbed land of much vegetative cover, freeing soils to erode and turning thousands of streams into muddy gullies. According to the U.S. Bureau of Land Management's own assessment, more than two thirds of its range is in less than "satisfactory" condition.[14]

Meanwhile, the economic benefits of extracting resources has fallen dramatically relative to the benefits of preserving them. Small-time miners and loggers have been replaced by multinationals—established companies that should be expected to stand or fall on their own. And these companies are automating, employing fewer and fewer workers. The average number of workers needed to fell and mill 9,400 cubic meters of lumber per year declined from 20 to 16 during the 1980s in the United States. And with the newest mills, it takes only 9 workers. Intact natural assets, on the other hand, are increasingly coming to be seen as economic assets. They draw settlers to a community, and where desirable workers go, companies often follow. In the United States, counties with open space now rank among the fastest-growing. Rather than workers following the jobs, jobs are increasingly following workers.[15]

As this dynamic strengthens, argues Thomas Michael Power, chair of the economics department at the University of Montana in Missoula, it is upending the conventional wisdom that extractive industries must form the bedrock of any rural economy. In the resource-rich states of Idaho, Oregon, and Washington and the province of British Columbia, only 1 in 25 workers made a living quarrying minerals, felling trees, or milling lumber in 1993, down from 1 in 12 in 1969. Service and manufacturing industries, from software to health care, now generate most job growth.[16]

Public attitudes reflect this economic shift. A recent poll reported that 59 percent of U.S. adults opposed expanding mining and grazing on public lands; just 26 percent supported it. Referring to the bitter early-1990s controversy over protecting the Northern Spotted Owl, the mayor of Springfield, Oregon, told a *New York Times* reporter in late 1994 that "owls versus jobs was just plain false. What we've got here is quality of life. And as long as we don't screw that up, we'll always be able to attract people and businesses." Springfield has thrived since logging was curtailed.[17]

*   *   *   *

In industrial countries, then, most resource subsidies are politically entrenched even though they are doing little good and much harm. They are generally benefiting companies that do not deserve special treatment from the government. Industrial countries have reached something of a dead end on the cowboy-style economic path.

But poorer nations have been following eagerly in their footsteps. As the colonial era ended at mid-century, new governments in Latin America, Africa, and developing Asia took over the reins of resource ownership and management from their former colonial rulers. They claimed 80 percent of the world's tropical forests from traditional residents and owners, equally high shares of the minerals and water within their borders, and much of the land. Many began cashing in these natural resources—either hoping to jump-start economic growth or, through giveaways of valuable assets, buy support from key business and military figures.[18]

From an environmental point of view, the price they have sold resources for has not mattered much— though the prices have often been extremely low. (See Chapter 7.) Rather, as with minerals on U.S. lands, the operative subsidy here has usually been the decision to transfer property rights from traditional owners to more-commercial interests. Unfortunately, as in industrial countries, the historical evidence strongly suggests that emphasizing resource extraction has not sped economic growth—a conclusion ironically exemplified by the extraordinary economic success of resource-poor nations such as Taiwan, Singapore, and Japan.

One indicator of the eagerness of developing countries to liquidate natural assets has been the rising output from resource-intensive industries. They now mine five times the copper they mined in 1955, pump six times the oil, and fell seven times the timber for paper and lumber production. (See Figure 3–1.)[19]

Although policymakers have often hoped that transfers of resources to commercial industries would stim-

Indexed to 1955

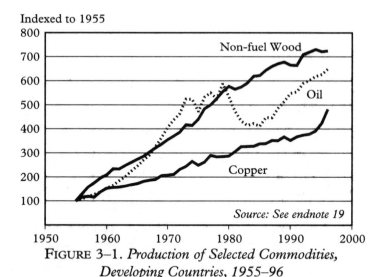

FIGURE 3–1. *Production of Selected Commodities, Developing Countries, 1955–96*

ulate economic growth, the results generally have been slower growth and more poverty. The more a developing country's economy depended on resource exports in 1971—the more it seemingly played off of its natural strengths, in other words—the less it grew in per capita terms between 1965 and 1990, according to a statistical analysis by Jeffrey Sachs and fellow economists at the Harvard Institute for International Development. On average among the countries sampled, a 10-percentage-point increase in resource exports as a share of gross domestic product in 1971 corresponded to a half-percentage-point fall in average annual growth over the 1965–90 period.[20]

During the years of expensive oil, for example, oil exporters experienced economic growth that was significantly below average, even negative. In Saudi

Arabia, economic production per person was actually higher before the oil boom than after it, despite a windfall of some $500 billion. As inherited wealth often does, this bounty seems to have blunted the drive for self-improvement rather than fueled it. Meanwhile, countries like South Korea and Taiwan, without major natural resource endowments, experienced robust growth.[21]

The apparent paradox of natural wealth leading to human poverty has seeded much debate among economists and political scientists. The consensus is that several factors contribute to the syndrome. One is that the leaps and dives of commodity prices can whiplash resource-dependent economies: episodes of high prices lead to ambitious, sometimes hasty investment plans; later, low prices force governments to choose between ruinous budget deficits and useless, half-finished projects.[22]

More fundamentally, modern resource extraction apparently does little to impart skills to the managers and laborers it employs—skills they would then be able to apply in other industries. Such knowledge transfers are central to sustained growth. Jane Jacobs, the great iconoclastic student of urban development, relates a classic example of this process. In the 1820s, the small town of Detroit's sole export was flour, which was milled and shipped across Lake Erie. By the 1840s, a handful of artisans who repaired and made parts for local flour mills and cargo vessels had accumulated enough expertise to venture into the boat business; eventually they turned the town into a major producer of small craft. Soon after, they transferred their skills to making steamships, and began exporting steam engines too. As in East Asian nations today, local entrepreneurs imported their parts at first, but quickly learned how to design and produce many themselves, spawning a bevy of new factories churning out gears, axles, pumps, and paints. By century's end, Detroit's dense network of machine shops and factories, the product of decades of local skills development, became the inevitable incubator for the U.S. car industry.[23]

Modern extractive industries, in contrast, usually fail to enrich the local economic fabric. The skills of the logger and the miner, it seems, do not transfer well to other industries. Nor does an extractive industry necessarily spur local growth in allied businesses such as mining machinery and meatpacking. These days, flour mills (and timber mills and oil refineries) are giant, high-technology affairs, and are imported from richer countries rather than made locally. "Everything you see here we brought here," says John Kazakoff, describing how his company, Canada-based Cameco, had hauled in goods ranging from food to heavy equipment to support its new gold mine in remote Kyrgyzstan. Most of the gold flows out of the country just as quickly, turning the mine into a sort of economic enclave. Thus when a mine plays out or a forest is depleted, extractive industries withdraw, leaving few constructive reminders of their presence.[24]

Another important dynamic behind the slow-growth paradox is that the resources sold have frequently ended up in the hands of a few timber tycoons or ranching barons, further concentrating economic power. Recent cross-country World Bank studies have found that concentration of landownership (a rough proxy for natural resource control) correlates with slower economic growth. Part of the relationship, the researchers suggest, is a version of the familiar tale of wealth gravitating to the wealthy. In Brazil, for example, where less than 1 percent of the population owns 50 percent of the land while the poorest 40 percent of the people own 1 percent, many peasants lack the collateral they need to obtain credit for investing in farm tools or their children's education.[25]

Wealth concentration also slows development through political channels. Resource-controlling upper classes usually gain disproportionate clout in government, leading it to underinvest in education, health care, and agricultural extension for the poor. Control of logging rights in the Philippines, for instance, has turned a few hundred well-connected families into the nation's nouveaux riches. Historically, the Philippine legislature has been heavily populated by members of these families and the lawyers who work for them, if only because they are among the few with the funds to run for office. Partly as a result, writes award-winning journalist Marites Dañguilan Vitug, "it has always been difficult for the House of Representatives to pass laws that would propel social and economic reform. Most of the members come from the elite and it would be anathema to legislate against their thriving prosperity."[26]

Since extractive industries are particularly hard on the environment, their longest-lasting effects in developing countries are often destructive ones. In Ecuador and Nigeria, oil production has poisoned the water and farmlands of local peoples, or completely displaced them. Metal mining has filled rivers in Guyana and Papua New Guinea with silt and tainted them with heavy metals, killing fish and contaminating riverside cropland. Fencing of grazing lands for commercial cattle ranchers in Botswana has cut into traditional range of native pastoralists. Most destructive have been the conflicts over forests, because of the vast areas they cover and the rich biodiversity they contain. From Brazil to Côte d'Ivoire to the Solomon Islands, government sanction of logging and incentives for forest clearance by ranchers and farmers have sped deforestation, species loss, and the disintegration of indigenous cultures.[27]

Experiences in the Indonesian province of East Kalimantan illustrate how an extractive industry can harm a regional economy. Logging companies obtained title from the government to indigenous lands, probably through backdoor channels, and employed 6 percent of the work force by the late 1980s. But they destroyed even more jobs by depriving cottage industries of forest access, according to the Indonesian Forum for the Environment in Jakarta. In 1989, for instance, the villagers in Jelmu Sibak found themselves encircled by two timber concessions. They were cut off from much of the land on which they normally cultivated rice, honey, fruit, rattan, and other crops. Under government pressure, the concessionaires gave residents modest cash handouts, a new road, and satellite television. A few villagers also got logging jobs. This did not compensate, however, for the substantial, permanent reduction in the village's main source of livelihood. As the trees fell during the late 1980s and early 1990s, so did the standard of living. Thus Jelmu Sibak's story is that of Dubois in reverse. But since the people affected are poorer, the stakes are much higher.[28]

In industrial and developing countries alike, resource subsidies have been routinely defended as promoting economic development, and they have routinely done just the opposite. Because they have hampered, even throttled, development, and because they have often only further impoverished the poor, these subsidies need to be scaled back worldwide. Their track record in terms of slow growth, environmental damage, and impoverishment and violation of the human rights of local peoples is abysmal. Justice and economic development will more likely be served if local peoples are granted more control over their lands, and if subsidies are dedicated to education, health care, and infrastructure—all vital ingredients in sustainable and equitable economic development. Natural resource management needs to be founded on a much more sophisticated understanding of the relationship between the environment and the economy—one that recognizes the economic value of intact ecosystems and that sees service and manufacturing rather than extractive industry as the major growth sectors in the twenty-first century.

4

Cash Subsidies

It is hard for people leading comfortable lives today to appreciate the desperation that farmers in the industrial world felt during the Depression of the 1930s. In the United States, the price a farmer could get for a bushel of corn plunged by half in the three years before Franklin Roosevelt's election in 1932. But many of the farmers' bills, such as loan payments, fell not a whit. Farmers found themselves squeezed between the cruel whims of the weather and the inflexible demands of banks, faraway commodities brokers, and families that needed food and clothing. Farm foreclosures became epidemic in the countryside, and the sight of a hardworking family's repossessed land being auctioned for a pittance drove some communities to violence. John Steinbeck captured the desperation in his *Grapes of Wrath*:

> Men stood by their fences and looked at the ruined
> corn, drying fast now, only a little green showing
> through the film of dust. The men were silent and they
> did not move often. And the women came out of the
> houses to stand beside their men—to feel whether this
> time the men would break. The women studied the
> men's faces secretly.... After a while the faces of the
> watching men lost their bemused perplexity and
> became hard and angry and resistant. Then the women
> knew that they were safe and that there was no break.
> Then they asked, What'll we do? And the men replied,
> I don't know.... As the day went forward the sun
> became less red. It flared down on the dust-blanketed
> land. The men sat in the doorways of their houses; their
> hands were busy with sticks and little rocks. The men
> sat still—thinking—figuring.[1]

Newly in office, President Roosevelt's response to
the farm crisis—the Agriculture Adjustment Act (AAA)
of 1933—was a blunt attack on the symptoms of the
problem. It was impossible to address the causes since
no one understood them. So the government simply
guaranteed higher prices for farmers. When market
prices fell, it would intervene with cash to fill the gap.[2]

The money pumped by the AAA into the farm economy—and by programs like it in other industrial countries—was gratefully received. But the farm crisis did not
go away. Over the next 60 years, the number of farms in
the industrial world eroded steadily as farmer after
farmer gave up in the face of the uncertainties and falling
profits in the business. Ultimately, the only way to compete was to replace people with machines; not even subsidies could refute the economic logic of automation.[3]

Meanwhile, the costs of the programs began to pile
up. Today, farm programs cost consumers more than
$1,000 a year per family on average in the industrial

world, through higher food prices and taxes to fund subsidies. Most of that money goes not to the small farms deemed most deserving, but to the minority of large farms that produce the majority of the food. In addition, the subsidies have helped lock in an industrial style of agriculture that depends heavily on pesticides and contributes to soil erosion and water pollution. One in four Iowans drinks water from wells containing pesticide residues at least part of each year; studies suggest that subsidies bear part of the blame for such problems.[4]

The passage of the AAA was a dramatic punctuation of a major twentieth-century trend. As industrial economies have grown, and as governments have grown even faster, political leaders gained the wherewithal to grant a kind of subsidy once relatively rare. In addition to channeling natural resources into certain parts of the economy, they began intervening by granting cash payments and tax breaks, setting prices and quotas, buying surpluses, and manipulating exchange rates—all cash subsidies from the recipients' point of view. Established industries with political finesse, populist clout, or both have won most of these supports. As a result, the subsidies have typically been used not so much to spur economic progress but to prevent change—to freeze certain industries in time. The rationales for the subsidies have thus included most arguments for maintaining the status quo: to stabilize communities and protect jobs, to sustain a way of life, to preserve the rural landscape, and to enhance national security (say, by reducing dependence on imported oil).

These are all good causes in themselves. Good intentions, however, do not always translate into good policy. Most subsidies grounded in these rationales—some $340 billion a year are documented here—have been unnecessary or poorly implemented. When they have done good, deferring the arrival of a few supertankers of oil or the disappearance of a few thousand jobs, it has almost always been at too high a cost for taxpayers, consumers, and the environment. One major problem, exemplified by the lion's share of farm subsidies going to large farms, has been poor targeting. But even when they are more sensibly targeted, protectionist subsidies face daunting odds. They oppose economic transformation in a world where the forces of change, such as automation, grow steadily. As a result, like dikes built against a rising sea, the subsidies have to climb just to stay even. Since taxpayers' pockets are only so deep, cash subsidies are ultimately doomed to failure. In the final analysis, they can only smooth change by assisting those who are most hurt by it.

*   *   *   *

Among people with vivid memories of spiraling heating bills and serpentine gas lines during the oil crises in the 1970s, one common rationale for protectionist subsidies—national security—requires little elaboration. And if domestic oil producers asking for government aid find sympathetic audiences, think how much more effective the appeal to national security can be coming from those who grow food, an even more essential commodity. The case for food production aid is particularly compelling in countries like the United Kingdom, where older people recall wartime scarcities and international supply lines cut off by German U-boats, and China, which saw 30 million starve to death during Mao's Great Leap Forward in the early 1960s.[5]

The national security argument has visceral appeal, but it seldom pans out in practice. Most commodities, from crops to copper, are more evenly spread about the planet than oil, making the dangers of import dependence in such goods less clear-cut. Indeed, diversity of supply is often the key to security in business. By operating in many parts of the world, mineral multinationals reduce their exposure to the risk of political unrest or nationalization of their operations in any one place. More broadly, trade increases economic interdependence among nations, potentially enhancing security by reducing the likelihood of war or trade embargoes. In this light, it is ironic that the European Union (EU), which was founded on the notion that trade begets security, dedicates most of its budget—some $70 billion a year—to one of the world's largest protectionist subsidy regimes, the Common Agricultural Policy.[6]

Most often, supporters of cash subsidies invoke another sort of security: job security. Fishers, loggers, and miners—like farmers—lead particularly insecure lives. During the twentieth century their jobs have proved vulnerable to the steady march of automation. Worse, the industries in which they work have sometimes literally run themselves into the ground by exhausting the resources on which they depend. Intensifying the insecurity is the rural nature of resource-based industries, which gives rise to small towns dominated by a single company—from the British Columbia woods to the Russian Arctic coal region of Vorkuta. If job bases shrivel, so too may the towns' economies, abruptly confronting many families with the stark choice of unemployment or emigration. The prospects a few years out are less bleak, as noted in Chapter 3, but economic insecurity is in large measure a lack of control over the near term.

Thus governments have often subsidized extractive

activities in the belief that community stability is worth paying for. The notion resonates especially deeply in the industrial world, where many people feel that work life has become less secure since the 1950s, even as inflation-adjusted incomes have more than doubled. In poll after poll, people do not report feeling twice as well-off, which suggests that there is more to economic well-being than maximizing wealth through an economic system undistorted by subsidies. Income stability should take some precedence over income growth—especially if the extra money would only buy a third TV or a slightly fancier car.[7]

Most security-seeking subsidies, however, have targeted those at risk only ineptly. One subtle but common problem is that they have rewarded output rather than employment. In Germany, Japan, and other countries, support payments for coal production are made by the ton, not the worker. Thus much of the subsidy ends up in the pockets of investors, not laborers, and there is no disincentive against replacing miners with machines. Similarly, only about 20¢ of every dollar in crop price support payments in industrial countries ultimately finds its way into farmers' pockets, according to researchers at the Organisation for Economic Co-operation and Development. The explanation for this low figure is that in order to earn crop and livestock subsidies, farmers have to grow subsidized crops and livestock—which means they spend more money on everything from fertilizer to interest on loans to buy tractors. Higher demand for these goods also causes their prices to rise. As a result, agrochemical companies, banks, and other parties in the agriculture business indirectly reap some 80¢ of each subsidy dollar.[8]

Furthermore, since the crop subsidies have been

based on output, most of the money goes to large farms, which grow most of the food, even though the programs are often supposed to aid small farms, as noted above. Not surprisingly, subsidies for production have boosted production rather than the number of farms. The number of U.S. farms has fallen two thirds since 1930, even as grain elevators have frequently bulged with surplus food. In 1996, 61 percent of U.S. agricultural support payments—$4.5 billion—went to the 18 percent of farms grossing more than $100,000 a year (and typically netting at least $50,000).[9]

And in stimulating overproduction, crop production supports have turned dreams of food self-sufficiency into nightmares of costly surpluses. In the European Union, subsidies had replaced wartime shortages with mountain-sized surpluses of butter, sugar, and grain by the late 1980s. Today chicken, sheep, pigs, and cattle eat 56 percent of the region's grain output (which would go much further if consumed directly by people). Another 9 percent is exported. Thus residents of the European Union are producing three times as much grain as they eat. Clearly the subsidies have gone far beyond ensuring basic food security for the region.[10]

In all western industrial countries, governments have attempted to limit surpluses they created and found themselves drawn into a quicksand of market controls. Historically, they began by buying up surpluses and then taking large losses by dumping the food in other countries' markets or destroying it outright. The dumping depressed global prices, however, raising the cost of domestic price guarantees even further. To control the losses, countries began requiring farmers to take land out of production, sometimes paying them *not* to farm. But constricting supply lifted prices, which cost domestic consumers. By 1996, governments in western industrial countries were spending $144 billion on agriculture every year and effectively transferring another $140 billion from consumers to producers through high prices, for an average total of $15,900 per farmer—with richer farmers generally getting even more. In other words, government policy inflated the annual food budget of a family of four in these countries by an average of $1,400. Similar transfers totaled $200 million in the Czech Republic, $2.1 billion in Mexico, $5.7 billion in Poland, and $13.8 billion in Turkey. And some developing countries spend billions more specifically subsidizing pesticide and fertilizer use. (See Chapter 8.)[11]

The rising complexity of agricultural policy has in turn burdened individual farmers with paperwork and regulations, making the profession with one of the most self-reliant images one of the most government-controlled. And some of that planning has played out absurdly at ground level. Brian Chamberlin, former head of the New Zealand Federated Farmers association, described a farm he visited in Scotland in 1992, where subsidies had shifted husbandry from good land to bad:

> The farm had originally been a beautifully balanced livestock unit, with easy rolling land in the front and higher [but poorer-quality] moorland at the back of the property. Grain subsidies came along and the better land was turned over to grain farming, while the livestock was consigned to the poorer land at the back.... [W]hen the set-aside arrived, with payments of [$270 per hectare] for doing absolutely nothing with the land, this area was taken out of production.... At the same time, hay and grain had to be brought in to feed the hungry (but heavily subsidized) stock on the hill section of the farm.[12]

For all the perversity of such situations, a more serious problem has been that much of the excessive harvest in industrial countries has come at the expense not only of consumers and taxpayers, but of future harvests. In western industrial nations and formerly communist countries alike, subsidies have encouraged environmentally destructive farming, including heavy use of chemical fertilizers and pesticides and the abandonment of traditional practices such as rotating crops and fallowing fields. This has accelerated soil erosion and the accumulation of chemicals in agricultural land and water, threatening agriculture's ability to keep pace with the skyrocketing increase in mouths to feed.[13]

Though the subsidy-sped erosion of the resource base is a long-term problem in agriculture, it has reached the crisis stage in fisheries. In many places, fishing subsidies are actually hurting the fishing industry. Thanks in part to tax breaks, low interest loans, and other handouts, there are now enough boats, hooks, and nets to catch roughly twice the available fish supply, a long-standing imbalance that has generated powerful pressures for overfishing.[14]

Fishing subsidies are significant in North America, heavy in Japan and Europe, and rising in ambitious maritime economic powers such as China and Viet Nam. Today, fishing subsidies total roughly $14.0–20.5 billion a year—some 14–28 percent of industry revenue—according to a conservative estimate by Matteo Milazzo at the U.S. National Marine Fisheries Service. Partly as a result, fish are being hauled in faster than they reproduce, causing the catch in 11 of the 15 major oceanic fisheries to stagnate at depressed levels or decline. Global oceanic catch today stands at 86 million tons a year, compared with the estimated 125 million that would be available under wiser management.[15]

In the increasingly vociferous battles over fishing rights, the world's 14–20 million small fishers stand in greatest peril. In Senegal, the government derives millions of dollars from payments that countries as far away as Canada and Japan make to guarantee their own citizens the right to fish along this West African nation's coast. Its latest deal with the European Union, worth $23.6 million annually, gives EU trawlers access to sardinella, horse mackerel, and other species that Senegalese fishers and consumers have traditionally depended on. Maguette Dieng, a 27-year-old Senegalese who makes his living in two small fishing skiffs, describes the effects: "When fish want to move closer to the coast, the big European boats catch them first. It's not good for us but it's very profitable for the Europeans." His father worries that such agreements are leaving traditional fishers, in effect, high and dry: "Life will be harder for my grandsons because of the reduction of fish resources. So they will have to try doing something else, and that will be very difficult."[16]

★   ★   ★   ★

Overall, the picture of subsidies dedicated to propping up farming and fishing businesses is rather dismal. By subsidizing production rather than people, governments have generally failed to help people much, and have even hurt them. One glimmer of hope does soften this picture: mistargeting can be fixed. By shifting subsidies from output to workers, governments can help intended beneficiaries much more while curtailing short-term overproduction. The United States, for example, has begun to do this with most of its crop subsidies. And most industrial countries have been expanding programs that reward farmers for practices that reduce soil erosion, preserve natural habitat, or protect traditional landscapes. (See Chapters 6 and 8.)[17]

But even when more sensibly targeted, cash supports for these and other resource-based industries face daunting odds, for the forces they oppose strengthen inexorably. First, the industries the subsidies support are inherently risky because of dependence on the weather and vulnerability to commodity price swings. Riskiness favors large companies, which can survive lean years more easily. That is why in industrial countries the small-time farmer and fisher appear increasingly only in history books.[18]

The second strike against security-seeking subsidies is the relentless advance of automation, which makes it ever cheaper to substitute capital for labor, and which exploits economies of scale. Not only does a modern combine harvester, for instance, let one pair of hands do the work of many, it also works most economically on large fields. Technologies like these contributed much to the rapid fall in the number of U.S. farms since 1930. Similarly, factory trawlers as long as football fields are leading to the demise of whole fishing towns.[19]

The automation threat to jobs and communities does not end there. Industries that do not automate as fast as the rest of the economy will shed jobs as surely as those that do. This is because the more efficiently other industries use workers—that is, the more income they generate per hour of labor employed—the higher pay those workers can demand. Resource-intensive industries with low worker productivity will eventually find themselves outbid by other industries. Unless they get more subsidies, they will have to scale back operations. This process of drawing labor to its most valuable use—essentially one of creative destruction—is precisely what has diversified and enriched industrial economies over the last two centuries. For better or worse, it is not easily resisted.

In industries consuming nonrenewable resources, there is a third inexorable trend undermining subsidies: the depletion of the resources themselves. In the United States, for instance, a clutch of tax breaks worth $1.4–3.3 billion a year to domestic oil producers has not kept companies' reserves from dwindling. As a result, their output has dropped by a quarter since 1970 and their domestic market share has fallen below 50 percent. About all that such incentives do is shift production from the future, when oil will be scarcer. Similar subsidies for oil and gas producers in Canada, currently costing some $5.9 billion annually, reduce that country's energy security in the long run too.[20]

The hard coal industry in Germany is experiencing some of these forces in combination. As miners have delved ever deeper into the country's sole hard coal deposit (snaking from the Ruhr River to the Dutch border), the costs in time and equipment needed to raise a ton of coal have climbed. In addition, productivity—output per worker—has lagged behind the national average, which is one reason wages in the industry have increased faster than earnings. In 1982, the government granted the industry $42 in subsidies for each ton of coal it sold in order to bring its prices within striking distance of imports; by 1996, the price of protection had nearly quadrupled to $153 per ton. Since total subsidies climbed about half as fast—from $4.1 billion to $7.3 billion—production had to fall 50 percent, and employment 54 percent. Overall, the cost of "protecting" a mining job with tonnage-based subsidies rose from a generous $21,700 a year to a lavish $85,800. (See Figure 4–1.) It would be cheaper now to shut down the mines and pay miners a handsome salary not to work. (All figures in 1997 dollars.)[21]

Sooner or later, Germany will have to cut back support, as some others who subsidize coal have done. Belgium has completely phased out coal production within its borders, and France and the United Kingdom nearly have. Similar pressures are operating in Japan, which granted its mines $780 million in 1996, and Spain, which handed out $1.2 billion. In the United Kingdom, where coal first powered the industrial revolution, the essential termination of subsidies— a drop from $1.9 billion in 1992 to $200 million in 1996—came suddenly, at the climax of a take-no-prisoners battle between Margaret Thatcher's Conservatives and the coal miners' union. Closing most of the

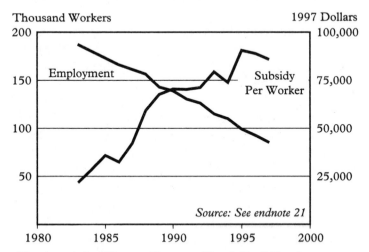

FIGURE 4-1. *Western German Hard Coal Employment and Subsidies Per Worker, 1982–96*

mines has been good for the environment and taxpayers, but many former coal towns are still struggling to recover economically, especially because of the sharpness of the cutoff. (See Chapter 6.) The probability of decline also stalks the former Soviet coal industry. The World Bank estimates that the Russian and Ukrainian coal industries would have to shrink by a third to become competitive without the aid that currently costs billions of dollars per year.[22]

Uncertain business conditions, automation, and resource depletion all erode the effectiveness of cash subsidies meant to stabilize resource-based industries. That in itself is a rather damning indictment—even before the destabilizing environmental and social costs are considered. For example, agricultural runoff and seepage of fertilizers and pesticides are major sources of drinking water pollution in many countries. The amount of subsidies going to farms has been found to correlate with the amount of chemicals used on those farms in the United States and Western Europe. Coal subsidies, meanwhile, are especially discordant in Germany, which has made a high-profile commitment to bring its greenhouse gas emissions to 25 percent below the 1990 level by 2005.[23]

A less appreciated side effect of protectionism is that subsidies meant to keep farmers on the land in rich countries often push them off in poor ones. Subsidizing one industry or one group of workers often ends up robbing Peter to pay Paul. In recent decades, subsidy-spurred overproduction of wheat, rice, and other staples in industrial countries has depressed food prices in the developing world. Lower prices have eased life somewhat for poor people who do not grow all of their own food—whether they live in cities or in regions where population has outpaced harvests—but it has been disastrous for unsubsidized Third World farmers.

The 1994 Uruguay Round of the global, trade-liberalizing General Agreement on Tariffs and Trade may have worsened their plight: it requires nations to reduce restrictions and tariffs on food imports but does little to curtail agriculture subsidies. (See Chapter 6.) On the corn-growing Philippine island of Mindanao, Oxfam International has warned, heightened exposure to competition from subsidized corn growers in the West could throw a half-million local farmers out of work—farmers who each earn roughly $1 for every $100 that western farmers receive just in subsidies. Simultaneously lowering incomes in the countryside and lowering living costs in cities has accelerated urbanization in the developing world, adding substantially to the mushrooming shantytowns that overwhelm governments from Manila to Mexico City.[24]

Trying to block change through subsidies indeed resembles the building of dikes against a rising sea. Even if the dikes are well made, which they usually are not, they can only work if they are continually built up. Meanwhile, the water held back washes onto less fortified shores. Risks and costs are not so much erased as shifted, and often onto those less able to absorb them. Prudence therefore calls for eliminating many such subsidies and introducing new ones with caution. Phasing the old subsidies out—or refusing to grant them in the first place—is an unenviable task for politicians. Losing a job is hard on a family, and losing an employer in a small community is even worse. But if the water will spill over the top of the dikes at some point, the sooner societies begin adjusting to the inevitable, the more gently they can do so.

5

Infrastructure Subsidies

If economies are organisms, infrastructures are their organs. Dams store; refineries digest; telephone lines signal; pipelines and power lines transport water and energy, the essences of life; sewage systems dispose; and along roads and rails, people and goods circulate.

Look closely at modern infrastructure, however, and you find a body economic in multiple-organ failure. In contrast with the finely tuned self-regulation of the human body, there are leaky irrigation systems where 70 percent of the water carried never reaches a crop, mighty rivers that have been subdued into reservoirs by dams that will never pay for themselves and that generate electricity to warm houses that leak heat like sieves, and spreading suburban roads that consume ever more land yet clot with traffic. At all turns, infrastructure is out of balance with its environment.[1]

What do the body's organ systems possess that human-made infrastructure lacks? Accurate feedback. Since an athlete's heart is stronger, for example, it beats slower at rest than a nonathlete's, thanks to an intricate web of hormonal and neural regulators. In contrast, governments often effectively hide much of the costs of infrastructure from users, passing them instead to the general taxpayer. As a result, when people turn on a tap, a light switch, or a car, the water, energy, and roads they use seem falsely cheap. Artificially low prices stoke artificially high demand among consumers, who then press politicians into building still more underpriced infrastructure, feeding a vicious circle.

From an economic point of view, infrastructure is an ambiguous combination of public and private activity. Set next to most businesses, it looks like a government program: government almost inevitably plays a major role in its management, either regulating or directly operating it (though the precise degree of involvement in oil refining or road construction does vary as waves of nationalization and privatization sweep the international scene). From this perspective, it seems natural to fund infrastructure out of general tax revenues.

But compared with other government services, like social security or weapons procurement, infrastructure looks like a business. It provides a distinct economic service to private citizens, which is often charged for. Seen this way, payments from the public treasury for infrastructure—not to mention exemption from the taxes that private industry pays—look like subsidies, and often environmentally harmful ones at that. Since the general public pays for infrastructure no matter what, and since the costs of mispricing some kinds of infrastructure are so great, it is generally fairer and economically sounder to charge people based on how much they use energy, water, and roads.

The subsidies that arise from underpriced roads, sewers, power lines, and so on are in effect aimed at everyone who uses infrastructure, which in most parts of the world is everyone. They amount to at least $300 billion a year worldwide, as documented throughout this chapter. To the extent that these subsidies really are meant to save everyone money, they are inevitably self-defeating, since many of the same people will have to pay at least as much in taxes to fund the subsidies.

When the subsidies are meant to help the poor in particular, they appear to stand on somewhat firmer ground. The poor typically spend proportionally more of their income than the rich on basic necessities such as fuel, drinking water, and irrigated crops, and so can benefit proportionally more from infrastructure subsidies. In Indonesian cities, for example, the poorest fifth of households spend 15 percent of their income on energy for lighting and cooking, while the top fifth spend only 8 percent. The weakness in this line of argument, however, is that although across-the-board price reductions often help the poor more in proportion to their meager incomes, the rich, who spend more on infrastructure services, still reap more subsidy. There are more effective and efficient ways to aid the poor— ways that hurt the environment much less.[2]

A stronger defense of infrastructure subsidies is that some of them—those for commuter rail and bus lines— can help the environment by luring people out of their cars. But mass transit subsidies account for only a few percentage points of the total in this giant family. (See

Chapter 8.) Overall, the subsidies are far too common. They deserve a role in national budgets, but not one nearly this large.

★   ★   ★   ★

Energy users get some of the most generous infrastructure subsidies—albeit less than they did a few years ago. In 1990–91, governments in the former Eastern bloc spent an elephantine $130 billion a year—roughly 10 percent of gross domestic product—to hold fuel prices to small fractions of what they were in the West. The region's electricity subsidies totaled another $34–39 billion, according to World Bank economists. (All figures in 1997 dollars. These figures have to be interpreted cautiously since hyperinflation made estimating fuel prices—and hence subsidies—extremely difficult.) Since prices governed economic decisions much less than in more-capitalist countries, cheap energy might not have induced waste. All signs, however, are that it did—ranging from grossly inefficient, pollution-belching factories to overheated apartment buildings that could only be cooled by opening windows.[3]

Since 1991, however, market reforms and budget squeezes have redrawn the region's subsidy map. For industry, energy subsidies have mostly ended, which is partly why energy use and air pollution have dropped sharply. In Russia, the subsidy rate for natural gas for industry fell from roughly 80 percent in 1990–91 to just 20 percent five years later. (Widespread nonpayment of energy bills, however, is creating hard-to-measure de facto subsidies.) Subsidies for household energy buyers have generally failed to fall, by contrast, with Poland providing the main exception. In 1990–91, Russian families paid only 10 percent of the world

price for natural gas. By 1995–96, that figure had barely budged: they paid 9 percent.[4]

But reflecting the cuts for industry, total fossil fuel
subsidies in the former Eastern bloc fell two thirds during this five-year period, to some $40 billion a year. The
World Bank has not updated its estimates of electricity
subsidies since the early 1990s, but if they shrank by
the same proportion, they would have approached
$10–12 billion in 1995–96. Overall, energy subsidies in
the region are down, but not out.[5]

Subsidies for energy use are also high in developing
countries. Popular objects of subsidy include kerosene,
a heat and lighting source for many low-income people,
and diesel fuel, which is used in public buses. But in
many of these countries as well, subsidies have fallen in
the 1990s, again reflecting the worldwide trend toward
a smaller role for government in the economy. In 1996,
for example, under pressure from the International
Monetary Fund, Venezuela slashed the $500 million a
year it once pumped into its popular gasoline subsidies,
which made gas so cheap (3.4¢ a liter, or 13¢ a gallon)
that some buyers used it to clean floors.[6]

China implemented particularly dramatic fuel subsidy cuts between 1990–91 and 1995–96, from $24 bil-
lion a year to $10 billion. Higher coal prices in particu-
lar have led to more-efficient energy use, one reason
Chinese economic output has grown 30 percent faster
than energy use since 1985, reversing the typical pattern
for newly industrializing countries. India, another coal
giant, also cut its subsidies, though less dramatically,
from $3.3 billion to $1.9 billion. In total, fossil fuel consumption subsidies in developing countries fell from
$72 billion a year in 1990–91 to $44 billion in 1995–96.[7]

More-fragmented data tell a similar story for electricity. In the 1980s, government fiat had driven electricity prices in developing countries down from an average 8¢ per kilowatt-hour early in the decade to 5.5¢ by 1988 (in 1997 dollars), roughly three fifths the cost of additional supplies. In 1991, developing countries had to grant power companies some $46 billion to compensate the losses from underpricing. But since then, power subsidies have probably declined, according to the World Bank—to $28 billion in 1995–96, assuming they fell as fast as fossil fuel subsidies. Still, electricity subsidies remain large in many countries. In the Indian state of Punjab, for example, the newly elected Chief Minister made power completely free for the state's farmers in 1997, a thank-you gift to his constituency for granting him power. Many Punjabi farmers already paid so little for electricity, like their counterparts in much of India, that they hardly saw the need to get rid of the remaining charges. "This is great," one told a visiting reporter for *India Today*. "I hadn't even asked for it."[8]

Western industrial countries also give energy consumers sizable assistance. And unlike poorer countries, they have not cut the subsidies much during the 1990s. In Italy, government appropriations and tax breaks costing $3.2 billion a year effectively cut the price of power a fifth. The United Kingdom imposes its value-added tax (sales tax) on energy at half the rate applied to most products (including energy-efficient appliances and insulation), a $1.2 billion-a-year subsidy that favors energy waste. In addition to granting private utilities free insurance against nuclear meltdowns, the U.S. government sells power from its own dams and nuclear plants so cheaply that it loses $4.4 billion annually.[9]

In western countries, as elsewhere, some of the most subtly decisive energy subsidies accrue through access to cheap capital. Publicly owned utilities often borrow funds from the government at below-market interest rates. As a result, they can more easily invest in capital-intensive technologies that take decades to pay for themselves, such as coal-fired and nuclear power plants. In the early 1980s, the U.K. state nuclear utility was required to generate a return of only 5 percent a year on funds it borrowed from the government. If it had been forced to pay the 10–11 percent more typical of private loans, it would have needed to hike its prices to customers 40 percent. In the United States, subsidized loans to extend power lines to customers scattered across rural regions now cost the federal government $1 billion a year. The loans also make it hard for small-scale energy technologies that can operate disconnected from the electricity grid, including solar panels and efficient natural gas turbines, to gain a toehold in what would otherwise be a promising market.[10]

★   ★   ★   ★

Subsidies for water use have similarly flowed freely worldwide, also leading to unhealthy infrastructure growth. Indeed, it is almost unheard of for a public water project to come close to covering its costs. In the basin of the heavily dammed Murray-Darling river, Australia's major agricultural region, most water charges are nominal. Hidden costs in the former Soviet Union were, and likely remain, massive. The U.S. government spent an estimated $47–99 billion more than it earned on public irrigation projects between 1902 and 1986 (in 1997 dollars). And that deficit continues to build. Projects administered by the U.S. Bureau of Reclamation, one of the two major U.S. irrigation agencies, today lose $2.5 billion a year, or $133 per irrigated hectare ($54 per acre), according to the government. In water-poor China, residents can buy piped water for a penny a liter, whereas factories can buy as much as 4,000 liters (1,050 gallons) for that price. In China, India, Mexico, and other developing countries, irrigation projects lose an estimated $23 billion annually and municipal projects another $14 billion (in 1997 dollars), according to rough World Bank estimates.[11]

The governmental behavior patterns that lead to these losses are remarkably universal. The U.S. government became the world's dam builder par excellence during the Depression, completing spectacular projects such as Hoover Dam on the Colorado River. But as it ran out of prime sites, ones with heavy water flows and steep drops, the economics of new dam projects deteriorated. In response, dam-building agencies—backed by congressional patrons—worked ever harder to bend the numbers to justify continued construction. Benefits of proposed projects were exaggerated, and costs underestimated. Once construction began, the projects often came in over-budget and behind schedule.[12]

Yet much of the world began to emulate the American style of water management, producing costly and destructive projects from the Aswan High Dam in Egypt to the giant Three Gorges Dam being built in China. Today, humanity has already diverted about a third of the Earth's accessible freshwater supply for use in factories, farms, and homes. Great rivers such as the Colorado, the Ganges, the Nile, and the Huang He (Yellow River) are so heavily tapped that for parts of the year almost none of their fresh water reaches the sea—though polluted runoff sometimes does.[13]

★   ★   ★   ★

Infrastructure subsidies also pave the way for drivers, leading to bloated, overused road systems. The difference between what road users pay to drive and what roads actually cost varies considerably from nation to nation, given different fuel duties, vehicle registration and purchase taxes, and road tolls. The gap is typically large in developing countries. In one survey of African nations, charges were found to cover only 25 percent of road maintenance costs in Tanzania, 20 percent in Kenya, and 4 percent in Cameroon—and those calculations excluded construction costs. In Japan, revenues from such levies fell $19 billion short of construction and maintenance spending in 1991. But in Western Europe, high fuel taxes go a long way toward covering road spending. In France, revenues exceeded expenditures by $11 billion in 1991. (All figures in 1997 dollars.)[14]

Roads are so enmeshed into the fabric of government policy, though, that these statistics only scratch the surface of the economics of driving. The shoebox accounting behind them—counting money only as it goes in or out of a highway department—hides large subsidies. The full costs of roads would quickly emerge if private companies were asked to run them, argues Douglass B. Lee, a U.S. government highway economist. If the "road industry" played by the same rules as its private air- and rail-based competition, for example, it would have to pay interest on funds borrowed from the treasury over the years to buy land and build roads and bridges. But public road-building agencies do not.[15]

A private road industry would also spread the cost of a road that lasted 30 years among users of the road for the entire period—rather than charging it all to people driving in the year it was built. In western industrial countries, where the golden age of highway expansion has closed, this change would substantially increase current costs by making people pay for roads that were built years ago but are still in use. In the United States, for example, thorough accounting turns what looks like a $23-billion deficit on a cash flow basis for 1991 into a $39-billion deficit (in 1997 dollars), based on data from an exhaustive study by transportation economics expert Mark Delucchi of the University of California at Davis.[16]

In addition, such tallies should include the tax breaks that governments in Canada, Germany, the United Kingdom, and elsewhere give automobile commuters. The U.S. government, for example, exempts $155 a month in employer-provided parking from personal income tax (compared with only $65 for mass transit coupons), costing it some $45 billion a year. And a tax break for ethanol fuel costs another $1 billion. Finally, as Douglass Lee points out, the road sector is exempt from profit, sales, and property taxes, exemptions worth roughly $26 billion a year. Altogether, U.S. road subsidies come to about $111 billion annually, equal to $400 a person. (All figures in 1997 dollars.)[17]

In the United States, passing all these subsidies on to drivers would require the equivalent of an additional 20¢-per-liter tax on gasoline and diesel (74¢ a gallon). In practice, however, a fuel tax is a blunt instrument for spreading road costs. It is better to erase tax breaks, such as for employer-provided parking, than to compensate for them with new taxes. As for general road expenditures, since the depth and width of a road primarily determine its cost, the main beneficiaries of this spending are operators of heavy tractor trailers (whose punishing loads demand thick pavement) and road-clogging commuters (who put the most pressure on width). The ideal charging regime thus consists of a system of weight- and distance-based fees for eighteen-wheelers, like the one New Zealand now uses, and rush-hour tolls for commuters. Of course, it would be impractical to plant a toll gate at the end of every country lane and neighborhood street, so taxes on gasoline and vehicle ownership probably deserve greater use too. However implemented, the money raised could be put toward cutting taxes or toward essential programs such as education.[18]

Until such charges are put in place, one of the body economic's most important circulatory systems, roads, will remain simultaneously bloated and clogged. But even these subsidies are not the whole story of hidden support for motor-vehicle-based living. Sprawled development often costs governments more than higher-density development because the sparser a development, the fewer people a local fire station, for example, can serve, and the costlier fire protection becomes per resident. Yet many, if not most, local governments pay for basic services such as fire stations and sewers out of property taxes and other general levies. Since developers do not pay these costs up-front, suburban sprawl appears cheaper, and continues as if it were.[19]

One solution is to charge developers "impact fees" to help pay for the new schools, water mains, and fire departments that come with growth. Some local governments have begun levying impact fees, but as with road user charges, full cost recovery is far from universal. In the United States, impact fees first took off in the 1970s in tandem with environmental awareness and resentment of rising property taxes. By the mid-1980s, some 190 localities, mostly in fast-growing Florida and California, had adopted the most usual kind of impact fee, one for sewers. But few of these charges fully covered the costs of new services. Even fewer used a formula that accurately reflected the relationship between cost and location. And most of the country's roughly 1,300 rapidly populating communities did not use impact fees at all.[20]

★   ★   ★   ★

In assessing subsidies for energy and water use, for roads and sewers, the philosophy that government should be run like a retail business can be taken too far. If everyone pays the same to have their trash taken away or their children taught, then the working poor will pay as much as millionaires. Deciding how far to take this concept is thus a complex task, requiring assessment of the social and environmental effects of different ways of funding government services.

On the side of raising charges to users is the argument that failing to do so hides the true cost of infrastructure, leading consumers to demand more even as they squander what they have. The organs of the economy become dysfunctional. Worldwide, low power and water charges have encouraged wasteful practices such as electric home heating and cultivation of thirsty crops in arid regions. The World Bank reports that as much as 70 percent of the water flowing into Third World irrigation systems leaks or evaporates before reaching a crop. Meanwhile, diverting large fractions of rivers has disrupted aquatic ecosystems around the world. Along the Pacific coast north of Los Angeles, for example, 55,000 steelhead trout once returned each year to journey up their ancestral streams; now just 500 do. The lands receiving the diverted water have been harmed too. Flushing large amounts of water through agricultural lands has caused widespread waterlogging and salinization. The long-term repercussions of this practice will tell particularly in Asia, where population is growing rapidly and farmers are already hitting the limits of regional water supplies.[21]

Likewise, energy subsidies have contributed to problems ranging from acid rain to global warming. Economists in Russia estimate that terminating the energy subsidies still provided as of 1994 would lower airborne emissions of carbon, nitrogen, and sulfur 15–25 percent by 2010. The industries most stimulated by cheap energy also tend to be hard on the environment in other ways, points out Douglas Koplow, an economist with Industrial Economics in Cambridge, Massachusetts. Energy subsidies make automation, petrochemical fertilizers, and long-distance transportation seem cheaper, thus giving an added boost to large-scale, industrial-style agriculture, for instance.[22]

Energy subsidies do the same for fishing, mining, chemical production, virgin paper manufacture, and virgin minerals processing. In the northwestern United States, $146–389 million a year in energy subsidies have benefited a handful of large aluminum smelters, members of one of the most energy-intensive industries. In recent years, subsidy receipts may have exceeded profits. Worldwide, aluminum smelters tend to congregate around sources of subsidized power, putting aluminum recycling, which is much less environmentally damaging than raw bauxite mining, at a disadvantage.[23]

Similarly, burying the costs of roads and sewer lines encourages sprawl and so contributes to pollution, oil dependence, and traffic jams that chew up billions of hours of people's time. In the United States, gasoline consumption recently reached an all-time high. One study put the costs of congestion there, counting the value of people's time and fuel wasted by idling engines, at \$40–160 billion a year, or \$150–600 per person. Central London's motor-powered traffic now moves as slowly as its horse-drawn traffic did a century ago.[24]

In developing countries, too, exploding metropolises are strangling in traffic. Perpetual traffic clots in Bangkok have contributed to severe air pollution and have turned the daily commute into a three-hour saga. Thai drivers have perfected the art of a life on wheels, doing business by phone, eating, and even relieving themselves without leaving their cars; meanwhile, police directing traffic at gridlocked intersections wear filter masks. The permanent crisis appeared to be scaring off tourism and foreign investment even before the crash of 1997, and prompted the government to consider banning new car registrations until 2001.[25]

If countries like the United States and Thailand want to repair such transportation problems, and if others are to avoid them in the first place, they could start by bringing drivers face-to-face with the full fiscal costs of roads. When driving costs rise, people not only drive shorter distances, they find other ways of getting around, such as taking the train, bicycling, or walking. A pair of rails can carry as many passengers as 16 highway lanes while generating 60 percent less air-polluting nitrogen oxide and almost no carbon monoxide or particulates. And taking cars off crowded roads actually increases the speed of those that remain more than proportionally, so that, in total, vehicles cover more distance in less time.[26]

This, then, is the case for full-cost pricing of infrastructure. But what about the concern that low charges for gasoline, power, and water are needed to help low-income people? Infrastructure subsidies actually often widen economic disparities. As noted earlier, people who are better off spend more on energy, water, food from irrigated lands, and driving, and so get more subsidy. In Argentina, Chile, Costa Rica, and Uruguay, for example, the richest fifth of the population receives 30–50 percent more in water subsidies than the poorest fifth. Electricity subsidies tend to skew even more toward middle- and upper-income brackets, since these groups have better access to electricity and more appliances.[27]

Even among the poor, the benefits of cheap resources often accrue unevenly. As a rule, the poorest of the poor get little subsidy. For instance, most public water projects in developing countries have delivered their benefits to fertile plains and valleys, which already have the best growing conditions and the most prosperous farmers. Two billion people in developing countries receive no electricity from the government, and so no electricity subsidies; a billion people still lack access to clean water at any price.[28]

People without access to subsidized resources face a tough choice. They can seek lower-quality alternatives: women can labor hours a day collecting water and wood and then carry them long distances to home. Or they can suffer without: limited access to clean water largely explains why waterborne infections still generate 7.6 percent of the disease burden in developing countries, three times as much as alcohol consumption and five times as much as tobacco use.[29]

Their third option is to buy the resources from people with access to them—but at unsubsidized prices.

One World Bank survey of 16 cities found that residents forced to buy bottled water from street vendors paid 25 times as much on average as those with access to piped supplies. Similar patterns emerge for agricultural electricity. Within a single village, rich farmers with large plots of land are best positioned to reap the benefits of low electricity prices because they have the easiest access to credit for investing in electric pumps and wells and can spread the costs over the largest harvests. In the village of Bhadresar in the Indian state of Gujarat, for example, upper castes owned 120 of 128 electric pumpsets in 1988. They got the lion's share of power subsidies—and the rapidly dwindling water reserve beneath their feet.[30]

And as Gujarat's rich have sucked aquifers dry with subsidized straws, droughts have often reduced the farmers without pumps to buying water from their fortunate neighbors, and at high prices, to quench the thirst of both their crops and their families. In the end, poor farmers, as well as poor food consumers in cities—the people in whose name such subsidies are usually defended—benefit little.[31]

The lesson is simple: unless governments see irrigation—or energy use or driving—as an end in itself, they should not as a rule subsidize it. Overall, across-the-board subsidies for infrastructure are badly misdirected. This conclusion seems to clash with the idea that expanding infrastructure is essential to economic development. But the issue at hand is not whether governments should spend money on infrastructure, but whom they should send the bill to. Hiding costs from users ultimately wastes water, energy, land, money, and people's time (through traffic jams). It turns development into maldevelopment.

Attuning the organs of an economy to their environment calls for ending infrastructure subsidies with major ecological side effects. Where people still lack access to power and clean water, government money would be much better spent extending access rather than subsidizing those who already have it. Where access is nearly universal, where subsidies for energy or water are particularly good at reaching low-income people, and where the reduction in poverty outweighs the environmental costs, the subsidies should be retained, but better targeted. For without effective targeting, subsidies meant to redistribute wealth toward the poor defeat their own purpose.

II

New Directions

6

Reforming Subsidies for the Polluter

Humanity stands on the edge of a century in which one of its greatest challenges will be to generate prosperity that is both widely shared among people and ecologically sustainable. Yet the main thing fiscal policies have to say about the environment is that "it pays to pollute." The clear mismatch between actions and goals points to two major policymaking tasks. The first is to reform environmentally harmful subsidies, eliminating or better targeting them in order to increase efficiency and effectiveness dramatically. If subsidies are tools, then those in place today—however well-intended—are blunt instruments applied to complex problems. Almost invariably, they produce more damage than gain.

The second major task is to think broadly about how to make fiscal policy and the environment mutually supportive. Avenues to pursue include using taxes and public resource pricing to tap into the economic windfalls that occur when natural resources appreciate, judiciously but emphatically subsidizing environmentally constructive activities, and, by far most important, charging for the right to pollute or deplete resources by levying taxes or selling permits. Together, these steps would turn an economic system that rewards unsustainable abuse of public resources with private profit into one that reaps collective profit from sustainable resource use. They would dramatically accelerate the ongoing economic shift toward service and light manufacturing industries, so much so that it would constitute an eco-industrial revolution. Chapters 7, 8, and 9 examine each step in turn.

It is tempting to say that the $650 billion or more being spent each year in environmentally harmful ways through government policy is being spent for no good reason. But that would be imprecise. The reasons commonly given for the subsidies—promoting economic development, protecting jobs, increasing equity—are almost inarguably good. As noted throughout Part I, however, these expenditures largely fail to serve their ascribed ends, and sometimes work against them. The ends cannot justify the means if the means undermine the ends. Mostly, the spending is a kind of fiscal fat. Getting it off and keeping it off will take hard work: it will cost some investors profits, some workers jobs, some consumers cheap goods, and some politicians key supporters. But spending money in ways that are more sensible and environmentally sound will make economies healthier in the long run.

The best that can be said for spending policies that do more harm than good is that there is huge potential for improvement. Reforming environmentally damag-ing subsidies would make them more useful, eliminate most of the $650 billion a year in direct costs to taxpay-ers and consumers, and help the environment. Money saved could be put toward more pressing needs, such as education and preventive health care, or used to cut taxes upwards of 8 percent on a global basis, which would reduce penalties for work and investment.[1]

The good news on the reform front is that these ideas are gradually penetrating the collective con-sciousness of some governments—particularly ones with little money to spare. Many developing countries have made major cuts in coal and pesticide subsidies in the 1980s and 1990s. And in the former Eastern bloc, governments have made even bigger cuts. The coun-tries that have taken these first steps and, sometimes, missteps toward reform have offered the rest of the world valuable lessons on how to proceed.

That said, many subsidies remain as entrenched as ever. No matter how much sense it makes in the abstract, reform confronts politicians with excruciating short-term tradeoffs. Russian housing and utility subsi-dies are a perfect example. Soviet-era concrete-box public housing is uniform, cramped, and sometimes dilapidated. But it is cheap: the average Russian family spends 6 percent of its income on housing and utilities, compared with 17 percent in the much wealthier United States. The subsidies that keep prices so low are offered to rich and poor alike, which is why they con-sume 3 percent of the country's economic output and up to a third of city budgets, crowding out other prior-ities. "The result is the crisis in education and health care," asserted Yegor Gaidar, President Yeltsin's former Prime Minister, in 1997. When *New York Times* reporter

Michael Gordon visited one well-to-do couple at home, he found an apartment filled with televisions, a satellite dish, a microwave oven, and more. Yet their monthly electricity bill was only $4.[2]

Yeltsin's First Deputy Prime Minister, Boris Nemtsov, had called for restricting the subsidies to the 25 percent of recipients who are poorest. (He has since lost his job.) But many families in Russia's "middle class," buffeted by inflation and job loss, fear the results. Muscovite Tanya Yesin, a kindergarten cook, and her husband, a military officer, live with their two daughters in a three-bedroom apartment; they spend a bit more than $12 of their $200–250 monthly income on rent and utilities. She calls Nemtsov's reform proposals "absolutely absurd." But in the next breath, she shows how to make the reform work: "They have to raise our wages and salaries if they want us to pay more." Indeed, that is essentially what other East European governments have done with the money saved through subsidy cuts.[3]

★   ★   ★   ★

Though the reform process will never be tidy, policy-makers and citizens should ideally approach it through a three-step analysis. First, they need to decide whether the benefits that subsidies promise are needed and whether subsidies can deliver on those promises. Second, they need to assess the potential gains from better targeting. Third, they need to determine whether the subsidies, once improved through better targeting, are worth keeping.

Some subsidies, as noted earlier, suffer in the first step of this analysis: they cannot do what they are supposed to do. Spending meant to boost production of food or oil for the sake of national security, to take one example, usually does not enhance national security in the end. Many countries find themselves with surpluses of these commodities, with deficits they can never hope to close, or with potential suppliers scattered around the world.

Many other subsidies, however, do some good, but with great inefficiency; they can benefit from sharper targeting. The U.S. government restricts its heating bill subsidies to poor households in order to hold down program costs and minimize the subsidy-bred incentive for energy use and pollution. Similar targeting would make sense in developing countries in many cases. In Indonesia, although across-the-board kerosene subsidies have reduced the cost of living for most families in the poorest one fifth of the population, 90 percent of the payments benefit people who are better off. If the subsidy were restricted to the neediest recipients, it could give them 10 times the benefit for the same cost, or the same benefit for one tenth the cost.[4]

Such targeting is relatively rare in developing countries, though, probably because most economic activity occurs off the books, making identification and targeting of the neediest a daunting task for government bureaucracies already stretched thin. But there are proven, cost-effective ways to sharpen, if not perfect, subsidy focus even in developing countries. These include targeting particularly poor neighborhoods and regions, and involving schoolteachers—government employees who know local communities well—in finding deserving families. Sri Lanka used such approaches to distribute "kerosene stamps" among the poorer half of its population in order to soften the blow of the 1979 oil shock. In the same spirit, this government, like at least a dozen others in developing nations, offers "lifeline" rates for electricity: discounts on the first 20 kilowatt-hours or so used each month, enough to power a couple of light bulbs every evening.[5]

Better targeting also requires changing not just who gets the money, but what they get the money for. Supports for growing grain or spending money on energy, for example, can be converted to simple income supplements—made into welfare payments, in effect. This aids those deemed deserving without artificially encouraging them to use more pesticides or energy. To compensate for large energy price increases in the early 1990s, for example, the government of Bulgaria began making fixed cash payments to all households, which it divided into three income brackets. Those in the lowest bracket received about enough to cover their energy bills while those in higher brackets received less. Since the payments were not keyed to how much individual households spent on energy, they created almost no incentive to waste energy. Similarly, Albania increased state wages, pensions, unemployment benefits, and welfare payments when it raised energy prices 75 percent in 1994.[6]

Such changes can be even more useful in reforming subsidies meant to protect jobs or a way of life. When governments subsidize farmers' income rather than their output, for example, farmers can pocket most of the aid rather than passing 80 percent of it on to their suppliers. (See Chapter 4.) The European Union moved in this direction in 1993 when it decreased guaranteed prices for major crops and instituted flat per-hectare payments. In 1996, the United States leapfrogged Europe on this path by abolishing price guarantees for most crops in favor of fixed payments based on farmers' past production levels.[7]

Both of these "decouplings" are intended to support farmers' incomes while ending the market manipulations that have burdened farmers with regulations, raised prices for consumers, and encouraged overproduction and environmental harm. Neither, however, explicitly targets the supposed primary beneficiaries of the programs—small farmers—which is not surprising given the political clout of large growers. In fact, by reducing or ending crop price guarantees and increasing farmers' exposure to the vicissitudes of the market, they may drive more small operators out of business. As it happens, these reforms have coincided with the highest crop prices in recent memory, so that farmers are actually getting more subsidy than they would have under the old systems. But if prices drop, the picture could change quickly.[8]

After assessing whether subsidies can do any good and, if so, how well they can be targeted, reformers can take the third step in the analysis—judging whether improved subsidies are indeed worthwhile. Two tests of worth apply. The cost-effectiveness test asks whether the gains in economic development, security, and equity are worth the financial, social, and environmental price tags. The fairness test asks whether some people deserve substantial assistance while others not only receive no help but pay the taxes that fund the subsidies. To take an extreme illustration, do Canadian seal hunters deserve government payments (about $4 per seal clubbed) to protect their jobs when mothers working minimum wage in garment factories besieged by foreign competition receive none?[9]

There are no universal formulas for performing these tests of worth or determining how fast to end spending programs that fail them. But in the halting manner of real-life policy formation, a few governments are grappling with the questions. In 1988, Brazil ended the generous investment tax credits it had once offered to ranchers and farmers who cleared land in the Amazon; officials there believe this change contributed to the temporary deforestation slowdown at the time. In the United States, the Congress has yet to reform the 1872 law that gives miners first dibs on millions of hectares of public land, but it has at least placed a temporary moratorium on new claims every year since 1994. And in another incremental step, in 1998 the Clinton administration announced plans to halt logging road construction in some still-roadless national forests—though it excluded from the ban Alaska's Tongass forest (see Chapter 3) and many old-growth areas in the Pacific Northwest.[10]

Of course, if the effectiveness of a given spending program is destined to fall over time, the operative question is not whether the scales of prudence will tilt against it, but when. Government spending then has to be seen, at the very least, as the wrong tool for holding back the economic tides. Such subsidies need, in other words, to be seen as transitional.

Ironically, however, when policymakers decide to end subsidies like these, it is arguably best if aid stops going to the affected industry, as distinct from the workers, immediately. Just as rising subsidies are politically hard to rein in, so are terminated ones hard to resurrect. Commitments to phase them out slowly may last only until the next election or change in leadership. Meanwhile, however, aid to affected workers can continue awhile, albeit in new forms, such as funding for worker retraining, tax breaks for new business startups, or bigger social security checks.[11]

New Zealand, remarkably, almost completely eliminated its farming supports in the mid-1980s—partly at the prompting of farmers themselves, through the agency of the national Federated Farmers group. The move was one in a rapid cascade of reforms that reduced government intervention in the economy—a level of intervention that had built up over several decades and had led to high taxes and inflation that hurt farmers as much as anyone. After some difficult years of adjustment, during which the government wrote off many loans it had made to farmers, the agricultural sector became much more efficient, and it rebounded. New Zealand is now one of the few industrial countries where the number of farmers is rising.[12]

Nevertheless, other experiences suggest that subsidy cutoffs cannot always be expected to work so smoothly. In the United Kingdom, where the coal cutback of 27.5 million tons (48 percent) in three years was by far the largest and the most rapid among industrial countries, social ills such as high unemployment and drug abuse have struck many former coal towns. Though British Coal offered severance packages and some retraining, these have not been up to the formidable task of engineering a wholesale transformation of dozens of local economies practically overnight. Mine-closing programs in continental Europe have often been slower, more generous, and more flexible. Miners in Baersweiller, Germany, for instance, will receive five years' notice if their pit is to close. In Belgian Flanders, the gradual mine closure program was once temporarily halted when local unemployment rose above the national average. Even on the continent, though, mine closings have often led to unemployment.[13]

★   ★   ★   ★

Though the judgment calls are rarely easy, the overall conclusions that arise from applying the principles of good subsidy policy (see Chapter 2) through this three-step analysis are nevertheless clear: withdraw almost all the resource subsidies that slow economic development; phase out cash subsidies that are or will be unnecessary, ineffective, or too costly; and charge users the full costs of infrastructure while helping the poor in other ways. (See Table 6–1.)

Of course, armchair analyses like this one have rarely hindered legislators from steering government spending toward favored interests. Most subsidies have only had their wings clipped once they have reached budget-busting heights. Consequently, the end for subsidies—when it has come—has often been precipitous. Belgium, France, Japan, and Spain, along with the United Kingdom, have all eliminated or radically reduced once-high coal subsidies since the mid-1980s. The environmental benefits have been equally sudden. The combined coal output of these five countries sank by half between 1986 and 1995. The imported coal that has replaced some of this output has generally contained less sulfur and ash, and its mining has entailed less environmental damage. In the United Kingdom, moreover, relatively clean natural gas, piped from the North Sea, has grabbed much of coal's old market share. The "dash for gas" has cut the country's carbon emissions during the 1990s even as its economy has expanded—a rare feat.[14]

The most dramatic subsidy cuts have taken place in the former Eastern bloc countries, where support for farming, fishing, and fossil fuel production reached

Table 6–1. Environmentally Harmful Subsidies:
Critiques and Remedies

Type	Ascribed Intent	Effects	How to Reform
Resource Subsidies	Stimulating economic growth.	Usually slow growth; often harm traditional resource owners; cause massive environmental damage.	Give traditional users more control over resources; sell resources above cost.
Cash Subsidies	Maintaining national security; protecting jobs or ways of life.	Often fail to enhance national security or stem job losses; hurt workers in countries unable to offer subsidies; cost taxpayers, consumers, and environment.	Convert subsidies to welfare for small operators; end where ineffective or too costly; provide transitional assistance.
Infra-structure Subsidies	Funding infra-structure out of general revenues; reducing cost of living for the poor.	Contribute to water and energy waste, air pollu-tion, traffic jams, and sprawl; usually benefit the poor least; hinder renewable energy use.	Pass full costs of infrastructure to users; expand access; offer "lifeline" rates or fuel coupons to poor customers; convert to wel-fare payments.

SOURCE: Worldwatch Institute.

untenable proportions along with much of the state planning system by the late 1980s. Prices that businesses there pay for agrochemicals and fuel have since shot toward world levels, causing fertilizer and energy use to plummet, and spurring jolting economic contraction. Joblessness and discontent are now rising in Russian farm regions in the wake of almost Draconian reforms, showing the danger in waiting for a crisis before instigating reform.[15]

Thus the unfortunate lesson from subsidy history is that things usually have to get worse before they get better. Rich countries especially can afford to carry heavy subsidies for many years, harming the environment and wasting money. So it is important to ask how supporters of reform, from individual citizens to the World Bank, can speed change. The sooner reform begins, the more orderly it can be, and the less pain it will inflict on subsidy-reliant families.

One key step supporters of reform can take is to measure and document subsidies: it is hard to reform what cannot be seen. Most governments have little idea of the magnitude and effects of the subsidies they offer. In the United States, taxpayer and environmental groups have joined forces to produce an annual *Green Scissors* report, which summarizes the environmental and fiscal arguments against more than a score of federal subsidies. The report and the coalition behind it may have played a crucial role in the prevention or elimination of several subsidies, including the cancellation of a money-losing dam project on California's American River.[16]

Ultimately, however, governments themselves are best positioned to measure subsidies. But few agencies have taken up the challenge, and even fewer have produced results that seem more than self-serving. The forest agency of the government of Victoria, Australia, for instance, has generally released accounting data to the public only stingily. In these data, it treats spending on road building as revenue to a forest, based on the argument that new roads increase the forest's commercial value, yet when forest value falls—when loggers haul out trees—no loss shows up on the expense side. These and other questionable practices make $170 million in annual losses look like only $10 million, according to Andrew Dragun, an economist formerly at LaTrobe University in Melbourne.[17]

Similar stories of obfuscation and resistance to disclosure abound worldwide. Far more useful have been the efforts of the intergovernmental Organisation for Economic Co-operation and Development (OECD) to measure agriculture and coal subsidies in western industrial countries, and those of the World Bank to gauge irrigation and fossil fuel subsidies in the rest of the world. In a telling demonstration of the political sensitivity of such documentation, in 1997 OECD canceled a nearly complete investigation of the economic and environmental effects of a variety of subsidies in member countries. The government of Canada and aluminum producers in several countries had argued that the study unfairly singled them out.[18]

Negotiations over trade treaties have provided another pressure point for reform. During the 10-year Uruguay Round negotiations that ended in 1994 with the creation of the World Trade Organization, agricultural subsidies were one of the toughest sticking points, both among industrial countries and between them and poorer ones that could not afford the same protection for their own farmers. The final deal, though modest—20-percent cuts in production incentives relative to high levels in the late 1980s—did at least establish that agricultural subsidies, like others, are fair game in the international trade arena. And it was the need for data during the negotiations that prompted OECD to begin measuring these subsidies.[19]

International aid institutions, which have too often ended up facilitating shortsighted resource giveaway policies, need to become stronger allies in the fight for subsidy reform. Under the rubric of structural adjustment, both the World Bank and the International Monetary Fund have pressed nations struggling to repay past debts to reduce public subsidies. But they often have allowed debtors to cut subsidies with the weakest political bases, such as ones mainly benefiting the poor, rather than those with the weakest policy rationales, such as for timber tycoons.[20]

Nevertheless, there are indications that these institutions are beginning to take environmentally destructive subsidies more seriously. In 1996, for example, the Bank conditioned a structural adjustment loan to Papua New Guinea on reforms of its loss-laden and corrupt Forest Authority. After several months of direct resistance, the government relented, passing a law to raise prices on forest concessions and to include representatives from environmental and indigenous groups on the agency's governing board. But when the Bank's credit is less needed, it wields less influence. In Indonesia, it tried with little success in the late 1980s to convince the government to rein in underpricing and overcutting of timber, and, implicitly, the rampant cronyism behind it. The only apparent result was Indonesia's loss of interest in Bank funding for timber projects.[21]

Domestic drives toward privatization and market liberalization have been more effective at squeezing subsidies out of budgets. Between 1989 and 1995, Mexico transferred control of two thirds of its irrigation systems to 300 local water user groups, in the process phasing out subsidies that had covered 43 percent of operating costs. (Large subsidies to cover past construction costs remain, however.) Though water prices nearly doubled, farmers also gained power over their systems. And irrigation managers became more responsive to the needs of the farmers who now pay their salaries, according to the World Bank. Meanwhile, farmers may be using water more efficiently since it costs more.[22]

Privatization and market reforms have also been at work in the coal industry. Poland, Hungary, and the Czech Republic have begun reforming their coal sectors, a painful job since it entails eliminating jobs in societies still picking up the pieces of the old communist system. In India, a program of market reforms begun in 1991 cut the consumer subsidy rate for coal from 32 to 27 percent, and ended net subsidies for diesel and other petroleum products altogether. China's reforms cut aid for state-owned mines from $750 million in 1993 to $240 million just two years later.[23]

These are promising trends, but there is still at least $650 billion to go on the path to full subsidy reform. And there is even farther to go before fiscal and environmental policies operate in harmony. Despite the importance of subsidy reform, societies will ultimately need to take more fundamental steps if they are to launch the eco-industrial revolution needed to attain environmental sustainability. While governments will still need to make careful use of subsidies to reward, they will also need regulations to restrict and environmental taxes to penalize. Yet environmentally harmful subsidies have so many strikes against them that if societies cannot reform them it is hard to see how they can ever take these other, more difficult steps. The indictment against the subsidies bears repeating: They do little good on their own terms. They hike the cost of government. The resulting higher taxes and prices burden economies. And they degrade the environment, undermining human health and long-term economic prospects. Citizens and policymakers determined to forge economies that are just and prosperous for generations to come would do well to start by getting government out of the business of paying the polluter.

7

Capturing Resource
Windfalls

The natural wealth of nations, from their forests to
their rivers, existed long before nations themselves.
From the point of view of the commercial economy,
natural wealth is an economic windfall. It is manna
from Earth, free for the taking—as if nature had set the
stage for the industrial revolution by sprinkling cash
across the landscape. Yet when industrial society has
bent over to pick up this found money, the collective
natural inheritance has usually ended up lining the
pockets of the few—from investors in mining companies who take free gold from public lands to timber
tycoons who use bribes to obtain cheap logging rights
in the rainforest.

This chapter considers various forms of economic
windfall generated by natural wealth and argues that

public institutions should use taxes and charges to capture much more of these financial gains than they do today. In practice, this suggestion distills down to two main policy prescriptions. First, when governments decide to transfer public resources to companies or individuals, they should at least sell the resources for what they are worth on the open market. They can spend the new revenues on essential programs or use them to cut taxes. Second, authorities should raise taxes on land in towns and cities and cut taxes on buildings on such land. Properly done, these fiscal shifts will aid economic development, make taxes fairer, and slow suburban sprawl.

★   ★   ★   ★

Economists since Adam Smith have understood the special virtues of taxing windfalls generated by natural resources. Historically, though, most economists have skirted around questions that make powerful people uncomfortable—such as whether timber tycoons and land speculators deserve the fortunes they have won. And they have been so dazzled by industrial economic growth over the last two centuries that they have tended to overlook nature as a source of wealth. Since economists rarely discuss resource windfall capture, the idea is also foreign to most laypeople. So it deserves careful explanation.[1]

Consider the example of the little-known American International Petroleum Corporation (AIPC). The company appears to have parlayed prime government connections in Kazakhstan into cheap and exclusive access to a mammoth oil field, 19,000 square kilometers (7,400 square miles) in area, that contains perhaps 2–3 billion barrels of oil. Indicative of how much wealth the government has given to AIPC, the company's stock market value shot from $9 million to $231 million in 1997.[2]

How did the tiny firm scoop companies like Exxon and Chevron, all eager to get their drills into the same concession? AIPC paid $23,000 a month in "consulting fees" to its local affiliate as soon as the deal was signed in 1997, an affiliate whose honorary chairman is the brother of the President of Kazakhstan. AIPC also issued special overseas shares of stock exempt from most information disclosure requirements in the United States; many of these may have gone to key Kazakh officials.

The true sources of AIPC's natural resource windfall are the oil buyers of the world and the biological and geological forces that created the deposit in Kazakhstan. Since nature and society alone made the oil fields valuable, if anyone deserves the windfall, it is the Kazakh public. AIPC invested almost nothing to earn this windfall, nor expended any labor—except on manipulating and exploiting a public institution. The firm has not added to Kazakhstan's wealth, but instead has removed it through a sort of creative parasitism. The natural wealth of Kazakhstan has become the private fortunes of a few.

If the Kazakh government wanted to claw back some of the windfall, it could revoke the deal and instead auction off pieces of the concession to major oil companies—exactly as AIPC is set to do. AIPC would lose its windfall, but the large oil companies would still get the same exploration rights at the same price. And the Kazakh economy would gain if the revenues from these new royalties went to increasing government investment in education, say, or cutting taxes.

It might seem that selling the oil rights rather than giving them away would slow Kazakhstan's economy the way a tax would. But up to a point, it would not. It would be as if the government asked AIPC or other companies to pay it $1,000—rather than nothing—for a $1,000 bar of gold. The companies would still buy the exploration rights, and still resell the extracted barrels at the same world oil price. A royalty charge would not slow the economy of Kazakhstan.

Losses from low or nonexistent royalties often anger environmentalists, who see them as subsidies for environmental destruction. From an environmental perspective, however, what mainly harms the Earth is the basic decision to have trees cut, oil extracted, or rivers diverted (as Chapter 3 describes). Once these basic decisions are made, for better or for worse, governments will do the public more good if they sell the resources at market rates and put the revenues to productive use. Royalty charges are thus not a substitute for environmental protection. But they are compatible with it. If Kazakhstan were to not only sell oil drilling rights for what they were worth, for example, but tax water pollution from oil drilling itself, it would shut down the least economic, most polluting wells in short order while extracting royalties from the rest.

Somewhat confusingly, economists call the windfalls won by speculators and politically connected concessionaires "resource rents." Alan Thein Durning and Yarom Bauman of the Seattle-based Northwest Environment Watch (NEW), explain: "Rent is windfall profit, profit that accrues to a company not as a result of its skill and hard work, but because it succeeds in gaining private control of a public good of exceptional value."[3]

In general, windfalls are pervasive in capitalist

economies—and have often been seen as particularly worthy of taxation. Every great fortune is partly a product of luck—had history gone slightly differently, for example, Andrew Carnegie and Bill Gates would not have become billionaires—which is one argument for taxing the rich at higher rates. But deciding just how much of a person's income is owed to luck or political manipulation is often impossible, making windfall taxation difficult. When natural resources generate the windfalls, however, an unusually precise line can be drawn. The word "windfall" itself contains this connection: it refers literally to fruit or tree branches blown down by the wind, which lie free for the taking by passersby.

What rent-capturing charges do offer—if political resistance to them can be overcome—is a way to raise revenue without slowing economic development, which is particularly valuable in developing countries. During the 1960s and 1970s, for instance, President Ferdinand Marcos granted cheap timber concessions to political and military allies. The logging that followed generated $42 billion in profits for 480 well-connected Philippine families, according to Maximo Kalaw, a prominent Philippine environmental activist, even as it impoverished millions of rural people by ruining their land. To the extent that the trees should have been cut, it is not hard to imagine how much more good the government could have done had it charged market rates for the timber and invested the billions in educating Manila's million street children or bringing electricity to rural villages. Indeed, the Harvard University study that found that emphasis on extractive industries slowed growth (see Chapter 3) also found evidence that spending on family planning, infrastructure, education, and

public health programs all speed development in developing countries. When resources are extracted, the study strongly implies, the windfalls could be well spent on such programs.[4]

*   *   *   *

Worldwide, governments charge much less than they could for publicly controlled water, timber, minerals, and other resources. In the process, they forgo major opportunities to raise funds without dampening economic activity. In Indonesia, loggers paid only $500 million in 1990 for rainforest logging concessions worth some $3.1 billion (in 1997 dollars), according to the Indonesian Forum for the Environment, an independent nonprofit group in Jakarta. For every dollar in development aid that flowed into government coffers, in other words, at least another dollar was effectively flowing out as windfall profits for a dozen or so timber magnates with ties to President Suharto. Concession prices have been similarly low in other tropical timber exporters, including Côte d'Ivoire, Ghana, and Malaysia, largely because of close ties between industry and policymakers.[5]

A few recent charge increases for logging rights offer some hope for change, however. Honduras experimented in 1992 with publicly auctioning timber concessions, and succeeded in raising sale prices from $5 to $33 per cubic meter of timber. The Philippines, too, began reforming timber pricing policies in the 1990s, and now captures about 25 percent of the value of its timber, up from 11 percent.[6]

A similarly mixed picture emerges for publicly controlled minerals. Hardrock mining is essentially free on a large fraction of public land in Canada and the

United States. In 1994 one Canadian firm bought 790 hectares (1,950 acres) of federal land in Goldstrike, Nevada, for $5,190; the tract contained gold worth $10 billion once mined—2 million times as much as the transaction price. Since 1873, U.S. taxpayers have forgone roughly $255 billion (in 1997 dollars) in mineral royalties on federal lands, equal to nearly $1,000 per U.S. resident, or one twentieth of the accumulated federal debt.[7]

Yet some countries have negotiated fairer deals with mining and oil companies, perhaps because minerals exploration and extraction is a risky and complex business, making it harder to extract the easy profits that make timber concessions so inviting for political patronage. (Though as AIPC's story shows, oil can corrupt too.) Here, in contrast to the situation with timber, Indonesia is an exemplar. In the 1960s, it charged oil companies a respectable 65 percent of the in situ value of its petroleum deposits; today it captures 85 percent, enough to generate a quarter of its tax revenues. Norway is also collecting substantial royalties from its oil reserves, and is investing much of the windfall in a fund whose value could climb to $25,000 per Norwegian by 2000. The fund will reduce the need for payroll and profits taxes to cover the pensions of the country's soon-to-retire baby boom generation. Alaska maintains a similar oil-funded rainy-day fund.[8]

Significant revenue potential also lies in charging more for water and power. In California's Imperial Valley, farmers hold rights to nearly a quarter of the flow of the Colorado River, and the federal government delivers the valuable water to the valley for free via a 129-kilometer (80-mile) canal. In Central Valley, to the north, the government charges many farmers only

$2.84 for a thousand cubic meters of water, enough to irrigate a few hundred square meters or yards of vegetables. But other farmers in the same valley already willingly pay 28–56 times as much for water from a state irrigation project, showing how much the federal water is really worth. Similarly, many publicly run or regulated utilities today sell power from well-situated dams at cost, which can be much lower than market value. The Norwegian government could capture $200 million a year in additional profits from its best-situated dams if it sold the electricity at the going rate, according to the official Norwegian Green Tax Commission.[9]

Royalties for fishery access are beginning to gain acceptance internationally. When European boats fish African waters, and when Japanese trawlers work the fisheries of South America, it makes sense for governments to charge admission to fisheries in order to retain more of the economic value of their resource at home. Some developing countries now charge industrial-country governments for fishery access. Worldwide, these fees total $500 million to $1 billion a year. Charges levied on fishers themselves are less common. But New Zealand does pass the costs of administering fisheries back to fishers through special charges. And the Russian government has granted Japanese fishers the right to catch salmon in its waters on the condition that they pay Russia 30 percent of the value of the catch.[10]

A few developing countries are exploring a novel royalty, charging for access to the genetic secrets of their biological wealth. Tiny Costa Rica, home to an extraordinary 1 in 20 of the world's terrestrial species, has begun pursuing this market aggressively. Its Instituto Nacional de Biodiversidad (INBio) struck a deal with the drug company Merck in 1991 to provide 10,000 biological samples for $1 million. INBio is also working with a British firm to derive a product from a substance found in a native tree species. The natural substance kills parasitic worms known as nematodes; a commercial derivative could protect banana trees without endangering banana workers. If a product is eventually developed, INBio will earn royalties. But the amounts involved in "biodiversity prospecting" deals to date suggest that such arrangements hold only modest revenue potential.[11]

Another modern natural resource—the airwaves used by the broadcast and communications industries—is a much larger potential revenue source. The U.S. government has become one of the first to sell pieces of the airwaves rather than give them away. A 1996 auction of frequencies for use in a new generation of wireless phones brought in a quick $10 billion, more than any other auction in history. One later auction ran into problems—small companies overbid and then went bankrupt—but overall, further sales have raised billions more.[12]

Thus charges for public resources could generate hundreds of billions of dollars a year in revenue worldwide without slowing economic development. The charges, moreover, would mainly tax the rich—whether they be irrigation interests, timber concessionaires, mining investors, or telecommunications tycoons. Whether the new revenue is put into health and education programs or into cutting conventional taxes, the human economy will benefit when natural wealth is used as a tax base.

*   *   *   *

Windfalls can flow not only from rivers, forests, and mountains, but from a resource found in a less natural setting—or, more precisely, under it. The land under towns and cities is also a natural resource, although it does not seem like it, in part because tax assessors lump land and buildings into a single category called "real estate." But from an economic perspective, land and buildings differ radically.

Mason Gaffney, a longtime resource tax analyst, explains the difference this way: the value of a piece of land that has a building on it is "what would remain after a good fire." It is what an investor would be willing to pay for the empty site in order to redevelop it. The more profitable the potential development, the more valuable the land. The land thus owes its value purely to societal factors such as the desirability of a neighborhood, convenient access to a subway station, or a healthy local economy—or as real estate agents put it, it is "location, location, location." Nothing the owner can do (outside the political sphere), in contrast, can affect the value. So if a parcel's value does rise—say, because a new park is built nearby—then the owner benefits from the work and investment of other people, work and investment that is often funded by taxpayers.[13]

The value of a building, on the other hand, is what would be lost during the fire. Buildings, unlike land, are easily destroyed—but also easily repaired and replaced. Thus while homeowners, for example, cannot raise the value of land, they can raise the value of their homes. They can repair roofs or insulate walls. They can add back porches or upgrade windows.

Since buildings and land differ economically, the standard property tax is really two contrasting taxes spliced together. Taxes on buildings are taxes on work and entrepreneurship. They reduce the supply of buildings, raising home and office prices and penalizing urban development and redevelopment. A seemingly modest 2 percent property tax on buildings, for instance, can ultimately raise the cost of erecting a new structure by 40 percent since it is applied every year.[14]

Taxes on land values, however, resemble fair charges for public oil concessions. Unlike most taxes, they do not penalize economic development. To see this, put yourself in the shoes of a London developer. You have limited funds that you can use to put an office building on a prime downtown site, now a parking lot, or in an inconvenient industrial zone at the edge of the city. Because you will only be able to charge low office rents at the perimeter site, you will have little money left over after construction costs and reasonable profits to pay for land. The right to develop on this land—which is to say, the land itself—would be worth little to you or any other developer.

Higher office rents on the downtown project, in contrast, would generate an extra $10 million in profits. So presumably the parking lot owner would demand $10 million as payment for the site. That $10 million represents the location value of the land, a product not of the current owner's entrepreneurship but of the health of the London economy. For the parking lot owner, it would be pure windfall.

Now suppose that a land value tax is levied throughout greater London. The taxes on the nearly worthless perimeter land would be negligible, and so would not noticeably raise the cost of building and operating an office complex there. But if you bought the valuable downtown lot, you would have to pay substantial land value taxes each year. As a result, you could only spare

$6 million up front for the land itself. If the current owner demanded more, you would develop on the perimeter. Thus the owner of the parking lot would have little choice but to sell the land for $6 million, fully absorbing the land value tax of $4 million. Then from your point of view, land taxes would rise but land prices would fall to compensate, so the downtown project's bottom line would stay the same.

In the end, the land value tax would not discourage you from building downtown. Nor would it affect office rents once the building was completed, just as fair royalty charges for Kazakhstan's oil deposits would not affect the price or amount of extracted petroleum. Those who reap the windfalls would pay the windfall taxes.

Thus the part of the standard property tax that applies to land does not discourage economic development. The part that applies to buildings does slow development. This is why towns and cities in much of Denmark and in parts of Australia, Colombia, Indonesia, Jamaica, New Zealand, Pennsylvania, South Africa, and South Korea have partly or fully shifted their property taxes onto land during the twentieth century. Many have found, not surprisingly, that this shift encourages more construction on central sites, adding vitality to downtowns and slowing the flight of jobs and homes to the suburbs. Higher land value taxes may also prompt land speculators, who by nature may be more interested in gambling with land rather than developing it, to embark on construction projects to help pay their tax bills—projects they had never noticed could be profitable.[15]

Yet careful examinations of land value taxation have been hindered by the conceptual underpinnings of modern economics. Pre-twentieth-century economics saw three factors of production: land, labor, and capital. Today's "neoclassical" economics, born of a civilization that sees itself as less dependent on nature, has in practice often banished land to obscurity as a subcategory of capital, in the process confusing natural assets with human-made ones. The great classical economists—Adam Smith, David Ricardo, John Stuart Mill—all saw land as the most deserving of taxation among their three factors of production. Adam Smith wrote that:

> [Land] rents ... are a species of revenue which the owner, in many cases, enjoys without any care or attention of his own. Though a part of this revenue should be taken from him in order to defray the expenses of the State, no discouragement will thereby be given to any sort of industry. The annual produce of the land and labor of the society, the real wealth and revenue of the great body of the people, might be the same after such a tax as before. [Land] rents ... are, therefore, perhaps, the species of revenue which can best bear to have a peculiar tax imposed upon them.[16]

In the twentieth century, Melbourne, Australia, has been one of the best laboratories for the study of shifts toward land value taxation. Half of the 56 local governments within the metropolitan area eliminated the buildings tax between 1919 and 1986 and increased the land value tax. Today, not surprisingly, districts that do not tax buildings have more of them. In fact, they have population and housing densities half again as high as those with conventional property taxes, even after controlling for distance from the city center, amount of industry, and other relevant factors; the difference is greatest for districts that switched earliest. And more construction within city limits has reduced pressure for expansion beyond.[17]

Pittsburgh, Pennsylvania, is another prominent land tax experimenter. It increased the land portion of its property tax in 1979 and 1980 as part of a policy package meant to launch a renaissance of commercial development in the city's core. During the 1980s the rate of new construction in central Pittsburgh exceeded that of the previous 20 years by 70 percent. The higher land value tax deserves some of the credit, argue Wallace B. Oates and Robert M. Schwab, economists at the University of Maryland, if only because it allowed the city to raise revenue in a way that did not discourage economic activity. In contrast, Philadelphia, at the opposite end of the state, has raised its wage tax in recent decades, chasing tens of thousands of jobs into the suburbs or other cities, according to several studies.[18]

When the economies and populations of land-taxing towns and cities have grown, or when municipal governments have built roads and other infrastructure, local land values have climbed. Land tax revenues have increased too, reducing the need for other taxes. After the government of Cali, Colombia, for example, announced plans to extend infrastructure to swampland on its current perimeter, land in the area (mostly owned by cattle ranchers and drug traffickers) shot up in value a thousandfold. In response to such private profiteering from public investment, the Colombian Congress decided in 1997 to allow local governments to apply stiff capital gains taxes on land to recapture the value increases for the public purse. Local officials are now working to implement the law.[19]

If a map of the world were drawn with each hectare scaled in proportion to its commercial value, cities would nearly fill the continents. The lion's share of land value, and hence the revenue potential from taxing it, lies in towns and cities. Nevertheless, shifting toward land value taxation may also make sense in rural areas, although it needs to be implemented with particular caution.

By itself, a high land value tax can put owners of land with development potential in a cash flow bind if they do not develop their commercially valuable land. In 1997, for example, Marylou Whitney, doyenne of upstate New York's high society, stirred controversy when she announced plans to subdivide and develop part of her family's 21,000-hectare estate within Adirondack Park in order to pay property taxes on the rest of it. Her real intention may have been to raise the state's eventual bid for the land, but Whitney's announcement highlighted a dilemma that a rising land tax could create for thousands of less affluent people who want to resist development pressure. It could give them no choice but to sell out.[20]

To reduce cash flow pressure, governments can allow cash-strapped landowners to defer tax payments until they sell, as many states in the United States already do. But containing sprawl also requires more direct solutions: even with low land taxes, development pressure is hard to resist. Zoning rules, such as the official development boundary around Portland, Oregon, will help. So will termination of infrastructure subsidies that make sprawl seem cheap. (See Chapter 5.) Also useful are tradable permit systems like the one New Jersey has deployed, which caps development in the Pinelands region and concentrates construction in town centers. (See Chapter 10.)[21]

Landowners can take initiative too, by donating or selling "conservation easements"—the right to build on their property—to private or governmental conservation agencies, which then agree to never exercise the rights. In the United States, a 1985 survey of 500 such programs found easements on 750,000 hectares (1.85 million acres), a quarter of which had been donated outright. Such charitable donations are deductible from U.S. income taxes. And by reducing development potential, all these restraints lower the market value, and hence the tax liability, of protected land.[22]

For different reasons, land value taxes also need to be applied with care in agricultural heartlands that are free of development pressure. Unlike town and city land, farmland owes its value to more than location. Though no amount of human effort could turn the tundra of Siberia into a breadbasket to rival Kazakhstan's, farmland owners can nonetheless influence the value of their tracts somewhat. They can lower values, for example, by farming in ways that deplete soil nutrients or speed soil erosion. Since farmers' liability for land value tax would fall as their land degraded, land value taxes can have the perverse effect of rewarding poor husbandry. One solution is to supplement taxes on land values with taxes on soil-harming practices—in essence royalty charges on soil mining. Alternatively, governments can subsidize soil-protecting activities, as most industrial countries already do. (See Chapter 8.)[23]

*   *   *   *

The revenue potential in charging full price for public resources and taxing land values has been little studied, and so is hard to estimate. One proposal put forward by the New Economics Foundation in London calculated that half the tax revenue in Great Britain—some $140 billion a year—could be raised through a land value tax set at a hefty 75 percent of annual rental value. Ninety-eight percent of this would come from land used for housing, offices, factories, or mining, not for farming. Combined with a sizable energy tax, this could fund the abolition of all taxes on income, payroll, sales, profits, and buildings, and also pay for a "Citizen's Income" in the form of stipend checks for several hundred or thousand pounds for each resident each year.[24]

Statistics on property taxes in industrial countries today give a sense of the revenue potential in more moderate, politically realistic rent-capturing proposals. In Western Europe, real estate taxation is light overall, generating about 5 percent of tax revenue, and it applies mainly to buildings, not land. Property is more heavily taxed in North America and Japan, yielding about 12 percent of revenue, but studies of several localities in Canada and the United States suggest that land values are underassessed relative to buildings, yielding effectively lower tax rates. If property taxes in North America and Japan were replaced with pure land value taxes and if land value taxes reached the same level in the rest of the world, they could generate 12 percent of global tax revenue, or $900 billion a year.[25]

Detailed regional proposals have yielded similar estimates. In a draft tax overhaul plan for the state of California, Clifford Cobb, an economist associated with the San Francisco–based group Redefining Progress, has proposed that the share of property taxes in local, state, and federal revenue be increased from 10 percent to 14 percent (a rise from 28 to 40 percent of state and local revenue only), and that the property taxes be gradually turned into land value taxes exclusively. The plan also proposes getting another 1.4 percent of the tax take through charges for water withdrawals from rivers. State and local taxes on sales, income, and profits would be terminated, with the remaining gap filled by levies on energy and pollution.[26]

Northwest Environment Watch has put forward a similar tax shift plan for Idaho, Oregon, Washington, and British Columbia. It envisions turning property taxes, which currently provide 10 percent of the tax receipts to all levels of government, into land value taxes that would raise the same revenue. NEW also calls for raising another 2 percent of revenue from taxes on resource rents from the region's minerals, fish, and cheap hydropower. And it proposes major increases in taxes on environmental damage. Together, the new taxes would nearly supplant other state and local taxes.[27]

★　　★　　★　　★

Refracted through the prism of the environment, tax and spending policies spread along a spectrum according to whether they are ecologically harmful or helpful. Subsidies for fishing and fossil fuel use, among others, occupy the damaging end. At the other extreme appear environmentally beneficial subsidies, such as those for renewable energy research, and environmentally beneficial taxes, such as those on pollution—the subjects of the next two chapters.

Resource royalties and land value taxes, however, cluster around the neutral center of the spectrum. Royalties do not discourage economic activity, but by the same token they do not protect the environment much either. Land value taxes are less neutral, but can swing in either direction depending on the context. Especially if combined with tax cuts for buildings, they can stimulate construction—which can be bad in rural areas, but is good for cities fighting to retain jobs and residents.

Thus although rent-capturing levies are promising—especially in developing countries—as a revenue source that does little economic harm, they need to be combined with strong environmental policies. On the other hand, even in a sustainable economy some water, timber, and minerals will be extracted, and land values will still rise, generating ample windfalls that can be diverted into the public purse to replace other taxes. Overall, to make maximum, responsible use of the environment as a revenue source, governments need to shift from the damaging end of the environmental impact spectrum toward the center and the protective end. The result would be tax policy that is good for both the environment and the economy.

8

Paying the Non-Polluter

Slashing environmentally harmful subsidies will begin to mend the damage that fiscal policy has done to the planet. But such activities as driving and pumping groundwater, even when they are not subsidized, impose hidden costs on this and future generations, and remain falsely cheap. So subsidy reform alone will not put the global economy on a sustainable footing. Likewise, capturing more resource rents will facilitate economic development by allowing cuts in conventional taxes. But even this shift will not take on environmental problems directly. Driving and water use will still seem falsely cheap.

How is fiscal policy to protect the environment more effectively? Two ways: either by paying people not to harm, it or by charging them for doing so. The second strategy—making the polluter pay—is ultimately the more effective of the two, and is discussed in the next chapter. The first strategy nevertheless merits careful use, especially to speed progress in clean technologies.

If traffic police handed out bonuses to people who stopped at red lights rather than ticketing those who did not, they would drive governments into insolvency. By the same token, any society that tries to subsidize itself into sustainability will bankrupt itself. Nevertheless, it will always be easier to win political support for environmentally protective subsidies than for taxes and regulations—as President Clinton found out to his chagrin in 1993. Just months before, a 1.5¢-per-kilowatt-hour tax credit for electricity from wind and biomass had sailed through the U.S. Congress, sped by the momentary oil scare Saddam Hussein had given the country. But Clinton's new proposal for an energy tax, which would have handicapped conventional sources by only 0.3¢ more—one fifth as much as the tax credit—fell victim to vociferous industry and popular opposition, giving the new president a rude legislative baptismal.[1]

In the short term, environmentalists are more likely to make progress by advocating subsidies for "good" behavior rather pushing for taxes on "bad" behavior. As Clinton discovered, subsidies for tiny industries tend not to ruffle political feathers the way taxes on established ones do.

Subsidies for environmentally protective activities have economic advantages as well. Contrast the impacts of an energy tax much larger than the one Clinton proposed—one that would double the price of fossil fuels and nuclear power—with a subsidy that would halve the price of wind power, a technology with only a sliver of market share. A tax big enough to double energy prices would have to be phased in slowly so as not to jolt an economy into a tailspin. The subsidy, on the other hand, would give wind power the same advantage without disturbing the economy much—most companies' energy bills would not change—so it could be ramped up quickly. And technologies, like children, benefit most from early nurturing. (See Chapter 13.) Thus for rapid, sustained environmental gain, the best strategy is to combine subsidies and taxes. Subsidies help launch the process of change; taxes assure its long-term continuance.

Environmentally protective subsidies can also make sense for reasons of fairness. To complement payments to low-income families to cover heating bills, for example, the U.S. government offers some funding to help them insulate their homes and upgrade the efficiency of their furnaces. In doing so, the government lowers the heating bills it is helping to pay. If it eliminated these conservation subsidies and relied solely on taxes to discourage energy use, many poor families would feel the pinch. By the same token, if policymakers in developing countries decide that energy subsidies are a good tool for mitigating poverty, they will succeed better by subsidizing all the forms of energy used by the poor that are practical to subsidize. That would include renewable technologies such as solar panels, which are safer and cleaner than kerosene and particularly appropriate in areas not reached by power lines.[2]

Nevertheless, environmentally "good" subsidies, like "bad" ones, deserve skeptical examination. It is just as easy to design wasteful subsidies as useful ones.

★   ★   ★   ★

To date, some of the largest ecologically beneficial subsidies have been offered to farmers. Industrial countries have begun to view farmers not just as producers of food but as potential stewards of the rural landscape. The 1996 U.S. farm bill, for example, authorized spending $2.2 billion between 1996 and 2002 on "agri-environmental" measures, including payments to farmers to keep highly erodible soils, wetlands, and other wildlife habitat out of production. Programs like these were credited with keeping soil erosion in the United States a substantial 1 billion tons a year below what it otherwise would have been in the early 1990s. Similar programs have proliferated in the European Union, costing $1.7 billion in 1995 alone. Historically, though, most such programs have fallen short of their full potential because they have emphasized reducing crop surpluses by idling the most productive land rather than the most fragile or ecologically valuable land. Moreover, though the funding levels for these programs are impressive, they equal less than 1 percent of the subsidies that stimulate crop production. Reforming those supports would probably help taxpayers and the environment much more.[3]

Subsidies for mass transit are similarly overwhelmed by powerful economic forces, including other subsidies. When governments spend more on sprawl-inducing infrastructure than they charge for it, when other costs of driving—from traffic jams to air pollution—are also hidden from drivers, and when zoning laws prohibit compact, pedestrian-friendly development, transit cannot compete unaided. In the United States, governments spend $13.5 billion a year subsidizing transit. The automobile industry spends nearly that much in the country just on advertising. Worldwide, it is almost unheard of for an urban transit system to pay its own way. Only a handful of city transit systems, including those in Hong Kong, London, and Santiago, manage to earn more in fares than they spend on employee salaries and day-to-day maintenance expenses—but even that comparison excludes spending on long-term investments such as new subway tunnels and buses.[4]

Overall, subsidies for environmental protection are likely to falter when they attack the economic status quo head-on. Trillion-dollar economies systemically biased against the environment by hundred-billion-dollar subsidies and subject only to patchwork environmental laws will not be disturbed by billion-dollar pinpricks. The best use of subsidies is more strategic: to speed the development and use of promising technologies to the point where they can compete better on their own—to the point where market forces can propel them much further than the subsidies alone can.

Several market biases against new technologies argue for government support. Commercial benefits from the most important scientific discoveries can take decades to materialize and may never accrue to the original researchers. As a result, many businesses, especially small ones, shy away from investing in basic R&D. Basic research, moreover, is only the first step on the difficult road to commercialization. New technologies like wind turbines often struggle to compete with established ones, such as fossil fuel power plants. It is harder for small companies with new technologies to survive price wars or business downturns, to invest in large factories that capture economies of scale, and to gain the confidence of investors and customers. On the other hand, big corporations with large sunk investments in current technology are often reluctant to innovate.[5]

Targeted government incentives, ideally transitional ones, can help makers of promising and environmentally sound technologies overcome such obstacles to viability. At their best, targeted subsidies work with the grain of culture, technology, and economics rather than against it, leveraging small amounts of money into enough innovation that the subsidies themselves become unnecessary. The strength of such subsidies lies not in the brute force of megabucks but in careful design and experimentation. They are more catalytic than coercive.

But in practice, unfortunately, technology development and commercialization subsidies have compiled a poor track record. An important example of both their strengths and their risks is provided by the Green Revolution—the high-output farming system that gained active government support in developing countries like Mexico and India in the 1960s. Pesticides, fertilizer, and water were practically given away, through favorable tariffs, subsidized loans, and government-funded irrigation projects. The Green Revolution did persuade millions of risk-averse farmers to grow new, high-yielding grain varieties, which reduced hunger even among rapidly growing populations. On the other hand, it also had serious environmental and social side effects, such as inequities in access to groundwater irrigation in India, as described in Chapter 5.[6]

And though the revolution is now largely complete, some subsidies that helped spawn it persist, distorting such decisions as when chemical applications are worth the costs and health risks. In a 1985 study, World Resources Institute economist Robert Repetto analyzed the effects of pesticide subsidies on farmers' decisions, using data from experimental rice plots in the

Philippines. He showed that without subsidies, heavy pesticide applications there were a losing proposition: an additional dose would cost 108 pesos more per hectare than it earned through greater rice growth. With a 50-percent pesticide subsidy, however, the cost turned into a gain of 434 pesos per hectare. Thus subsidies can tip the balance toward practices that, though potentially useful in moderation, also endanger farmers and their land.[7]

Although pesticide and fertilizer supports are still found in many countries in Africa, Asia, and Latin America—India, for example, spent $1.7 billion subsidizing fertilizer use in 1995—many nations have also reduced their supports. Indonesia slashed its pesticide subsidies, which covered 85 percent of pesticide costs in 1985, to zero in 1989. Some pests had actually thrived after evolving resistance to the chemicals— while their predators did not. In 1976, for instance, a brown planthopper infestation destroyed enough rice to feed 2.5 million Indonesians for a year. Stung by such experiences, many Asian countries now support integrated pesticide management, which minimizes chemical use in favor of techniques such as planting insect-resistant crop strains and manipulating pest-predator populations. After Indonesia's subsidy termination, pesticide use fell two thirds, but rice production did not skip a beat.[8]

One realm in which subsidies for environmentally beneficial technologies have worked fairly well is that of energy efficiency. Three of the most successful technologies supported by the U.S. Department of Energy (DOE)—heat-reflecting windows, electronic ballasts for fluorescent lights, and variable-capacity supermarket refrigeration systems—are now saving enough energy to easily justify DOE's entire $425-million efficiency R&D budget.[9]

Though tiny, the $23.7-million public investment in these three technologies was pivotal to their development. In all three cases, small companies that would have had difficulty embarking on such risky research on their own vied for the initial grants. Only when their efforts bore fruit did established firms take notice. Most likely, then, it would have taken much longer for the technologies to have developed without government help. The efficient windows, ballasts, and refrigerators already sold will save $8.9 billion in fuel costs over their lifetimes—375 times what DOE spent developing them.[10]

A key circumstance behind these impressive numbers is that with businesses and consumers spending so much on energy—$500 billion per year in the United States alone—an R&D grant that cuts energy bills only one part in a thousand can quickly save enough money to make up for dozens of failed grants. Public investments in new ways of producing, rather than saving, energy have not paid off nearly as well. Western industrial countries alone spent $55 billion (1997 dollars) on energy R&D between 1990 and 1996. Forty-three percent of that was devoted to a single technology: traditional nuclear fission. Another 22 percent went for advanced fission and fusion technologies, which have been forever on the horizon. Only 9 percent went for renewable energy technologies, whose use is exploding in percentage terms. Thus the energy sources that are the most polluting and slowest-growing received the most support. (See Figure 8–1.)[11]

The heavy funding for nuclear fission in particular has amounted to a permanent subsidy for the adoption of a new technology, a paradox that hints at failure. The global nuclear market has foundered since the 1970s on high costs and concern about nuclear accidents and radioactive waste disposal. In the United States, the last time a plant order was placed and not subsequently canceled was 1973. The U.S. government has spent $35 billion (in 1997 dollars) on fission R&D since 1948; despite this and other subsidies, only 1 in 50 American utility executives would now consider buying the technology, according to a recent survey. Worldwide, nuclear power generation is set to decline early in the new century as utilities decommission existing plants.[12]

Funding for renewable energy research has met with its share of failures too. DOE, for example, has sunk $1.4 billion over the last 20 years into the development

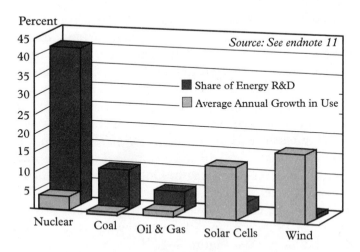

FIGURE 8–1. *Energy R&D Funding Priorities versus Trends in Commercial Use, Industrial Countries, 1990–96*

of a solar "tower of power": an army of 2,000 computer-controlled mirrors arrayed in the Mojave Desert, all bouncing sunlight toward a steam generator atop a 100-meter tower. The technology may find a place in the country's energy mix someday, but it will probably have trouble competing with simpler rooftop solar panels, which can be mass-produced and exploit one of sunlight's great advantages as an energy source: that it is naturally dispersed. Wind power research has suffered from a similar top-down mentality. Most publicly funded wind research in Germany, Sweden, the United States, and elsewhere has been performed by agencies and aerospace giants culturally predisposed toward pursuing technical sophistication rather than practicality. Their prototypes have usually been neither reliable nor commercially viable.[13]

Tellingly, the world's most successful wind power industries have arisen in countries where governments are spending much less on R&D than on across-the-board production and investment incentives. Germany, for example, requires its utilities to buy wind power at 90 percent of the retail price, guaranteeing a hefty premium of 10¢ per kilowatt-hour. Its wind power industry has flourished since the rule became law in 1991. To the north, Denmark instituted subsidies for wind turbine investment and power generation in 1979, leaving technology choice to turbine buyers. It retired the investment credit in 1989 after advances had driven prices down and pushed installed capacity from next to nothing to nearly 300 megawatts. And the industry continued to thrive.[14]

More recently, Denmark helped India spark a wind revolution of its own. Inspired by a demonstration windfarm built by the Danish foreign aid agency, and spurred by generous tax breaks from the Indian government, local companies jumped into the wind business. At first they imported most of their components, but gradually they drew on the country's own manufacturing strength and its cheaper labor to bring most of the turbine production business within its borders. By 1997 the Indian wind industry had created hundreds of new jobs and had placed fourth in the world in annual capacity additions, behind Germany, Denmark, and Spain. The striking contrast with India's stagnant, problem-plagued nuclear program suggests that wind technology is easily a better fit for much of the developing world.[15]

People working at the grassroots level, who have less money but a better sense of what is needed, have also achieved more success in catalyzing change. They too have worked not so much to push technologies out of the laboratory but to pull them into everyday use. A U.S.-based nonprofit called Enersol, for example, founded by a former nuclear and coal plant engineer, has parlayed modest grants from the World Bank, the Rockefeller Foundation, and other donors into the creation of a nearly self-sustaining solar industry in the Dominican Republic.[16]

Enersol's customers are rural peasants beyond the reach of the nation's electricity grid. The nonprofit does not pay for the imported solar panels, but instead has established a revolving loan fund that lets buyers spread payments over several years. The subsidy in this case is modest: some funding to train marketers and system installers, and the willingness to risk losing seed money should buyers default. Nevertheless, the readiness to take risks that conventional banks will not gives the program tremendous leverage. By 1993, Enersol had brought solar power to 4,000 families and put local people to work. Other organizations are now copying this approach in China, Honduras, Indonesia, Sri Lanka, Zimbabwe, and elsewhere.[17]

These forays into technology development and commercialization hold several important lessons. The first is that building expiration dates into subsidies for specific technologies is often warranted to guard against their becoming entrenched despite failure—or successful to the point of obsolescence. The second is that bottom-up technology commercialization typically works better than top-down because it tends to respond better to practical imperatives such as making equipment reliable and meeting customer needs. The last lesson is that, given governments' poor track records in picking winners, it often makes more sense to favor broad-gauge subsidies over R&D. By focusing more on results, governments can lessen the risk of subsidizing failures, and leave it to the market to pick winners.

★ ★ ★ ★

Another kind of environmentally protective subsidy is for pollution control and environmental cleanup. Brazil, India, Mexico, and most western industrial nations and former Eastern bloc countries offer tax breaks or accelerated depreciation (which allows companies to defer some taxes to later years) for spending on smokestack scrubbers and water treatment plants.[18]

The Netherlands has developed pollution control incentives perhaps to the fullest. Its tax breaks apply specifically to purchases of 400 or so technologies officially listed as cutting-edge, whether they recycle concrete or generate ozone for use as a chlorine-free bleaching agent in papermaking. When these technologies become commonplace, they get bumped off the list by newer entries, creating a steady prod for industry to push the technological envelope. In another path-breaking step, the Dutch government now grants complete tax exemption for mutual funds that invest in "green" projects such as wind farms and pollution control R&D.[19]

The Dutch programs again illustrate how subsidies for environmental protection have both strengths and weaknesses. The subsidies won political support with relative ease and are doing environmental good, but are ultimately less effective than direct regulation and taxation of pollution. They make some polluting activities—though low-polluting ones—seem artificially cheap. More worrisome, they sometimes foster an incremental, end-of-the-pipe mentality in pollution control.

Yet the best, most cost-effective way to clean up pollution is usually to avoid generating it in the first place. The top pollution prevention strategies often do not involve advanced add-on technologies like sophisticated water filters, but simple steps like fine-tuning equipment and switching to safer chemicals. In the early 1990s, for instance, a Martin Marietta plant in Denver, Colorado, that builds spacecraft decided to stop using an ozone-depleting degreaser called TCA. The substitute it eventually settled on, trade-named Daraclean 282, does not deplete ozone, is reusable, and is biodegradable. Studying alternatives and making the switch cost $270,000, but materials and waste disposal costs dropped $200,000 a year, providing a quick, environmentally sound payback. The company boosted its bottom line further by replacing a toxic solvent with a more natural chemical: essentially, diluted orange juice.[20]

The very difficulty of envisioning such ad hoc, often low-tech environmental solutions makes designing subsidies to support them nearly impossible. The only practical way for fiscal policy to make this kind of pollution prevention more profitable is to make the absence of it more expensive—by taxing pollution directly. Indeed, one spur to Martin Marietta's quick decision to drop TCA was that the step would also cut its annual tax bill by $400,000, because the U.S. government has taxed ozone-destroying chemicals since 1990. Environmentally protective subsidies are politically popular and are good at incubating technologies, but among fiscal policies, only taxes can attack head-on the fundamental problem that environmental harm is one of the cheapest, most socially costly activities any business can engage in.[21]

9

Taxing the Polluter

Since the beginning of civilization, tax codes have been both artifacts and instruments of history. Just about the earliest snapshots we have of the birth of writing, numbers, and money—5,000-year-old clay tablets unearthed in Iraq—appear to have recorded tax payments. Like the priest-kings of ancient Sumeria who extracted crop surpluses from farmers to support their cities, latter-day legislators have relied on effective taxation to maintain government power and stability, and thus to preserve civilization. Rulers' overriding concern has almost always been to perform the unpopular act of taxation with the least risk to their own careers. "The art of taxation consists of plucking the goose so as to get the most feathers with the least hissing," observed

Jean Baptiste Colbert, the finance minister charged with keeping Louis XIV's opulent court afloat.[1]

For the governed, meanwhile, the goal has usually been to avoid as much plucking as possible—or at least make sure everyone is being equally plucked. Public demands for fairness have in turn injected a note of principle into the politics of tax policy. Like history books, today's tax codes were written by the winners of countless policy battles, both political and ideological. What has resulted is a mix of principle, pragmatism, and anachronism. As John Kay and Mervyn King, two authorities on the British tax system, succinctly put it, "No one would have designed a tax system like this, and no one did."[2]

Tax codes, in other words, make about as much sense as history—which is not to say no sense, but not complete sense either. Among their greatest failings is that they barely penalize activities that do economic harm, including pollution, while heavily taxing ones that do economic good, including work and investment. Indeed, more than any other shortcoming in the world's fiscal policies—more than the high subsidies for destructive activities, the low subsidies for relatively benign ones, and the low capture rates on natural windfalls—this lopsidedness is what makes fiscal policies so destructive of human health and the environment today.

* * * *

What has most shaped modern tax codes is the need to raise historically unprecedented amounts of revenue in ways that are perceived as broadly fair. Especially since World War II, public budgets have mushroomed in western nations, reflecting the climbing cost of weapons and war, the expansion of social welfare programs, and the introduction of subsidies for industries such as agriculture and energy. To fund this growth, public officials haltingly adopted broad-based taxes on income, profits, wages, and sales—all taxes with little historical precedent, all designed at least in principle to spread the cost of government according to people's ability to pay.[3]

Austria, the Netherlands, and Great Britain, for example, made early use of a tax on personal income to fund wars against Napoleon. In Britain, the House of Commons reintroduced the tax in the 1840s and cut import duties on grain, butter, and cheese in order to quell unrest among city dwellers verging on starvation. It was again a supposedly temporary measure, but food riots and rising demands on the treasury made the tax shift permanent. In the United States, the income tax was first pressed into service during the Civil War, later struck down by the Supreme Court, and finally backed by constitutional amendment in 1913. Broad-based taxes have since ballooned to generate the majority of government receipts in industrial countries, equal to some 30–50 percent of total economic output. (See Table 9–1.)[4]

In developing countries, broad-based taxes on income and profits tend to be less practical because most incomes are low and unrecorded, while widespread corruption often impedes tax enforcement. As a result, typically 3 percent of the population in developing countries pay income tax, compared with 60–80 percent in industrial ones. Instead (though generalizations are almost impossible), developing-country governments get more of their revenue from taxes on trade and sales of certain products, particularly easy-to-track imports.[5]

Table 9–1. Tax Revenue, Total and by Source,
Selected Countries, 1994

| Country | Total Revenue | | Sources[1] | | |
	Per Person	Share of GDP	Profits, Wages, and Income[2]	Sales and Trade[3]	Property
	(dollars per year[4])	(percent)	(percent share of total tax revenue)		
Germany	7,512	39	69	29	3
United States	7,040	28	70	18	12
Japan	6,235	28	73	16	12
Russia	1,621	37	58[5]	30[5]	12[5,6]
Thailand[7]	1,202	17	34	62	3[6]
Brazil[7]	1,136	18	66	29	7[6]
India[7]	121	9	58	37	4[6]

[1]Some rows do not total 100 percent due to rounding. [2]Includes employee and employer contributions to social security funds. [3]Includes taxes on turnover, sales, and value added, on specific products, and on imports and exports. [4]Converted from domestic currencies on the basis of purchasing-power parities. [5]Data for 1993. [6]Includes other taxes, and, for Russia, nontax revenue. [7]Central government only.
SOURCE: See endnote 4.

Of course, just because there are reasons tax codes are the way they are does not mean they are beyond criticism. The question too rarely asked about taxes is this: What are the best things to tax? The obvious answer is that societies should start by taxing things they want less of—like resource waste—not things they want more of—like employment. Benjamin Franklin observed that taxation is as inevitable as death. But there is freedom in what to tax. So why should tax codes discourage job creation, for example, any more than necessary if other parts of government are striving to stimulate it? Why shouldn't taxes discourage pollution, especially since large bureaucracies are already being funded—with tax dollars—to do the same thing? The idea that people should bear responsibility for the harm they do others is the cornerstone of most moral and legal codes. Yet it is remarkably absent from the world's tax codes.

Remedying that absence is the single most important step policymakers can take in conforming fiscal policy to environmental principles. Only taxes can bring consumers and businesses face to face with the full costs of the environmental harm they cause. And only when they face those costs can they realistically be expected to make choices that also make sense for society.

Famed British economist Arthur Cecil Pigou was the first to advocate taxes on environmental harm. In his 1920 classic, *The Economics of Welfare*, he pointed to the hidden costs of smoke pouring from factories and fireplaces in Manchester, England. Costs of extra laundry cleaning, of artificial lighting necessitated by darkened air, and of repairs to corroded buildings had been estimated at £290,000 per year (about $10 million at today's prices). As a result, a steelmaker might have made £100 worth of steel with a furnaceful of coal, and done £200 in damage in the process—a gain for the company, but a net loss for the city. In effect, pollution victims were subsidizing pollution causers, and making society as a whole poorer.[6]

Modern parallels abound. Fertilizers and manure from farms in the American heartland drain, along with industrial effluents, into the Mississippi River and from there to the Gulf of Mexico, where they produce an oxygen-depleted "dead zone" the size of New Jersey, in which few fish survive—and no shrimper can thrive. Ozone pollution, particularly from cars, sends 50,000 people to the hospital each year in the Washington, D.C., area. And for every dollar spent extracting natural gas in one Malaysian project, roughly another dollar of harm is imposed on future generations by depriving them of cheap energy at a time when it will be scarcer.[7]

In all these cases, it is inconceivable that the winners and the losers—who number in the millions or are not even born yet—could resolve the problems on their own, through courts or over the bargaining table. The solution to such problems, Pigou argued, is for governments to intervene, by using taxes to make people who create environmental problems absorb the costs of the harm they do. Then when they tally up the costs and benefits of environmental harm for themselves, they would have to take society's interests into account. If a £100 worth of steel suddenly cost more than £200 to make because of pollution taxes, any sensibly run company would cut pollution to protect its bottom line. An additional benefit, appreciated more recently, is that taxes can alert managers and scientists to new markets—for solar panels or pollution prevention devices, for instance—helping to steer technological development in an environmentally sound direction. (See Chapter 13.)[8]

Many people accustomed to thinking of taxes as a necessary evil will be surprised to learn that some taxes can do economic good. But when it comes to environmental harm, it is economically better to tax than not to tax.

Pigou's sensible prescription became received wisdom within economics, but most of the bricks in the environmental policy edifice built during the last 30 years have been fired from the stuff of regulations, not taxes. To be sure, regulations have scored important successes. In Western Europe, for example, regulators can point to a 47-percent reduction in sulfur emissions between 1970 and 1993, due substantially to rules requiring scrubbers in coal plants. In the United States, tightened tailpipe emissions standards for new cars and light trucks made catalytic converters universal over the same time span, cutting nitrogen oxide emissions 6 percent, carbon monoxide 33 percent, and volatile organic compounds 54 percent, all despite a 44-percent increase in driving.[9]

Nevertheless, regulations are increasingly being pushed beyond their limits. Because they often focus on means rather than ends—for example, by prescribing the use of particular kinds of water filters—they tend to discourage innovation. And though they often work well when there is a front-runner solution (such as catalytic converters for cars), they tend to break down in the face of complexity. A joint study by the U.S. Environmental Protection Agency (EPA) and Amoco Corporation documented one telling absurdity at the oil company's Yorktown, Virginia, refinery. Regulations required Amoco to spend $31 million on a wastewater treatment plant to stop airborne emissions of benzene, a carcinogen. Meanwhile, the rules failed to cover benzene emissions from a nearby loading dock— emissions that could have been reduced as much for just $6 million. As one exasperated refinery official put it, "Give us a goal to meet rather than all the regulations....That worked in the 1970's, when the pollution problems were much more visible and simpler. It's not working now."[10]

The growing use of environmental taxes is one response to that plea. One of the best and earliest examples is the system of water pollution taxes in the Netherlands. Since 1970, gradually rising charges on emissions of organic material and heavy metals into canals, rivers, and lakes have spurred companies to cut emissions—without dictating how. Between 1976 and the mid-1990s, emissions of cadmium, chromium, copper, lead, mercury, nickel, and zinc into waters managed by regional governments (which adopted the charges earliest) plummeted 72–99 percent—primarily because of the charges, according to statistical analyses. (See Figure 9–1.)[11]

The Dutch example illustrates the strengths of environmental taxes at their best. Companies that could

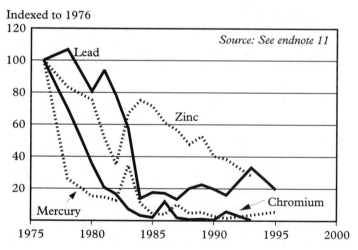

Indexed to 1976

FIGURE 9–1. *Industrial Discharges of Chromium and Zinc, 1976–93, and Lead and Mercury, 1976–95, into Regional Surface Waters, The Netherlands*

prevent pollution most cheaply presumably did so most. Firms would also have passed part of the taxes on to their customers through higher prices, causing them to switch to less-pollution-intensive products. And demand for pollution control equipment has spurred Dutch manufacturers to develop better models, triggering innovations that regulators could never have planned, lowering costs, and turning the country into a global leader in the market. The taxes have in effect sought the path of least economic resistance—of least cost—in cleaning up the country's waters.[12]

★   ★   ★   ★

As an alternative to taxes, governments can auction off limited numbers of permits for the right to pollute or deplete resources. A company that then decides to pollute or deplete more than it is initially entitled to has to buy extra permits from firms that agree to do so less. This approach, suggested by ecological economist Kenneth Boulding in 1964, began to be used in the 1980s. To phase out the use of ozone-depleting chlorofluorocarbons (CFCs), for instance, in 1989 Singapore began to distribute on a quarterly basis declining numbers of permits for producing or importing the chemicals. It gave half the permits to companies for free, based on past CFC use, and auctioned the rest to the highest bidders. It does essentially the same for new cars, to control the crowded city-state's automobile fleet. In 1992, the cost of a permit represented about a quarter of the price of a new Honda Civic. That is a steep charge, but Singaporeans have it to thank every time they catch a bus downtown at rush hour and find the streets unclogged.[13]

The United States has become a leader in permit

trading. In 1990, it created the world's largest system in order to control emissions of sulfur dioxide, a contributor to acid rain. The system is capping emissions after 2000 at half the 1980 rate. Trading activity started slow, but has "doubled every year," according to Brian McLean, EPA's top acid rain official. The volume of trades—some $1.2 billion a year—now exceeds that for some more mainstream commodities, such as soft red winter wheat.[14]

During the legislative battle over the bill that started the trading system, industry had predicted the permit price would settle at $1,650 per ton. EPA put the figure around $660, and environmental groups estimated $330. All were wrong. Today the price is about $100. Cutting emissions, in other words, has proved far cheaper than almost anyone expected, so companies have been unwilling to spend much in the permit market in order to emit more. Even companies that do not trade have more flexibility in meeting emissions requirements than most regulations give them. They can install sulfur-filtering "scrubbers," switch to low-sulfur coal, or opt for natural gas. "You don't need a large volume of trades to have an impact," observed James Potts, a vice-president of the Potomac Electric Power Company in Washington, D.C. "When we went out for competitive bids for lower sulfur coal...those bids came in very, very competitive." Sulfur scrubber prices have tumbled, and so have rail freight charges for coal delivery (though railroad deregulation deserves some of the credit for that). The U.S. General Accounting Office, the federal government's auditing arm, has predicted that the trading system will save power companies $1.9–3.1 billion a year by 2002.[15]

But the system has a downside. Rather than auctioning off the permits, worth billions of dollars, the U.S. government has taken the politically easier—if more usual—course of giving them away in proportion to how much each company emitted in an earlier year. In doing so, the government is subsidizing established firms for past emissions even as it taxes them for current ones. That handicaps newcomers not grandfathered into the system, and slows the economy by forgoing a chance to cut taxes on work and investment.[16]

Also worrisome have been the effects of the most common strategy for cutting emissions—switching to low-sulfur coal. Some parts of West Virginia coal country, already struggling to cope with the industry's long legacy of landscape destruction and shrinking payrolls, sustained new layoffs as mines containing high-sulfur coal were shut down. (Providing some assistance, Congress has granted these communities special grants for job skills training.) Meanwhile, the coal industry in West Virginia has shifted its operations to low-sulfur deposits—but they tend to lie in broad, thin layers that require destroying much more land to reach. The heightened appetite for low-sulfur coal could lead industry to lop the tops off of half the mountains in West Virginia.[17]

But any acid rain policy would face such tradeoffs—and would ideally minimize them with additional rules. The essential lesson remains that tradable permit systems, much like taxes, allow societies to put the market into service for the environment. Permit systems fix the amount of environmental harm and then let the market set the price. Taxes set the price and let the market decide the amount. (Because of their kinship, these approaches are often referred to collectively as "environmental taxes.") Both can raise revenue with which to cut other taxes. And both allow governments to do what they do best—essentially, set targets for reducing environmental damage—while letting the market in turn do what it does best: find the cheapest ways to get there.

* * * *

The idea of businesses buying and selling the right to pollute strikes some people as morally repugnant. Cartoonist Ruben Bolling lampooned the idea in a strip called "Tales of Market-Driven Crimes." Hero Martin Ryder catches a burglar in his house. Instead of shooting him, he holds him at gunpoint and calls the local crime broker to sell his justifiable homicide. Moments later, a loan shark calls the broker, buys the credit, and puts it to use on an unfortunate client. "The same number of deaths result, but with a more efficient allocation." Many environmentalists argue that since environmental protection should be a moral responsibility, not a commercial opportunity, permit trading is immoral. "Most of us... do care about the motives of our fellow citizen; it matters if someone seeks to protect the community and its land base because they actually care, as opposed to doing it to protect their pocketbooks," write Thomas Michael Power and Paul Rauber in *Sierra*. Strangely, most people who challenge trading endorse its cousin, taxation, even though paying a pollution tax is equivalent to buying the right to pollute from the government. They usually favor regulations too, which also grant rights to pollute—just ones with stipulations.[18]

Nonetheless, the moral skeptics are on target in an important way. Economists usually argue that governments should allow environmental harm just up to the point where the costs to society begin to outweigh the economic benefits. But environmental problems, like most important issues, involve more than costs and benefits: they also involve values and vision, rights and wrongs. Yet if the crime of pollution pays, cost-benefit analysis endorses it. In Pigou's era, London smogs are thought to have taken thousands of lives—2,000 between 1873 and 1892. Today, air pollution affects 1.1 billion city dwellers worldwide, prematurely ending 300,000–700,000 lives a year and causing chronic coughing in at least 50 million children.[19]

Likewise, resource depletion can carry a hidden moral cost: that of depriving future generations of limited natural resources. Today's financial markets force human-made and natural capital to compete on equal footing, even though one is easily replaceable and the other is not. Fish and forests that cannot grow as fast as investments in corporations should be liquidated, the market says, consumed as if there were no tomorrow. As a result, we are on a path to bequeath generations hence a world full of factories, suburban houses, and superhighways—but empty of fish and old-growth forests. No doubt, future generations can develop substitutes for many disappearing resources, but this likelihood does not justify foreclosing their options. How much moral weight to give future generations' claims to topsoil and natural gas is ultimately an ethical question, not just an economic one.

These imponderables are in a sense nothing new: whenever policymakers regulate, or tax, or decide to do nothing, they make difficult tradeoffs between some people's jobs and other people's health, between profits today and profits tomorrow.[20]

Since a society that does not respect people's rights to a safe environment is fundamentally immoral, ethics seriously applied demands that pollution and resource waste be banned now. But abolition is impractical in the short run, for it would freeze the pollution-spewing industrial economy in its tracks. The only way to reconcile morality and practicality is to work steadily toward environmental soundness as a long-term goal by, for example, developing cars powered by solar electricity or building bicycle-friendly neighborhoods. In the short run, policymakers must strive to make the tradeoffs pragmatically, in rough accordance with collective values. The problem with the moral argument against pollution trading is that it does not focus on what matters most—that people have a right to breathe air and drink water not contaminated by other people's wastes. If market-based policies have economic or political advantages in service of protecting these rights, then they should be used.

In practice, pragmatism means not worrying over the exact tax rate or permit allocation. Instead, policymakers can start taxes low and permit allocations at generous levels, and can tighten the constraints over time, in order to send a clear but minimally disruptive signal that economies must move toward configurations that respect people's rights to a healthy environment. Since the full value of human life and health cannot be expressed in dollars, there can in many cases be no right price for pollution and depletion, only a right price trend: upward.

How fast taxes should rise depends on the seriousness of the environmental problem at hand and the difficulty of solving it. The U.S. Congress, for example, set its tax on CFC-11 at $3.02 per kilogram in 1990 (with comparable rates for other ozone depleters) and quadrupled it stepwise to $11.80 by the time CFCs were phased out six years later. Both the urgency of the ozone problem and the increasing availability of CFC substitutes sped the rise. In contrast, curtailing fossil fuel dependence in order to halt climate change will take decades, so a more gradual rise in the price of carbon emissions will be appropriate. That would give carmakers, for instance, breathing room to develop vehicles powered by solar electricity or hydrogen, and give developers and planners time and incentive to make neighborhoods where people can walk more than drive. It would also allow coal companies to shed jobs through attrition and give governments a chance to help low-income people insulate their homes. Whatever the time frame, the sooner tax and permit phaseins— like subsidy phaseouts—begin, the more gradual and less disruptive they will be.[21]

The decision on whether to tax or issue permits should also depend on the problem at hand. Permit systems have been used most when policymakers wanted to ensure that pollution or depletion stayed below certain levels. Iceland, New Zealand, and the United States have all used such systems to regulate fishing, in part because once boats start hauling in fish faster than they reproduce, a fishery can collapse in short order. Likewise, forests are thought to be able to withstand some acid rain; but beyond a "critical load," trees start dying quickly.

Taxes, on the other hand, can make sense when the long-term trend, for example in greenhouse gas emissions, matters more than the precise quantity emitted each year. Predictability of amount is sacrificed for predictability in price, which is something that businesses value highly. Notably, the European Organization for Packaging and the Environment, which includes

DuPont and Philip Morris, backed a solid waste tax in a recent position paper, "provided it is first introduced at a relatively low level but with a clear commitment to a steady increase in the tax rate. This will give industry time to adjust and an economic incentive to ensure that companies do adjust."[22]

★   ★   ★   ★

As revenues from environmental taxes and permit auctions rise, other taxes can fall. Since the total tax burden would not rise with this seesaw-like tax change, the cost for economies overall would probably be quite small or nil—and that is before counting the economic benefits of a healthier environment. (See Chapters 12 and 13.)

The economic and rhetorical appeal of tax shifting—"taxing bads, not goods"—began to dawn on West European environmentalists in the 1970s. In 1975, for example, Norwegian economist Agnar Sandmo argued in the *Swedish Journal of Economics* that an "optimal" revenue code would make substantial use of Pigouvian taxes in order to pass the costs of pollution back to polluters and reduce the need for other taxes. In the mid-1980s, analysts in the German-speaking world began to discuss in less abstract terms the idea of taxing energy—rather than wages—to fund social security. A few years later, the prominent German environmentalist Ernst Ulrich von Weizsäcker seized on the idea of tax shifting. Von Weizsäcker's name—his father a well-known physicist and philosopher, his uncle the president of Germany—brought almost instant legitimacy to the proposal. His 1992 book, *Ecological Tax Reform*, became a best-seller among environmentalists and dramatically raised the profile of the tax shifting concept in

Western Europe.[23]

But though the proposals appeared in German-speaking countries, they were implemented elsewhere, especially to the north. One of the world's most environmentally proactive nations, Sweden, became the first to take up the idea, in 1991. The government took $2.4 billion from new taxes on carbon and sulfur dioxide emissions, equal to 1.9 percent of all tax revenues, and used it to cut income taxes. As concern grew over unemployment in Western Europe, more shifts in the mid-1990s—in Denmark, Finland, and the Netherlands as well as Spain and the United Kingdom—focused more on cutting wage taxes. (See Table 9–2 and Chapter 12.)[24]

Eventually, environmental tax and permit systems could bring in far more than the few percentage points of revenue they garner today, allowing for much larger cuts in conventional taxes. One way to see this possibility is by leafing through the many studies on the economic costs of environmental harm. The hidden costs of driving in the United States, for example, include lung disease, climate change, injuries and deaths from accidents, and wasted time in traffic jams. They totaled $120 billion to $1.0 trillion in 1991 (in 1997 dollars), according to a study by transportation economist Mark Delucchi. That translates to anywhere from $480 per person to $4,000—the higher number being comparable to what Americans spend on car payments, insurance, and fuel each year. The full costs of driving, in other words, may be as much as twice what they appear to be. Passing these costs back through a fuel tax would take a tax rate of between 21¢ and an extraordinary $1.76 per liter (80¢ to $6.67 per gallon). But those revenues might suffice to eliminate, say, the employee-paid

Table 9–2. Tax Shifts from Work and Investment to Environmental Damage

Country, Year Initiated	Taxes Cut On	Taxes Raised On	Revenue Shifted[1]
			(percent)
Sweden, 1991	Personal income	Carbon and sulfur sulphur emissions	1.9
Denmark, 1994	Personal income	Motor fuel, coal, electricity, and water sales; waste incineration and landfilling; motor vehicle ownership	2.5
Spain, 1995	Wages	Motor fuel sales	0.2
Denmark, 1996	Wages, agricultural property	Carbon emissions; pesticide, chlorinated solvent, and battery sales	0.5
Netherlands, 1996	Personal income and wages	Natural gas and electricity sales	0.8
United Kingdom, 1996–97	Wages	Landfilling	0.2
Finland, 1996–97	Personal income and wages	Energy sales, landfilling	0.5

[1]Expressed relative to tax revenue raised by all levels of government.
SOURCE: See endnote 24.

payroll tax in the United States, giving most workers an 8-percent raise. Similar studies have concluded that even in Western Europe, where they are already lofty by world standards, motor fuel taxes would need to go even higher to pass the full costs of driving back to drivers.[25]

Some studies have measured the economic costs of a suite of environmental problems at once. To arrive at their bottom lines, they count everything from the cost of replacing the water purification services of destroyed wetlands to that of building dikes against a rising sea. Various studies have tallied environmental costs at 2 percent of gross domestic product in Australia and Japan, 12–15 percent in China, 23 percent in Germany, 40 percent in Sweden, and 45 percent in the United States. The spread is wide because different studies count different damages or the same damages in different ways. Most important, climate change and fossil fuel depletion—which account for two thirds of the costs reported for Germany, Sweden, and the United States—are not considered in the other studies.[26]

Since environmental tax and permit auctions work by raising revenues comparable to economic damage done, their revenue potential is similarly huge. The damage estimate for Germany, for instance, equals 58 percent of tax revenues there; those for Sweden and the United States exceed public revenues. In practice, taxes would raise much less than this suggests, since taxing environmental damage will reduce the amount that occurs. And especially once taxes reached their final rates—in some cases, well into the next century—revenues might decline with time. In counterpoint, conventional taxes on work and investment could fall at first but might eventually have to rise again. Since taxes have long fluctuated at this slow tempo, the adjustment stresses would not be high by historical standards.[27]

In fiscal and environmental impacts, tax or permit systems that effectively addressed carbon emissions would likely loom as the giants among environmental revenue raisers. On 10 December 1997, delegates at the Kyoto conference on climate change agreed to a landmark treaty that made modest progress toward erecting such systems. The accord proposes to create the largest pollution rights trading scheme ever, one that would involve all industrial countries. Moreover, it makes modest progress on shrinking and dividing the international greenhouse gas pie—on deciding who would get how many permits, in other words. The United States agreed to a 7-percent reduction below its 1990 level by 2008–2012 while the European Union agreed to an 8-percent emissions cut and Japan, a 6-percent cut.[28]

For all their import, the treaty sections allowing quota brokering contain only a handful of sentences and leave for subsequent conferences the task of filling in the details. As written, the treaty permits only countries, not businesses, to trade emissions rights internationally. European Union members might be allowed to levy carbon taxes within their borders—a proposal they have long discussed—and then, if they overshot their quota, to buy credits from the United States, Japan, or Russia.[29]

It is hard to estimate how high the price for a ton of carbon emissions will eventually have to be to protect the atmosphere. A survey of several global economic models by the Energy Modeling Forum at Stanford University suggests that if the price started at $22.50 and gradually climbed over 50 years to $250, global emissions might roughly plateau through the middle of the twenty-first century. For comparison, a $250-per-ton tax would add 18¢ to the pump price of a liter of gasoline (69¢ for a gallon) if fully passed on to consumers. It would double the price of natural gas, and increase that of coal sixfold. If the tax continued rising after 2050, emissions might almost halt by 2100. Climate models suggest that the amount of carbon dioxide in the air would stabilize at about 65 percent above where it was before the global fossil fuel binge began. Revenues would peak mid-century at roughly $700 billion to $1.8 trillion a year.[30]

★   ★   ★   ★

Studies like these indicate the potential dimensions of environmental fiscal reform. Today the major family of environmentally beneficial taxes consists of gasoline and diesel duties. Along with a handful of more modest energy and carbon taxes, these raised some $243 billion in 1994 in western industrial countries, or 3.8 percent of total tax revenues. Gasoline taxes are especially high in Southern Europe (accounting for 5–10 percent of tax revenues), where a culture of tax evasion forces governments to lean particularly heavily on difficult-to-dodge motor fuel taxes. But since industrial countries spend comparable amounts building and maintaining roads, the net tax, if any, is considerably lower. (See Chapter 5.) Other environmental taxes raise another $63 billion a year in western industrial countries, or 1 percent of total revenue. In a few countries, they raise more. Denmark got 4 percent of its revenue from nonenergy environmental taxes in 1993, and the Netherlands, 5.1 percent (excluding carbon taxes, which are here grouped with energy taxes). As a liberal estimate, then, environmental taxes generate perhaps 3 percent of global tax revenues.[31]

In addition, small amounts are raised from the rent-capturing charges discussed in Chapter 7—royalties on public oil deposits, timber, and minerals, and taxes on land values. Since land taxes are by far the largest revenue source in this family, and since property taxes (which apply to buildings as well as land) generate 8 percent of revenue in western countries, rent-capturing charges are here estimated to provide 4 percent of global tax receipts. That leaves roughly 93 percent of the $7.5 trillion a year in tax revenue to be raised from taxes on work and investment.[32]

The Stanford Energy Modeling Forum results suggest that carbon taxes or permit auctions could eventually supply about 15 percent of government revenues worldwide. Cutting environmentally harmful subsidies 90 percent could free up another $600 billion, or an additional 8 percent of current revenues. The remaining subsidy funds could be targeted at truly deserving recipients, from developers of clean technologies to low-income people who have trouble paying the energy taxes on their utility bills. Land taxes and resource royalties could generate another $900 billion each year, or 12 percent of total revenues. (See Chapter 7.) Taxes on wages and profits would therefore need to supply only some 65 percent of that $7.5 trillion revenue pie, nearly a one-third cut from today's 93 percent. (See Figure 9–2.) In many countries, income and profits taxes—or sales taxes, or payroll taxes—could be eliminated. The changes would stimulate economic development even as they guided it toward environmental sustainability.[33]

Of course, the magnitude of the tax shift would vary from nation to nation, and from household to household. But applying these representative percentages to the per-person tax bills in Table 9–1 suggests that in industrial countries, taxes on pollution and resource use would rise $2,000–2,500 a year per person (some of which would be reflected in higher prices for resource-intensive products) while taxes on income

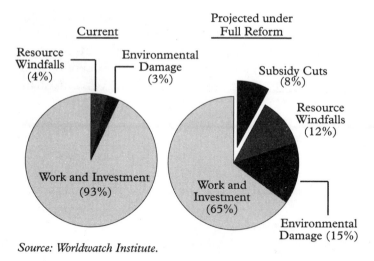

Source: *Worldwatch Institute.*

FIGURE 9–2. *Approximate Composition of Global Tax
Revenues, Current and Projected under Full Reform*

would fall the same amount. In developing and former
Eastern bloc nations, the change would be $40–500 a
year per person.

What this simple picture of reform belies is that the
shift to environmental taxation will be a complex historical event. "Polluter pays" makes sense, and is perhaps the most important solution to one of the greatest
problems of our age. But as policymakers are discover-
ing, the devil lies in the details. As a result, like the early
income tax innovators, today's policymakers are adopt-
ing environmental taxes in halting, patchwork fashion,
confronting and accommodating considerations of
practicality, fairness, and politics. What matters most is
that the learning process has begun. Lawmakers and
tax writers are now participating in a process as old as
civilization: adapting the tax code to the times.

III

From Theory to Practice

10

Environmental Taxes: Practical Limits and Potential

The main planks of environmental fiscal reform—cutting payments to polluters, capturing more resource rents, judiciously subsidizing environmental protection, taxing environmental harm, and cutting conventional taxes—can be powerful tools precisely because they are designed according to incisive principles. Those who harm society should be taxed rather than subsidized. Human labor and entrepreneurship should be taxed less, and exploitation of nature should be taxed more.

Yet many people, whether new to the ideas in this fusion of environmental and fiscal policy or expert in them, see serious flaws in the approach, especially in the tax increases. Columnists and radio talk show hosts often condemn the ideas from public pulpits, as do lobbyists in the privacy of politicians' offices. And in doing so, they generally reflect widespread misgivings among citizens. They call the ideas impractical. Or unfair. Or sure to raise taxes. Or destructive of jobs and the economy. Or a political dead end.

Naturally, there is some truth in these five objections, to various extents. The twentieth century has shown how overreliance on central planning and overreliance on markets are both dangerous—thus the collapse of communism, and the heavy regulation in the West of everything from workplace safety to stock trading. Just so, market-oriented environmental policies can be overused as well as underused. Few things are as dangerous as a principle applied with untempered zeal.

Part III offers five chapters that examine these challenges, then rebut or accommodate them as appropriate. They will focus particularly on the step with the most weighty implications—the use of taxes that "make the polluter pay." Taken to their fullest, such taxes will engineer nothing less than another industrial revolution. They will change how things are made, where people live, and how they travel, in order to rebalance economy and environment. Precisely because environmental taxes can change so much, they must be investigated most carefully.

★   ★   ★   ★

One blunt objection to environmental taxation is that it will not work, or at least not work nearly as well as environmental regulations. A general response to that assertion, by J. Andrew Hoerner, a tax analyst at the Center for a Sustainable Economy in Washington, D.C., is that environmental taxes can in fact work better than conventional regulations, since they are often administered by revenue collection agencies. These bodies typically have more enforcement authority and personnel than environmental regulatory agencies, which in rich and poor countries alike are often hobbled by underfunding. And poor enforcement compromises even the best laws. The U.S. Internal Revenue Service, by contrast, brought down Chicago gangster Al Capone. It is hard to imagine an environmental agency doing that.[1]

Nevertheless, there is no question that however elegant environmental taxes are in theory, and however enforceable, they rarely work so neatly in practice. For one, taxing pollution or resource depletion requires measuring it, and that is not always easy. There are no affordable technologies, for instance, for tracking automobile emissions of carbon monoxide and smog-causing nitrogen oxides (NO_x) and hydrocarbons. Even if there were, setting taxes perfectly according to the economics textbooks would require knowing exactly how much damage the chemicals will do at a given time, and that depends on how many other cars are around, the temperature and humidity of the air, the number of people breathing the air, and the health effects of the pollutants. Estimating these variables with precision would require sophisticated mathematical models and impossibly detailed knowledge of local car use patterns, smog chemistry, and human biology.

The response to this problem is straightforward: we should not let the perfect be the enemy of the good. In many cases, governments can tax rough proxies for pollution. Sweden, for example, has taxed fertilizer sales rather than the amount of fertilizer that drains into surface and groundwater, since that is impractical to gauge. It also exempts small power plants from its NO_x tax because they cannot afford pollution monitoring equipment. As for the exhaust spewing unmonitored from millions of cars, governments could require odometer readings and emissions tests during annual car inspections, and use them to estimate a car's pollution over the past year, providing a rough base for a tax.[2]

That said, the more policymakers latch onto what is easiest to measure rather than most relevant, the less effective taxes become. An inspection-based emissions tax, for example, applies equally to cars driven on days when smog is a problem and cars driven when it is not.

As a result, like government trust-busters who intervene in the market in order to make it work better, environmental policymakers would often do best to summon regulations and other policies to the aid of market-based approaches. The taxes can even fund some of these steps. The Swedish government credits a drop in fertilizer use during the 1980s both to the taxes on fertilizer sales and to education programs, funded by the new revenues, that raised farmers' awareness of the financial and environmental costs of fertilizer overuse.[3]

World Bank economists Gunnar Eskeland and Shantayanan Devarajan recommended a similar blend of market and regulatory ingredients after studying pollution control in Chile, Indonesia, and Mexico. In Mexico City, one of the world's smoggiest cities, administrative expense and corruption make it nearly impossible to institute taxes based even on annual car inspections. The practical palliative, they concluded, was to require catalytic converters in new cars. But while converters can dramatically lower emissions per kilometer driven, they do nothing to reduce the number of kilometers driven. That is where a motor fuel tax would come in.[4]

Having chosen practical tax bases, policymakers then run into another problem: even when meaningful tax signals can be sent, there is no guarantee that consumers and businesses will respond. But experience with gasoline taxes in industrial countries offers hope. The United States has by far the lowest gasoline taxes, averaging 10¢ per liter (38¢ per gallon) in 1995, while taxes in Australia, Canada, Japan, and New Zealand lie in the range of 20–35¢ per liter (76¢–$1.32 per gallon). In Europe, taxes of 50–90¢ per liter ($1.89–3.41 per gallon) push pump prices two to four times higher than in the United States. Of course, many factors shape people's decisions about what size cars to buy and how much to drive them—including population density and convenience of public transit. But the influence of gas price is obvious to any visitor to the United States or Italy: where gas is cheap, minivans and sport utility vehicles roam the roads in droves; where it is pricey, petite autos vie with mopeds for road space. (See Figure 10–1.)[5]

On the other hand, *Homo sapiens* is clearly only distantly related to *H. economicus,* the mythical species that populates most of the economics literature. *H. economicus* knows every product and every price and is driven only by profit maximization and material accumulation. Real people, by contrast, miss large opportunities to save money. Efficiency standards adopted in the United States during the last 10 years, for instance, on refrigerators, fluorescent lights, and other appliances have pushed the average efficiency of new models up sharply by pushing inefficient ones off the market and forcing companies to innovate. They will eventually save households an average $250 a year on energy bills. That consumers and companies did not switch to the

Use (liters per person)

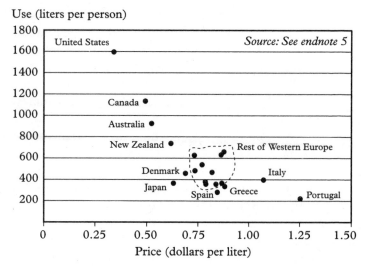

FIGURE 10–1. *Gasoline Price versus Use, Western Industrial Countries, 1995*

money-saving models on their own shows that although people respond to market signals, they do not do so nearly as nimbly as economists tend to wish.[6]

The general lesson is that making the industrial economy operate efficiently within environmental limits will require integrating environmental taxes with other kinds of policies, using the strengths of each to compensate for the weaknesses of the other. If governments of especially sprawl-afflicted countries such as the United States and Australia want motor fuel tax hikes to work well, and work fairly, they need to give people better alternatives to driving. They will need to spend more on mass transit, as much of Western Europe already does, and rewrite zoning laws to foster neighborhoods that more closely mix schools, homes, and shops. Together, these changes can lure people from behind the wheel and onto sidewalks, bike paths, or bus lines. Meanwhile, to the extent that government policies force people to drive, and to the extent that people already drive efficient cars, taxing gas will not so much discourage gas use as punish it.[7]

More generally, many nontax policies are essential to building environmentally sustainable societies. Laws—not market forces alone—are what will protect endangered species, manage nuclear waste, and ban pollutants deemed unacceptable in any amount, such as DDT or dioxins. Unless communities have the legal means to protect themselves, waste incinerators (as long as they exist) are likely to be built with disproportionate frequency in poor and minority neighborhoods. And to control population, governments need to give couples universal access to birth control. They also need to step up programs that increase the literacy, education, and economic independence of women in order to reduce their dependence on numerous sons for social security.[8]

*   *   *   *

On balance, the question of practical import is not whether market approaches work, but when they are useful. Whenever environmental goals can be expressed in significant part in a single number—how many tons of benzene should be permitted into an airshed each year, how much water pumped from an aquifer, how many hectares developed—and whenever actual pollution or depletion rates can be estimated, market mechanisms offer a way to protect the environment while exploiting the market's flexibility.

The problems that market tools are today helping to alleviate include air and water pollution from large factories and power plants, where measurement equipment is relatively affordable; household trash generation, since municipalities can tally a family's trash by requiring the use of government-issued bags; overfishing, where tonnages caught are already measured in the course of business; carbon emissions, which are easy to predict based on how much coal, oil, and natural gas people buy; groundwater overpumping; and large-scale conversion of farms and forests into suburbs. Indeed, the best argument for the viability of environmental tax and permit systems is that they are already taking root around the world. (See Table 10–1.)[9]

Surprisingly, some of the historically least market-reliant countries levy what are, on paper, the world's most sophisticated environmental taxes. In China, Poland, Russia, and other traditionally communist countries, tax regimes now cover hundreds of air and water pollutants, toxic and radioactive waste, and even noise. The systems developed out of a communist tradition of using fines to at least nominally enforce environmental standards, and in response to the ruinous environmental toll of central planning. The taxes are used mostly for funding environmental protection agencies, as well as for grants and subsidized loans to industry for pollution control investments.[10]

These pollution levy systems are, however, generally more impressive in theory than in practice. Emissions below officially permitted levels are usually exempt from taxation. And corruption and inflation have wiped out much of the taxes' incentive effect. In addition, many companies still hold monopolies and so can pass their costs on to the government or customers, making them unresponsive to market signals.[11]

Nevertheless, the charge systems are a foundation

for what could eventually become a set of robust environmental taxes. In Poland and the Czech Republic, revenues are relatively high at 1 percent of total tax receipts, which suggests that significant taxation of a wide variety of pollutants is practical in traditionally communist nations. The government of China seems particularly keen to press forward. It has announced plans to extend existing taxes to emissions already within permitted levels by 2001, and to establish new taxes to attack acid rain and water pollution.[12]

Some developing countries have shown that they can use environmental taxes with more effect, even if with less sophistication. Malaysia adjusted its gasoline taxes to make leaded fuel 2.8 percent more expensive than unleaded. Partly as a result, unleaded gasoline has grabbed more than 60 percent of the market. Since lead has been linked to brain damage in children, there is little doubt that the modest charge has paid for itself. Thailand and Turkey also favor unleaded fuel with lower taxes. Costa Rica lays a 15-percent duty on oil products and uses a third of the proceeds to pay small farmers to plant trees, which soak up heat-trapping carbon dioxide as they grow, partly compensating for emissions from driving. And the Philippines launched an industrial water pollution tax system in 1997, to complement existing regulations.[13]

Tradable permits have also proved useful in developing countries. Chile has auctioned permits to regulate fishing of some species as well as agricultural water use. Farmers in parts of Algeria, Brazil, India, Mexico, Morocco, Pakistan, Peru, and Tunisia trade water rights. Many of these systems developed without formal government involvement and are quite old. In the southern part of the Brazilian state of Ceará, farmers

Table 10–1. Experiences with Selected Environmental Tax and Permit Systems

Policy, Country, First Year in Effect	Description, Effect
Overfishing Tradable fishing permit systems, New Zealand, 1986	Overfishing reduced. Many stocks appear to be rebuilding. Fishing industry is stable and profitable despite lack of subsidies.
Excessive Water Demand Tradable water rights, Chile, 1981	Existing users grandfathered in. Rights to new supplies auctioned. Total water use capped.
Solid Waste Toxic waste charge, Germany, 1991	Toxic waste production fell more than 15 percent in 3 years.
Solid waste charge, Denmark, 1986	Recycling rate for demolition waste shot from 12 to 82 percent over 6–8 years.
Water Pollution Fees to fund wastewater treatment, Netherlands, 1970	Main factor behind 72–99 percent drop in industrial discharges of heavy metals into regionally managed waters.
Fertilizer sales taxes, Sweden, 1982 and 1984	One charge, 1982–92, funded agricultural subsidies; other tax funded education programs on fertilizer use reduction until 1995. As of 1997, only nitrogen is taxed, cutting use about 10 percent.
Acid Rain Sulfur oxide tax, Sweden, 1991	One third of 40-percent emissions drop during 1989–95 attributed to charge.
Sulfur permit system, United States, 1995	Permits allocated free to past emitters. Capping emissions after 2000 at half 1980 level; compliance costs unexpectedly low.
Global Atmospheric Disruption Ozone-depleting substance tax, United States, 1990	Smoothing and enforcing phaseouts.

Policy, Country, First Year in Effect	Description, Effect
Chlorofluorocarbon permit system, Singapore, 1989	Half of permits auctioned, half allocated to past producers and importers. Smoothing and enforcing phaseout.
Carbon dioxide tax, Norway, 1991	Emissions appear 3–4 percent lower than without the tax.
Uncontrolled Development	
Tradable development rights, New Jersey Pinelands, 1982	Land use plan sets development limits in forested, agricultural, and designated growth zones. Developers may exceed limits in growth zones if they buy credits from landowners agreeing to develop less than they could. Owners of 6,400 hectares (15,800 acres) in more-protected areas have sold off development rights.
General	
Linking of investment tax credits to environmental and employment records, Louisiana, 1991	Tax credits reduced up to 50 percent for firms that pollute most and employ least. Twelve firms agreed to cut toxic emissions enough to lower the state's total by 8 percent. Repealed after one year.

SOURCE: See endnote 9.

have traded water rights for at least a century.[14]

Western industrial countries have made the greatest use of environmentally beneficial tax and permit systems. In addition to motor fuel and other energy taxes, governments in these nations have implemented hundreds of less conventional tax, permit, and deposit-refund systems, applied to everything from beverage containers in Belgium to car batteries in Canada.[15]

Some of these taxes are levied by local authorities to solve local problems. Others are applied by national governments to address global ones. Like the United

States, Denmark and Australia combined regulations and taxes to phase out chlorofluorocarbon sales by 1996. Between 1990 and 1997, the U.S. tax raised $4.24 billion, and appeared to have accelerated the phaseout beyond what was required. Sweden's Environmental Protection Agency attributes 12 points of the 40-percent drop in sulfur emissions between 1989 and 1995 to a sulfur tax adopted in 1991.[16]

Sweden's NO_x tax, applied only to large power plants, cut emissions from those facilities in half (though that amounted to a cut of only 1 percent from all sources). Interestingly, it also led to rapid innovation and price cutting in emissions measurement equipment. As those costs dropped, the country extended the charge to smaller power plants in 1996 and 1997. After Denmark instituted a solid waste charge, the share of demolition refuse that went unrecycled crumpled from 88 to 18 percent. And Denmark is also one of the few countries to directly tax the depletion of a natural resource—sand and gravel, the most valuable grades of which are rapidly being used to make roads and buildings.[17]

While Europe has used taxes the most, other industrial countries have developed more experience with tradable permits, and found them also to be useful in many contexts. In the mid-1980s, the United States established a trading system to give oil refineries flexibility in complying with laws banning lead from gasoline. Companies were allowed to phase lead out of their products more slowly than the national timetable required if they bought permits from others phasing out faster—a successful model that later informed the design of the U.S. sulfur trading system. (See Chapter 9.) Authorities in Massachusetts and southern

California are instituting permit schemes to reduce local air pollution from factories and power plants. Tradable permits now govern almost all of New Zealand's fisheries, and a few in Australia, the United States, and Canada. In Alicante, in Spain's dry southern half, villagers have traded water rights since the mid-1200s.[18]

Some of the most innovative environmental tax and permit systems to date have been developed by state governments in the United States. Arid Arizona instituted one of the world's few groundwater depletion tax regimes in 1991. New Jersey has used permits to add flexibility to its plan to protect the Pinelands, a 445,000-hectare region of wildlife habitat, berry farms, and small towns under strong development pressure. After extensive consultations with residents, the state set limits on building density in designated forest, farm, and town zones. Since the state believed that the character of the region was threatened not just by the rising number of buildings but also their dispersion across the landscape, it then established a trading system to facilitate more-concentrated development in existing town centers. Developers in designated growth areas can exceed local construction limits if they buy credits from landowners in other areas who agree to build less than they could. Since 1982, owners in more-protected zones have traded away in perpetuity rights to build on 6,400 hectares (15,800 acres).[19]

Another creative market mechanism appeared in the heavily polluted state of Louisiana in 1991. The government there began grading companies on compliance with environmental laws and on the number of people they employed for the amount of pollution they generated. Firms with low scores lost up to half the standard tax deduction for new investment. In the first year, 12 firms agreed to cut toxic emissions enough to lower the state's total by 8.2 percent. Many of the pollution reduction plans cost the companies more than they earned in tax credits, showing that the fear of a tarnished public image was giving the tax system added kick—no company relished the prospect of being branded with a "B-minus" on the evening news. Unfortunately, businesses disliked the program so much that they fought successfully for its repeal in 1992.[20]

The environmental problem for which tax and permit systems are tailor-made is the control of emissions of heat-trapping carbon dioxide. On the one hand, energy is used in so many ways that government could never dictate through regulation all the changes that will needed to ratchet down fossil fuel use. On the other, the amount of carbon pumped into the air by burning coal, natural gas, or oil products depends almost exclusively on the quantity and type of fuel burned, and so is easy to assess for tax or quota purposes. Energy retailers—from gas stations to power companies—can be required to pay taxes or buy permits based on how much fuel they sell; they would then pass part of the costs on to consumers.[21]

In an important environmental tax development of the 1990s, five countries—Denmark, Finland, the Netherlands, Norway, and Sweden—have introduced duties on carbon emissions. They have partially or fully exempted the most carbon-intensive industries, however, such as steelmaking, which seriously blunts the taxes' effect. Overall, the Norwegian tax seems to have cut emissions 3–4 percent compared with what they would have been, and the Swedish tax has slowed emissions 2–3 percent. In Sweden, the use of wood in district heating plants—which, much like power plants, generate heat in a central location and then pipe it to a town's buildings—doubled between 1990 and 1995, to 42 percent of the fuel used in these plants.[22]

Taxes alone will not create a sustainable society. Regulations, education programs, and family planning services are needed too. But because environmental tax and permit systems directly address one crux of the environmental problem—the mismatch between individual and collective interests—and because they have substantial, demonstrated potential to address many major environmental issues, it is hard to imagine how humanity can achieve sustainability without them.

11

Making Reform Fair

The intersection of Franklin and Norris Streets in North Philadelphia looks to be generic American ghetto. There are no trees. Shards of glass crunch underfoot on the concrete. A brown brick elementary school with security-grated windows occupies the northeast corner of the crossing, centered in a small sea of asphalt. Across Franklin, a parking lot fills the northwest corner. On the southwest side, a crack house gutted of anything of value has structural timbers falling out its front door. On the southeast corner stands a modest stone church that not long ago underwent repairs to prevent the tower from collapsing. The church looks abandoned, left to die by the flight of whites to the suburbs.[1]

But like any neighborhood, this one is more complex

than it appears, housing hope as well as desolation. And the church is the source of some of that hope. In the early 1990s, it arranged with a man named Bobby to keep a protective eye on the cars in the parking lot. Richie Gonzalez ran a busy car repair shop on a barbed-wire-ringed lot on church property. And on Wednesday afternoons, the church's doors would open to bright-faced third-graders from the school across the way. Some children would spring across the street in a burst of energy; some would approach more quietly. The after-school program was part of an array of services provided through the Methodist church by the Reverend Frank Kensill and his wife Winifred. Frank died in 1996, but Winnie and many of the programs have stayed on.

The neighborhood will probably never see anything like the Kensills again. They were just about the only whites in an area now predominantly black and Hispanic. Frank was a mechanical genius and, with his wife, blended knowledge from engineering, psychology, and sociology with practical experimentation to develop programs that attempted to help neighborhood residents, especially children, overcome the many pressures of poverty.

One pressure that occupied Frank's attention for many years—and that foreshadowed a danger in current proposals to raise environmental taxes—was the burden of high fuel prices on low-income neighborhoods. The strategy he devised for reducing that strain typified the church's approach: using limited funds, he tried to address that and other problems at the same time by drawing on the neighborhood's main resource, its people. After oil prices rose in the late 1970s, he invented a cheap way to upgrade home oil heaters and cut fuel use 20 percent. Collaborating with state and federal agencies, he then developed a program to train and employ people from neighborhoods like his in performing the upgrade in low-income homes. Thanks to government funding, hundreds of technicians were eventually trained in two dozen states, and tens of thousands of upgrades were performed. Energy was saved, bills were cut for poor households, and people who needed it got training and paid work.

In the 1970s and 1980s, poor people in many countries were confronted with the choice "to heat or to eat." In the United States, the pressure was particularly great on poor senior citizens living in the Northeast's old housing stock. Not only were the walls and windows of the houses porous to heat, but older people need warmer homes in order to live comfortably. According to one U.S. study, energy bills consumed a substantial 18 percent of the income of low-income elderly households in 1986, compared with 5 percent for all elderly households.[2]

OPEC's hold on the global oil market has since weakened, but the episode of expensive energy still shapes debate over environmental tax policy, giving rise to one of the most cutting attacks against environmental taxes—the charge that they are unfair. The essence of the market-oriented approach is to auction the right to exploit the environment to the highest bidder. But the highest bidders are not necessarily the most deserving. Climate protection policy would be unacceptable if, for example, it allowed British executives jetting to vacations in Tuscany to outbid poor Londoners for oil to heat their homes. Similarly, market-oriented policies are also problematic if they turn a cold shoulder to steel workers thrown out of work by competition from untaxed overseas steel plants, or if they make traditional fishers pay for the shortsightedness of newcomers who overexploit their waters. If the overarching goal of environmental policy is to allow future generations to meet their basic needs, it is inconsistent to make it harder for people today to do the same.[3]

Fortunately, just as governments can make environmental taxes more practical through compromises such as measuring rough-and-ready proxies for pollution, they can also make them fairer. As in North Philadelphia, appropriate adjustments can help prevent fiscal policies from becoming just one more pressure on people whose options are already limited. Compensating subsidies can be targeted at needy groups. Exemptions can be worked into taxes. Permits can be given for free to people deemed particularly deserving. Like any policy, environmental fiscal reform can be implemented unfairly, but it need not be.

* * * *

Though low-income consumers are not the only group that has trouble adapting to price hikes for natural resources, they are the largest. In most countries, they spend disproportionately high shares of their income on energy, water, and resource-intensive products, which is why these products are often subsidized. (See Chapter 5.) In the United States, a carbon tax on fossil fuels of $100 per ton (equivalent to 7¢ per liter of gasoline, or 27¢ per gallon) would take 2.3 percent of the spending budgets of the richest 10 percent of households, but 3.7 percent among the poorest 10 percent, making it "regressive." And within the poorest tenth, certain groups would spend even more, including elderly pensioners in cold cities and low-income people forced by lack of public transit to drive old, gas-guzzling cars. In developing countries, the urban poor could also be hit hard. Manila provides a representative example: the richest fifth of households devote 5 percent of their income to energy, while the poorest fifth spend 12 percent.[4]

Thus proponents of environmental taxes (and subsidy cuts) ignore the issue of regressivity at their peril. In the United Kingdom, for example, the Conservatives attempted in 1993 to abolish the exemption for energy used in the home from the value-added (sales) tax. In the end, they succeeded in levying a tax of 8 percent, about half the normal rate, but only after provoking a sharp public backlash, watching their standing plummet in the polls, and agreeing to use most of the revenue to compensate low-income and elderly households.[5]

A better-thought-out plan, assert Stephen Tindale and Gerald Holtham of the Institute for Public Policy Research in London, would have incorporated several carefully designed measures from the beginning to prevent regressivity. The government could help the poor pay their heating bills, and cut those bills by putting insulation and efficient heaters into their homes— something particularly needed in the United Kingdom, a country with housing stock so drafty that curtains sway indoors when the wind blows. And they could hire and train unemployed workers to perform the upgrades, as Frank Kensill did in Philadelphia. They could also expand bus service in low-income neighborhoods: in many southern European cities, convenient mass transit (along with short heating seasons) reduces energy spending among the poor enough that energy taxes there would tend to be "progressive" rather than regressive. Finally, governments could assist low-income consumers with unrelated expenses such as food. In general, these measures will reach distinct but overlapping populations, so they need to be combined carefully to reach as many people as possible.[6]

A more direct antidote to tax regressivity is to adjust the taxes themselves. The coastal town of Setúbal, Portugal, for example, recently "terraced" its new water taxes. Households can buy 25 cubic meters a month tax-free, enough to meet most basic needs; but above that threshold, the levy kicks in, rising in three stages. The Netherlands did the same with the new duties on natural gas and power in 1996. This technique may merit wide application for taxes on residential energy and water use.[7]

Another option is to make nonenvironmental taxes more progressive. The Netherlands, for instance, increased its standard income tax deductions in 1996, especially for senior citizens, and lowered the tax rate on the lowest income bracket. As a result, most low-income people came out just about where they started under the shift toward energy taxation.[8]

Progressivity can also be increased by raising taxes on wealth (as opposed to annual income). In the United States, for example, the richest 20 percent reaps 55 percent of income each year—but owns 80 percent of the wealth. That means wealth taxes, such as estate taxes, can be extremely progressive. Yet in recent decades, taxes on the wealthy in industrial countries have been falling. As the world's economies have become increasingly integrated, corporations and the well-off have become more able to shuttle their assets across national borders in order to shield them from taxation. In response, governments have often cut taxes on profits and capital gains—which dominate the tax returns of the rich—hoping to lure investment back. That has forced a shift toward taxes that land mainly on sales and wages, which are rarely very progressive, and often regressive.[9]

One logical way to reverse this trend and compensate for the additional regressivity of taxes on environmental damage is to increase taxes on resource rents, as discussed in Chapter 7, and then put all the revenue into cutting taxes on sales, wages, or buildings. Since a plot of earth can never sidle across a national border to avoid taxation, natural resources give governments a sort of protective barrier against the corrosive forces of international tax competition. The richest 10 percent of Americans own 60–65 percent of private land by value, calculates economist Clifford Cobb at the group Redefining Progress in San Francisco. In Brazil, the wealthiest 1 percent hold title to half the countryside. Statistics like these indicate that taxes on land values can be quite progressive. Similarly, those who reap windfalls by winning access to cheap public resources are also wealthy as a group, ranging from Malaysian timber tycoons to major shareholders in Australian mining companies.[10]

Taxes on resource rents raise their own fairness issues, however. John Stuart Mill, the brilliant nineteenth-century economist and philosopher, was one of the land tax's most thoughtful supporters. But one facet of such a tax that troubled him was its potential for arbitrariness. When a land tax hike is announced, the people worst affected are those for whom landownership is a primary form of savings. Land values suddenly drop a notch, and from their point of view, some of their savings simply evaporate. Recent sellers of land, on the other hand, escape unscathed. Of course, the same can be said for a payroll tax hike, which reduces the earnings value of an education, or a profits tax increase, which hurts stock prices. But that will not reassure retirees, say, whose main asset is their home.[11]

The solution Mill proposed was for tax assessors to treat past land value rises—up to current levels—mostly as water under the bridge and tax them moderately. With due warning from the government, however, future land appreciation would be taxed much more heavily. To take a modern example, if a speculator bought farmland just beyond the suburbs for $10,000, held it for 10 years, then sold it to a developer for $20,000, a tax could extract 50 percent of the windfall profit.[12]

Another partial solution is to exempt senior citizens from some part of any land tax increase—say, on the first $30,000 of land value. The exemption could then be phased out over several decades.[13]

But where buildings are still taxed, the best approach may be the one cities such as Melbourne and Johannesburg have already taken (see Chapter 7): cutting taxes on buildings while raising taxes on land. Then when land values fall, building values will rise. According to the mayor of Harrisburg, Pennsylvania, when his city increased its land tax and decreased its buildings tax, assessments fell for 90 percent of property owners. The explanation is that a few people, generally wealthy people, owned much more land than building—large estates or empty, underused downtown lots. But most people, including typical homeowners, owned relatively more building than land. Carefully used, therefore, rent-capturing charges can make environmental tax shifts more progressive.[14]

*   *   *   *

Potent questions of fairness also arise along axes other than that dividing rich and poor. In New Zealand, indigenous Maori had been fishing for centuries before westerners joined them in the 1930s. After World War II, larger boats became more common and total catch shot up, leading to overfishing by the 1970s. When the government put fisheries under permit trading systems in 1986, it based allocations on how much each fisher had caught in the early 1980s. Since total catch had to be scaled back—up to 80 percent for some species— many Maori received shares too small to live on, despite their ancestral claims. Meanwhile, relative new-comers ended up ahead of where they had started a few decades earlier. Fortunately for the Maori, they could turn to the courts, where in 1989 and 1992 they fought successfully to increase their permanent allocations.[15]

A different divide emerged after the U.S. govern-ment launched fishing permit systems in the early 1990s off the coast of Alaska—a rift between boat own-ers and workers. The government's North Pacific Fisheries Management Council (NPFMC) gave all $800 million worth of permits (known as Individual Fishing Quotas, or IFQs) to boat owners, whose repre-sentatives dominated the Council's board. Local boat workers, who have some moral claim to the windfall generated by local resources, received no permits. Since then, the local industry has moved toward large, automated trawlers, which support fewer and lower-paying jobs. The NPFMC has effectively transferred control of much of the fish resource, and the earnings from it, from local communities to investors else-where.[16]

Like the U.K. government's attempt to raise the sales tax on energy, the NPFMC's slighting of equity considerations ultimately backfired loudly. Angry fishers organized. After pressing their case with the agency and in court without effect, they went to the top. Testifying in Anchorage, Alaska, during field hearings of a U.S. Senate subcommittee, Paul Seaton of the boat workers group Alliance Against IFQs made clear the group's opposition to the present system but said it might reconsider if major changes were made. The government would have to allocate many of the permits to boat workers and other locals, who could then sell or lease them to boat owners, in the process garnering a share of the fishery's wealth. Or the government could auction the licenses instead of giving them away, and then pass the revenue back to local people. (The State of Alaska does this with its oil royalties, mailing each Alaskan a check for some $1,000 every October.) Until such changes were made, they urged a moratorium on the establishment of new tradable quota systems in the United States. "We do not want to be the Nation's guinea pig and staging area for this large corporate welfare scam." On this last point, Seaton got his wish: Congress enacted a four-year moratorium on such plans in 1996, casting doubt upon the future of a new approach to fisheries management.[17]

Another market-oriented policy has engendered opposition by violating the physical geography of the problem it was meant to solve, rather than the cultural geography. The U.S. sulfur dioxide trading system is nationwide, though it aims to solve what is better seen as a set of regional acid rain problems. As a result, some regions may see smaller acid rain reductions than others. One New York utility embroiled itself in controversy in 1993 by deciding to cut emissions and sell its unneeded permits upwind to midwestern utilities. The trade provoked a lawsuit from the state government on grounds that it would, ironically, increase acid rain back in New York. To avert such outcomes, the sulfur trading system could have been broken into a group of regional permit markets, each with its own cap. Or restrictions could have been placed on upwind trades. In the event, however, emissions have fallen quite uniformly from region to region, and the state has dropped its suit.[18]

*   *   *   *

The question of how to divide the costs of environmental protection also plays out on the international stage. In Kyoto, in December 1997, industrial countries agreed in principle to develop a greenhouse gas emissions trading system. The treaty also gives preliminary endorsement to a system through which countries can create new permits and then sell them for cash. Costa Rica, for example, could earn credits by planting trees, which pull carbon out of the atmosphere as they grow, and then sell the permits to Canada for less than it would cost Canada to scrap one of its coal plants. The same amount of carbon would be kept out of the air, but at lower cost.[19]

Many people in developing countries, however, are profoundly suspicious of these ideas, fearing that industrial countries will use a trading system to codify into international law the current, highly unequal pattern of fossil fuel use, capping emissions and throttling economic development in developing countries while allowing rich countries to defer reducing their own emissions by buying credits. Developing-country governments point out that until industrial countries put their own greenhouses in order, they cannot expect others to do so. But industrial nations, particularly the United States (buoyed by the relative success of its sulfur trading system), argue that it will be almost impossible for nations to restrain their emissions without using permit systems (or else taxes) to raise the price of fossil fuel use.[20]

The clash between these points of view is more apparent than real. What is actually at stake in the climate negotiations, regardless of the policy tool chosen to protect the climate, is who should bear the costs of protection. This question can be translated into the terms of a trading system, where the issue becomes how many permits each country should receive for free at the start of trading—and how many they should have to buy.

Developing countries, home to 80 percent of the world's people yet the source of only 20 percent of carbon emissions to date from fossil fuel burning, have argued that since the atmosphere belongs equally to all people, any global climate accord must give developing countries most of the rights to emit greenhouse gases. Industrial countries that wanted to keep some of their coal plants and cars running would then have to buy or rent billions of tons worth of permits from poorer countries, which would generate a trillion-dollar cash transfer from rich to poor countries. Developing countries could then invest these funds in their own development. The U.N. Development Programme has put the case this way: "Such flows would be neither aid nor charity. They would be the outcome of a free market mechanism that penalizes the richer nations' overconsumption of the global commons."[21]

Such a huge transfer of wealth seems unlikely to many, but quick, decisive progress toward averting the risks of climate change will be diplomatically impossible without at least some transfer via permits. Rising carbon emitters like China will never abide an arrangement that gives industrial countries most emission rights in the future simply because they have emitted most in the past. Moreover, the money would represent only a few percentage points of rich countries' economic output—a small price to pay for the economic benefits of climate stability.

Conventional economic wisdom until recently denied any link between the questions of how much to cut emissions and who should pay for those cuts—that is, until an independent-minded Columbia University economist, Graciela Chichilnisky, overturned the wisdom with a mathematician's rigor. The essence of her argument, perhaps more surprising to her colleagues than to laypeople, is that when it comes to climate change, we are all in the same boat, rich and poor alike. The boat is heading toward a fork in the river: one way lies the calm waters of climate stability; the other, a deadly waterfall. We are so close to the precipice now that only if rich countries bear more of the costs of a major environmental course correction—by donating large oars to the poor—can we together paddle to safety. It is in the self-interest of rich countries, in other words, to recognize the fairness argument of poorer countries by agreeing to bear much of the costs of climate protection.[22]

*   *   *   *

The fairness argument against fiscal reform that perhaps resonates most deeply with the public hinges on fears about international competition. Seemingly, a country that levied a stiff environmental tax, say on carbon emissions, would end up sending steel and chemical makers abroad to pollute, throwing people out of work and doing the environment no good. Conservative commentator Paul Craig Roberts pursued this line of argument in the U.S. magazine *Business Week*. A carbon tax, he wrote, "will merely redirect energy, capital, technology, and industry away from the U.S., Europe, and Japan to China, India, Mexico, and other Third World countries ... there will be no reduction in greenhouse gases, only in living standards in the few industrialized democracies."[23]

More than any other fairness argument, this one threatens to stymie proposals for market-oriented policies. Before the Kyoto conference, for example, the U.S. Senate voted 95-to-0 to oppose any treaty that obliged the United States, but not developing nations, to control greenhouse gas emissions—even though developing countries emit far less per person. Since the Senate has the final say on whether the world's champion greenhouse gas emitter will agree to any international climate accord, this parliamentary maneuver was both a shot across the bow of U.S. negotiators and a shot heard around the world. The Senate's sentiment threatens the entire international effort to protect the atmosphere.[24]

This is all the more unfortunate since the competitiveness attack is overblown. Among environmental policies, regulations have been used more than taxes and permits, and hence more studied. And there is remarkably little evidence that regulations handicap businesses, or chase them into "pollution havens," countries with lax environmental rules. For example, between 1970 and 1990, U.S. industries making and exporting the most pollution-intensive products, such

as paper and chemicals—all big spenders on regula-
tion-required pollution control—fared better as a
group in global competition than less-polluting industries, according to Robert Repetto at the World
Resources Institute.[25]

A 1992 World Bank analysis surveyed a slew of
reports and concluded that "the many empirical studies which have attempted to test these hypotheses [of
harm from regulation] have shown no evidence to support them." Evidently, factors such as labor costs, prox-
imity to consumers, and prevalence of corruption have
influenced businesses' fortunes and location choices
much more than environmental policies. In addition,
complying with regulations has almost invariably
proved cheaper than predicted. Sometimes it has even
led businesses to uncover money-saving opportunities.
(See Chapter 13.)[26]

Nevertheless, the trade-based fairness argument is
rhetorically effective, and well founded to the extent
that an environmental tax meant to engineer change
more profound than regulations have to date will leave
its mark on economies. Some industries, and thus
workers and investors, will lose, though probably
less than critics predict. This is arguably why the
Nordic countries and the Netherlands, all small nations
heavily dependent on trade, partially or fully exempt
energy-intensive industries from their carbon taxes,
and why most energy taxes worldwide fall primarily on
consumers.[27]

The ironic upshot of such concessions, though, is
that the most polluting industries are taxed least. A
more precise way to protect companies from untaxed
foreign competitors is to apply "border corrections" to
environmental taxes. This entails rebating taxes on

exports and taxing imports as if they had been made domestically. The United States took half of this approach when it backed its duty on ozone-depleting substances with tariffs on imported products made with or containing the chemicals.[28]

Border corrections, however, face their own obstacles: international agreements such as the Maastricht Treaty, which further integrated the economies of the European Union (EU), and the General Agreement on Tariffs and Trade, which set up the World Trade Organization (WTO). Both treaties work to prohibit protectionism, but are ambiguous on border corrections for environmental taxes. The European Commission, the administrative arm of the Union, set an important precedent in 1995 by approving Danish carbon tax rebates for energy-intensive industries, even as it acknowledged that they apparently contravened EU trade laws. Similarly, in 1994, the WTO's predecessor court upheld the U.S. "gas guzzler" tax although it mostly affected inefficient Japanese- and European-made luxury cars. The court argued that the tax was intended to protect the environment, not restrain trade.[29]

Nevertheless, the conventional wisdom is that the WTO will eventually prove unfriendly to border corrections. Meanwhile, the uncertainty itself deters their use. But until economic superpowers such as Germany, Japan, and the United States confront the carbon problem, for example, in deeds as well as words, the freedom of small, pioneering countries to apply border corrections will be crucial to the development of tax or permit systems worldwide.[30]

In the long run, the best solution would be for trading partners to avoid competitiveness concerns by harmonizing environmental tax and permit systems, especially when they address international problems such as acid rain and global warming. An international forum in which such tax changes were negotiated and coordinated could therefore speed progress, suggests Barbara Bramble at the National Wildlife Federation in Washington, D.C. There is as yet no ideal candidate. What is needed is an institution with the authority of the WTO but without the bias toward viewing environmental policies as little more than impediments to international trade.[31]

The ultimate goal of environmental policy is to fashion a society in which people do not harm each other and their descendants simply by getting up and going to work each day. No one can dispute the basic fairness of this vision. But getting there will require major economic changes. Unavoidably, some people will feel the costs of change more than others. "Polluter pays" seems transparently fair unless the "polluter" is a poor woman in North Philadelphia who needs heat to live, a fisher with a 500-year-old claim to local waters, or a wage laborer in a business undercut by untaxed foreign competitors. In fact, environmental issues, like most important issues, contain moral complexities. Good policy—and politically acceptable policy proposals—must recognize that. Good fiscal policy can.

12

Tax Cuts

Earlier chapters have raised a number of challenges to environmental fiscal reform. But perhaps the most obvious objection of all is simply this: an environmental tax increase is a still tax increase. Many people, especially in the United States, tend to see fiscal reform as just another government revenue grab. But this objection overlooks something equally simple: the billions of dollars from new taxes on environmental harm, along with those on resource windfalls, can be put toward cutting conventional taxes. Even better, slashing obsolete, environmentally harmful subsidies can shrink government and pay for an additional tax cut.

Though the potential revenue shift is large, it would probably not suffice to end conventional taxes in most countries. (See Chapter 9.) Nor would ending all standard taxes necessarily be desirable, since some, such as on income, are important for ensuring progressivity. So an important decision confronts designers of environmental fiscal reforms. Which taxes should be cut? It is a decision with weighty implications, both economic and political.

Conventional taxes apply to two main sources of wealth: capital and labor. Levies on corporate profits, capital gains, and built property apply mostly to capital; taxes on payrolls target labor; and sales and income taxes effectively apply to both. Not surprisingly, many business executives argue that the best way to stimulate the economy and create jobs through tax cuts is to reduce taxes on capital. In direct contradiction, labor groups contend that if governments want to increase payrolls, they should cut payroll taxes.[1]

In a sense, both camps are right. What distinguishes rich countries from poor ones is the quality of not only their physical assets but also their human capital, consisting of workers' skills and knowledge. Spending on education is an investment in an economy's future, just as expenditures on factories and rail lines are, since it makes workers more valuable in the long run. Thus whereas taxing profits makes physical investment less worthwhile, taxing wages can make education investment less worthwhile, by reducing post-graduation pay. And just as investment in factories creates opportunities for workers, investment in human capital creates opportunities for businesses. A well-educated work force is one reason Intel can consider putting a new chip plant in South Korea, but not in Viet Nam. A healthy economy therefore needs steady investment in both computer plants and computer engineers—in both tools and people. Cutting taxes on either part of the economic dynamo helps both to an extent.[2]

The tax cut question then becomes this: Which needs more stimulation today—the use of workers or the use of machines? In almost all countries, the answer is workers. In the United States, the economy is placing less and less value on minimally skilled workers, which is depressing their wages. Partly as a result, the share of U.S. households with at least one child that were living below the poverty line despite having a full-time worker rose from 8.3 percent in 1975 to 11 percent in 1996, for a total of 3.65 million families. (See Figure 12–1.)[3]

In Western Europe, meanwhile, stronger unions, labor laws, and traditions of lifetime employment are protecting many jobholders against falling wages. But like a squeezed balloon, employers there are finding

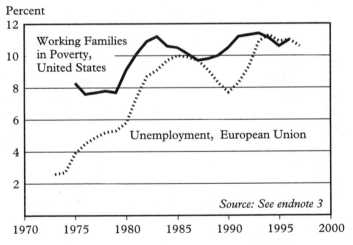

Percent

Working Families in Poverty, United States

Unemployment, European Union

Source: See endnote 3

FIGURE 12–1. *Working Families in Poverty, United States, 1975–96, and Unemployment, European Union, 1973–97*

other ways to release pressures building on them. Wages held high by well-organized workers are spurring some employers to move abroad, automate, or simply not expand. Instead of seeing workers' pay fall, Western Europe is seeing jobs disappear. The unemployment rate in the European Union climbed from 2.6 percent in 1973 to 10.6 percent in 1997, meaning that 17.9 million people in the 15 member nations were looking for jobs. Here, too, the problem is concentrated among less-skilled workers.[4]

And worldwide, 100 million people out of a labor force of 2.8 billion are classified as unemployed, and another 750 million as "underemployed"—able to find odd jobs and seasonal work, but not enough to meet even basic needs. The well-paid, employed majority suffers from these developments too, through everything from higher taxes to pay for social programs to skinhead violence and urban unrest.[5]

Debate rages over the causes of the trends. Analysts have pointed to international capital mobility, trade-induced competition, immigrants willing to accept low wages, and the rise of information technologies, each perhaps with some cause. But taxes contribute as well. Wage taxation has been rising in almost all western industrial countries in recent decades, for example. Between 1970 and 1995, the share of what companies spent on wages that actually went to taxes climbed from 30 to 43 percent in Germany, from 18 to 26 percent in Japan, and from 20 to 26 percent in the United States. And most of those increases occurred through rises in flat-rate levies, not in the progressive income taxes that bear less heavily on low-paid workers. Meanwhile, taxation of profits and capital gains fell.[6]

Economic researchers in western industrial countries have been reasonably consistent in concluding that the tax shift from capital to labor has added to joblessness. One study found that wage tax increases explained 0.5 percentage points of the unemployment rise in France between 1956–66 and 1980–83, 1.3 points in Canada, and 2.0 points in the United Kingdom.[7]

If policymakers want to boost demand for workers, they should seriously consider using the revenues made available by environmental fiscal reform to reverse the rise of the tax burden on wages. In the United States and many developing countries, most of the tax cut would probably translate into higher paychecks. But in the long run, businesses would benefit too: with higher wages on offer, workers would have more reason to invest in their own education. Higher pay could buy better workers. In Western Europe, by contrast, more of the savings would go to businesses at first, according to economic models. But cutting the cost of workers could also stimulate job creation. And studies suggest that targeting wage tax cuts at the lowest-paid workers, which would make wage taxes progressive, like income taxes, would create the most jobs. Demand would rise for the least-skilled service workers, who are having the most trouble finding employment.[8]

Economic models are the best tools for predicting the effects of environmental fiscal reform. Most modeling to date has assumed that revenues to pay for tax cuts would come mainly from greater taxation of environmental damage. They would show even better economic results if they also included higher rent-capturing charges and subsidy cuts. Nonetheless, even in their current forms the models generally show modest but significant benefits for workers. One study, commissioned by the Institute for Public Policy Research (IPPR) in London, modeled the effects of a tax package that would transfer 6 percent of the tax burden in the United Kingdom from labor to environmental damage. (For the sake of progressivity, the energy taxes are applied only to gasoline and diesel fuel and to businesses' utility bills, not to home heating oil. Thus while U.K. citizens would on average break even under this revenue-neutral tax shift, those with lower incomes would generally come out ahead.)[9]

The IPPR's modeling results are a rough guide to what would happen under an environmental tax shift. (See Table 12–1.) Since some taxes rise and others fall, there is essentially no effect on total economic output. (The model does not attempt to count the economic benefits of environmental protection.) Looking more closely, the cost of the environmental taxes is shared among investors and workers in environmentally damaging industries—profits fall and jobs are shed. In effect, part of every pound of tax increase applies to capital, and part applies to labor. Meanwhile, however, the full pound is dedicated to the wage tax cut, which benefits labor exclusively. Overall, more jobs are created in cleaner industries than are lost in the dirtiest ones. Investment, however, falls somewhat. The model, which assumed that the government would start phasing the tax changes in during 1997, projected that employment would rise 717,000 by 2005, or 2.56 percent.[10]

Along the same lines, a European Commission study estimated that levying carbon/energy taxes in the European Union as a whole equivalent to $10 per barrel of oil and using the money to pay for wage tax cuts could create 1.5 million jobs, reducing unemployment 0.9 percentage points. And modeling by Dale

Table 12–1. Projected Effects of IPPR Environmental Tax Shift Plan for the United Kingdom, 2000 and 2005

Tax Measure/Economic Indicator	Effect[1] 2000	2005
Average Effect on Family of Four[2]	(dollars)	
Tax on energy use by businesses	−481	−869
Landfill tax increases	−110	−188
Acceleration of planned gasoline and diesel fuel tax increases	−240	−790
Tax on quarrying of sand and gravel for construction	−84	−207
Tax on office parking spaces	−30	−51
Termination of tax breaks for company car use	−37	−34
Total costs of tax increases	−982	−2,140
Savings from wage tax cut	+982	+2,140
Economic Effects	(change from business-as-usual scenario)	
Gross domestic product[3]	+0.44%	−0.03%
Jobs	+0.95%	+2.56%
	(+253,000)	(+717,000)
Solid waste generation	−6.00%	−16.00%
Carbon emissions	−3.67%	−9.14%

[1]Model assumed tax changes phased in starting in 1997.   [2]Taxes paid by businesses would be passed on to individuals through higher prices, lower wages, or lower stock dividends. Tax costs and savings are estimated as four times the per capita revenue effect of each tax measure. Actual average effects for families of four would differ somewhat from these figures. Few households would break precisely even. Lower-income households would generally gain.   [3]Model did not count economic benefits of a healthier environment.
SOURCE: See endnote 10.

Jorgenson at Harvard University found that a tax shift in the United States, differing in details, could improve economic welfare fairly evenly across the income spectrum, but slightly more at the bottom.[11]

The tax cuts made possible by environmental fiscal reform will not end unemployment and wage declines in rich countries nor make economic miracles in poor ones. But they can help. Even if 10 million new jobs are needed, 1 million would still be a blessing for 1 million families and their communities. Worthy ends in themselves, the benefits also open up new avenues for building political support for a tax shift—support that could be crucial to achieving the primary aim of fiscal reform: a dramatic transformation of how the global economy uses and disposes of resources.

13

An Eco-Industrial Revolution

Global climate change is not the only environmental
problem humanity faces, but it is one of the most serious. Even the most widely quoted greenhouse skeptics
agree that the atmosphere will heat up—they disagree
only on how much and how soon. The consensus among
most scientists is that unless worldwide emissions of carbon slow to less than 2 billion tons a year (from more
than 6 billion today), climate change will likely continue.
That estimate is "conservative," in a perverse sense: even
at 2 billion tons a year, humanity would be playing dice
with the atmosphere. True conservatism argues for min-
imizing human interference in the planetary life-support
system by cutting emissions at least that much.[1]

But the 2-billion-ton target is already ambitious
when viewed from where we stand today. Divide it by

the 10 billion people projected to be living in 2100, and it gives a per person quota of about half a kilogram (a pound) of carbon emissions a day. In a Range Rover, you could drive 4 kilometers (2.5 miles) on that amount before having to stop for the night.[2]

Few major nations have emissions this low. In India, where many people use traditional fuels such as dung and wood, per capita emissions from fossil fuel burning were 30 percent above this level in 1996. China, with its growing use of coal in homes and power plants, exceeded it by a factor of three. Oil-producing Iran surpassed it sixfold. Japan and Germany, with their wealth of chemical and steel plants, their cars and fast trains, emitted at 12 and 15 times this rate. And in the United States, where the good life is increasingly defined as a sport utility vehicle in every three-car garage, emissions were 27 times this projected quota. Thus as western-style industrialism spreads, global carbon emissions are headed to overshoot a "safe" level by a factor of 12 to 27.[3]

Similar stories can be told for other environmental problems. Billions of tons of topsoil wash off farmlands each year, which is the main reason that since World War II, agricultural land equal in expanse to 38 percent of currently cultivated area has been degraded so much that it has reduced or halted local food production. Farms, factories, and households now use 35 percent of the accessible freshwater supply and another 19 percent is claimed in-stream to run hydropower dams or keep rivers navigable. Human activities consumed a fifth of the world's forests in the twentieth century and turned half of what is left into fragments or uniform tree farms. And billions of people suffer from air and water pollution. All of this has happened with only a minority of global society industrialized.[4]

To phrase these statistics differently, industrial economies need to make dramatic cuts in the use of fossil fuels, water, and materials, as well as in pollution, if they are to offer an environmentally sound economic model for the rest of the world in the new century. In the case of carbon emissions, a 90–95 percent reduction per person is needed. It will be nearly impossible for industrial countries to reach such targets unless they steadily raise the price of environmental harm through subsidy terminations, tax hikes, and tradable permit systems. Residents of industrial countries are just beginning to grasp what this means: much less wood to make their houses and their paper; less meat in their diets; less coal for their power plants; less gasoline for their cars. Seemingly, it would spell an end to life as they know it.

No wonder, then, that environmental salvation so often seems built on economic damnation. No wonder that industry-commissioned studies easily stir public concern with predictions of lost jobs, forgone economic growth, and high prices. A recent study of the effects of capping U.S. carbon emissions at 1990 levels, for instance, commissioned by the American Automobile Manufacturers Association (AAMA), forecast a 40-percent job cut in the U.S. coal industry by 2010, and economic damage equal to $1,250 a year for a family of four nationwide.[5]

Previous chapters addressed three common attacks on environmental fiscal reform: that it is impractical, that it is unfair, and that it will raise taxes overall. As with the other indictments, the thinking behind this fourth one, that fiscal reform is economic poison, is understandable. But it is also simplistic and dangerously misleading. The attack dramatizes how raising environmental taxes will hurt some industries while discounting how cutting conventional taxes will help others. It ignores the economic benefits of a healthy environment. And it equates change with cost. In sum, it assumes the price of change will be high, and the benefits low. These assumptions are all questionable.

*   *   *   *

Making the global economy environmentally sustainable will require nothing less than another industrial revolution. As has been the pattern for two centuries, some industries would rise, some would fall, and most would evolve. Though lifestyles would change dramatically in certain respects, it is far from clear that overall economic prosperity would decline, even as measured by the unreliable yardstick of gross domestic product (GDP). On the face of it, an economy that devotes less energy to damaging its own foundations, an economy with lower taxes on work and investment, should prosper more, not less.[6]

An eco-industrial revolution would propel the global economy into a configuration that can be outlined today, if not detailed. Several European environmental groups, including the Wuppertal Institute in Germany and Friends of the Earth in the United Kingdom, have perhaps peered farthest into a sustainable future. They have estimated how much pollution and resource use each planetary citizen would be allowed on average in a sustainable world, and have then explored the consequences of the limits for everyday life. Not surprisingly, the groups find that in the industrial west, per capita consumption of virgin materials and fossil fuels would have to fall 80–95 percent, as would pollution. Freshwater use would have to slow too, though how much would vary more from region to region.[7]

To meet these targets, the studies conclude, the circulation of resources within the global economy would have to rise dramatically, through reuse and recycling. People would have to draw energy mainly from the sun or the Earth's hot interior, wood and fruit from sustainably managed forests, and water from sustainably managed rivers and aquifers. Manufacturing industries would need to be reengineered to minimize production of goods—but maximize the services provided by them. Builders would need to insulate homes so well that the inhabitants' own bodies would generate much of the heat in winter. Everything from buses to refrigerators would be designed for easy repair, disassembly, and recycling. One factory's waste would become another's feedstock—making pollution nearly obsolete. Neighborhoods would have to be laid out to make walking, biking, mass transit, and even carpooling easier than solo driving. People would spend less on BMWs and beef and more on information, education, and entertainment.[8]

As the economy's makeup shifted, society as a whole would gain. There would be fewer acid-rain-corroded buildings to repair, for instance, and fewer children sent to the emergency room with asthma attacks. Topsoil and groundwater would be better husbanded for a time when there will be more mouths to feed. Insurance executives would be relieved of their fear of freak storms caused by global climate change, storms that could turn half their clients into claimants in a matter of months.

Yet these gains are rarely counted in economic models. A study led by the World Resources Institute's Robert Repetto, for example, demonstrated how failure to count environmental benefits has biased assessments of environment policies already on the books. Air pollution regulations, the authors found, were one reason the

U.S. electric utility industry's costs rose 8 percent between 1970 and 1991 for the amount of power sold—one reason its productivity, in other words, apparently declined 8 percent. But adding in the economic benefits of cleaner air, including lower doctors' bills for people downwind, turned the decline into an 8–15 percent productivity increase from the point of view of society as a whole. The potential for gains like these is not surprising: it is what led economist A.C. Pigou to advocate environmental taxation back in 1920.[9]

The transition to a sustainable economy will in fact greatly accentuate a long-standing economic trend. Since the nineteenth century, when almost all laborers in industrial countries worked the land, employment in the businesses that consume the most resources—and also pollute the most—has been falling steadily because of automation. (See Chapter 4.) Between 1983 and 1994 alone, employment in farming, fishing, logging, mining, and oil and gas production fell from 24 million to 18 million in western industrial countries, even as output held steady or increased. Jobs are shifting to service and light manufacturing industries, ranging from solar cells to medical care—industries that are not intrinsically as hard on the Earth. Such companies expanded their payrolls in the same period from 290 million to 340 million jobs. As this trend shows no signs of slowing, many of the layoffs predicted by the AAMA study and others like it will occur anyway.[10]

The industries that would generate the fastest job growth are the ones that offer alternatives to environmentally damaging products. They in fact stand to benefit twice over. First, costs for their unsustainable competitors would rise as strong environmental policies, including taxes, took hold. Second, they would benefit from the cuts in wage or profit taxes made possible by environmental fiscal reforms.

Consumer pressure, regulations, and even a few taxes are already giving a taste of what may come. Sales of organically grown food rose 19-fold in the United States between 1980 and 1996, from $180 million to $3.5 billion. They grew similarly in the European Union. The chlorofluorocarbon (CFC) phaseout, hastened by taxes in some countries, has created billion-dollar markets for ozone-safe alternatives and for refrigerators and air conditioners designed to use them.[11]

Global wind power capacity additions quintupled between 1990 and 1997, with Denmark, Germany, Spain, and India installing the most, thanks in part to strong subsidies. The wind industry now employs 20,000 in the European Union, up from practically zero in the 1970s. The latest doubling of global solar cell sales, which are made from silicon, took four years, a growth rate worthy of silicon computer chips. The international market for "environmental" goods and services that monitor and control pollution, recycle, and conserve energy amounted to roughly $408 billion in 1994, and is projected to reach $572 billion by 2001—comfortably larger than the global aerospace business. (See Table 13–1.)[12]

Thus under environmental fiscal reform, for every declining coal industry, there would be a rising solar or wind power industry. Raising taxes on environmental harm and cutting subsidies for it would hurt some businesses, but the resulting tax cuts would benefit others. And greater reliance on rent-capturing taxes on public resources and land values—taxes that do not discourage industry—would give economies a modest boost overall.

Not surprisingly, industries that would stand on the

Table 13–1. Global Market for Environmental Protection Goods and Services, with Projection for 2001

Region	Sales	
	1994	2001
	(billion dollars)	
North America	176	233
Latin America	7	15
Western Europe	127	168
Eastern Europe, Russia	6	11
Africa	2	4
Middle East	4	6
Australia, New Zealand, Japan	72	92
Developing Asia	14	43
World	408	572

SOURCE: See endnote 12.

losing side of fiscal reform are working hard to fight such a balanced outcome. If they must pay carbon taxes, for example, they want the revenue returned to them in proportion to their past fossil fuel use. They want tradable permits to be given to them, not sold. Indeed, the ability of permit giveaways to assuage politically powerful polluters is a major reason that the United States has pushed hard to include permit trading in the international climate change treaty. But by handing out trillions of dollars worth of permits, governments would be rewarding companies for earlier emissions—the more a company emitted in the past, the more free permits it would get—rather than using the potential revenue to cut taxes that penalize current activity. From the standpoint of economic growth, the money would disappear into a black hole—ironically, in just the manner assumed in industry-funded studies that make tax and permit systems look so costly.[13]

★   ★   ★   ★

The great bulk of the industrial economy actually lies between these environmentally benign and destructive extremes. Most industries will see neither massive shrinkage nor massive growth. But many will have to evolve in order to survive. A sustainable economy will still need paper, chemicals, and steel, for example, but makers of these products will have to redouble their searches for ways to pollute less and recycle more.

If experience is any guide, devising these new ways of making things will cost much less than is often predicted. When Hart Hodges, an economist with the City of Portland, Oregon, did a literature survey on the costs of environmental protection, he found a dozen policies in the United States, affecting everything from asbestos to vinyl chloride, for which costs had been estimated both before and after entering into force. All but one policy turned out to cost half or less of what was originally projected, mainly because of unforeseen technological advances. Such advances are a major reason, for instance, that the price of permits in the U.S. sulfur trading system fell to $100 a ton, less than a third of what even the system's optimistic defenders originally predicted. (See Chapter 9.)[14]

The U.S. phaseout of CFCs provided the exception to the "half or less" rule in the Hodges study—but for a good reason. In 1988 the U.S. government predicted that halving CFC use by 1998 would cost $3.55 per kilogram. But five years later it pegged the price of complete elimination by 1996 at $2.45 a kilogram— only 30 percent less, but for a much more aggressive target. The outlook had brightened because companies and public agencies, unencumbered by regulations but propelled by an imminent ban and a rising tax, had found CFC substitutes in most major uses.[15]

Electronics giants such as AT&T, General Electric, and Texas Instruments, for example, worked together to find alternatives to CFCs for cleaning new circuit boards. Eventually, they settled on a more radical approach: soldering components together so neatly that they needed no cleaning. By 1992, they had refined the technique and halted CFC use. One company, Nortel, spent $1 million on the switchover, but saved $4 million in CFC purchase and disposal costs (and CFC taxes). The new process also raised efficiency and product quality.[16]

Michael Porter of the Harvard Business School has won a name in some circles and notoriety in others by arguing that money-saving outcomes like these are the rule rather than the exception in environmental policy. The prod of new regulations and taxes often stimulates companies to change and innovate, making them more, not less, competitive, he asserts, pointing to a dozen instances of this pattern. Pollution and resource waste, Porter suggests, are often signs of financial waste.[17]

Economists generally respond to Porter's thesis the way the Pope greeted Galileo's news of moons around Jupiter. It contradicts their worldview, so they reject it. To make their computer models work consistently, economists tend to assume that the market is not just powerful but perfect. No cost-cutting opportunity, the models say, is ever missed. Thus, in the words of Voltaire's Doctor Pangloss, we live in the best of all possible worlds. Any regulation or tax that pushes the economy away from this point of perfection must cost money.

But a small band of economists is arguing with increasing credibility that real economies can easily get stuck in money-wasting ruts and never find their way onto more efficient development paths nearby—unless nudged by some force, such as an environmental tax.

The layout of the keyboard now found on most of the world's computers is a classic example. A Milwaukee, Wisconsin, printer—Christopher Latham Sholes, "the fifty-second man to invent the typewriter," according to economic historian Paul David—purposely designed the layout known as QWERTY in the 1870s for inefficiency. He spread the most common letters over the keyboard, instead of grouping them in the center, in order to overcome a serious shortcoming of his "type writer"—adjacent keys struck in succession tended to jam. Thanks to quirks of history, his model gained an early lead in the market. By the 1890s, the United States found itself locked into the odd arrangement. If typists had to learn one layout, this was it; thus if manufacturers had to provide one layout, this was it. The U.S. Navy demonstrated in the 1940s that typists could work faster with more sensible arrangements, once they learned them—but few have. In this case, Doctor Pangloss was wrong.[18]

In general, dissident economists list several factors—in addition to standards that perpetuate themselves—that can lead economic development into inefficient ruts. For one, drawing on the insights of Nobelist Herbert Simon, they point out that companies never have enough people with enough time to investigate the millions of process changes they could make. Nortel, for example, for years stuck to circuit board cleaning techniques that it later found to waste money simply because the techniques had worked reasonably well in the past. The CFC phaseout, however, focused its corporate mind. Engineers were put on the job of finding affordable alternatives, and in a matter of years they succeeded beyond expectations.[19]

The dissident economists point to other factors that can fool modelers into overestimating the costs of environmental policies. The more widgets—or water purifiers, or solar cells—a company makes, points out W. Brian Arthur, the better the company becomes at making them, which allows it to bring down prices, stoke demand, and make even more widgets. It was Henry Ford's genius to appreciate the power of this dynamic. Whether he was reusing wood from shipping crates or inventing the moving assembly line so that workers would spend less time walking around, Ford obsessed over reducing costs. As a result, he was able to cut prices the way Intel does today. Between 1909 and 1923, Model T production shot from some 10,000 a year to more than 1 million, prices dropped 70 percent, and the car went from being a rich person's novelty to the signature consumer item of the middle class. (See Figure 13–1.)[20]

This virtuous circle can arise in any manufacturing business where change is afoot, which is why technologies often develop in unpredictable waves and pulses. Between 1975 and 1997, for instance, the price of a kilowatt of solar cells dropped 30 percent for every doubling in cumulative sales worldwide. (See Figure 13–2.) At this rate, another tenfold increase in cumulative sales would bring prices to $1 per watt, often considered the threshold for competitiveness with coal and natural gas. Every $1,000 that governments spend on solar cells today nudges the industry along its learning curve and lowers prices of future solar cells enough to save buyers

List Price

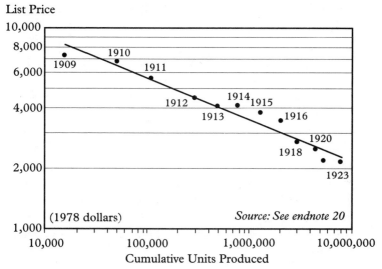

FIGURE 13–1. *Ford Model T: Price versus Cumulative Production, 1909–23*

Dollars per Watt

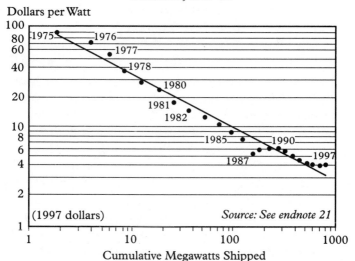

FIGURE 13–2. *Photovoltaic Modules: Price versus Cumulative Production, 1975–97*

about $400, estimates a World Bank study by economists Dennis Anderson and Robert Williams.[21]

But there is no guarantee that environmentally sound technologies will win on their own. When two technologies compete, the overwhelming advantage usually goes to the one with the head start, precisely because it has had more time to move along its learning curve. Solar power, for instance, must compete with oil- and coal-burning technologies on an economic playing field that has been tilted in favor of fossil fuels for a century by subsidies and the lack of environmental taxes. As a result, for every dollar that has been spent developing renewable energy technologies, a hundred or a thousand have been spent refining their polluting competitors.

Overall, this historical perspective has double-edged implications for the costs of an eco-industrial revolution, argues Michael Grubb at the Royal Institute for International Affairs in London. On the one hand, industrial economies have fallen deeply into an economic rut characterized by fossil fuel dependence, wastage of water, and throwaway consumption. Climbing out of this rut could be expensive at first. Neighborhoods built around the automobile could become almost unreachable as the true cost of driving was passed back to drivers. Poorly insulated office towers could become unrentable. Solar cells could start out pricey.[22]

But if governments apply enough policy muscle to tip the market toward environmentally sound technologies, compensating for decades of imbalance the other way, the newcomers could eventually develop their own momentum in the manner of the Model T. Substantial subsidies could be targeted at the technologies to speed their development early on. Taxes, phased in more slowly, could help sustain the development. (See Chapter 8.)[23]

Once governments lifted economies out of the environmentally destructive rut and onto the neighboring ridge, falling into the environmentally sound valley on the other side could be easy. Change in the long run would cost much less than at first. And in many cases, as with CFCs, the "long run" could be surprisingly short. Production costs for solar cells and efficient drip irrigation systems could fall fairly quickly. In other cases, such as in making neighborhoods in industrial countries more pedestrian-friendly, change would take longer. Thus developing countries, which have fewer suburban highways and virgin paper plants to leave behind, may make the transition more easily—just as they got a jump on the West in the use of mobile phones.

In sum, there are many reasons to believe that industrial economies are much more flexible in the long run than they appear from where we stand today. What makes perceiving the capacity for change hard is the difficulty of imagining any development path that is not a simple extrapolation of past trends, any world that is much different from our own. Yet the past is a notoriously poor guide to the future.

Alan Kay, whose vision of the notebook computer in the 1960s inspired engineers to realize it decades later, has said that "the best way to predict the future is to invent it." Though change always exacts some cost, a sustainable future is to a great extent ours for the making. Given the economic benefits of intact resources, healthy air and water, and a stable atmosphere, an environmentally sound economy will probably not generate any less prosperity than the status quo. It will not be smaller in dollar terms, just different.[24]

14

The Political
Marketplace

Proponents of environmental fiscal policy reform often depict the arrows of influence between the government and the market as running one way: government sets the rules for the market, and businesses and consumers obey. The prescription that flows from this picture is straightforward. All policymakers need to do is get the tax and subsidy signals right, and the global economy will be on an environmentally sustainable, prosperous course. But any realistic assessment of the global environmental predicament must recognize that markets influence governments as well as the other way around. Fiscal policy is nothing if not political.

Indeed, the hard part is not figuring out what reform should look like. The preceding chapters have argued that environmental fiscal reform—cutting environmentally harmful subsidies, capturing more resource rents, and implementing environmentally protective subsidies and taxes—can provide multiple benefits. It can protect the environment, boost economies, even make existing subsidies work better on their own terms. And the chapters have drawn on real-life examples to show that these reforms can be designed to be workable, fair, and revenue-neutral.

The greatest challenge for reformers lies in making change a political reality. The biggest losers under environmental fiscal reform—from middle-class buyers of subsidized electricity to investors and workers in resource-based industries—usually enjoy more legal recognition and are better organized and financed than those who would gain, which includes low-income or indigenous people, city dwellers who cannot tell what is polluting the air they breathe, and generations yet unborn.

As a result, opponents of fiscal reform are more practiced at exploiting avenues of influence such as public protests, campaign contributions, family and other connections, and even corruption in order to thwart change. The process of policy formation itself is a sort of market, but a complex one with multiple currencies: votes, campaign money, and kickbacks. Mapping a route through this rocky political terrain to a sustainable society will not be easy. To the extent that environmentally blinkered tax and spending policies are held hostage by special interests—and they are to a considerable degree—fiscal policy reform and continuing progress toward environmental sustainability are bound up with the broader task of making government more accountable to all the governed. But to the extent that representative government is working the way it is supposed to in reflecting, for example, widespread hostility to gasoline taxes, the prime task is to educate people about why reform is in their best interest.

*   *   *   *

The intertwining of policy and politics is easily seen in subsidies. Whatever its purpose, a subsidy calls into being a well-defined group of beneficiaries. The subsidized and the subsidizers usually support one another in a resilient feedback loop. Makers and enforcers of policy use the power of their office to hold up their end of the political bargain; recipients use votes or money to deliver on theirs.

The best-studied instances of the symbiosis between subsidies and one form of influence-peddling—corruption—occur in the management of public resources. Backroom timber deals are rife in the Asia-Pacific region, for example, the world's major supplier of tropical wood. Several characteristic features stand out in such situations. First, the recipients of the extraction rights are few. In Indonesia, there are 584 logging concessions, owned by roughly 50 conglomerates, which appear to be controlled by as few as 15 business leaders, including several billionaires. The most powerful figure is Bob Hasan, a trusted aide of President Suharto. Through his control of the Indonesian Plywood Association (APKINDO), which holds an export monopoly, Hasan is able to hold down the market price for the raw logs used to make plywood and to capture much of the billions of dollars in windfall created by the liquidation of Indonesia's forests.[1]

The second common feature in these examples is that relations between politicians, military officers, and logging tycoons are complex and close. Three key figures engineered much of the logging of the Philippine island of Palawan in the early 1990s, according to local environmentalists: the Speaker of the House of Representatives, who represented part of the province; the principal shareholder in the province's two biggest logging firms; and the director of the Palawan Philippines National Police. Local environmentalists have reported seeing military escorts for trucks carrying illegally cut logs; the Speaker, meanwhile, was widely understood to be "involved in everything" that happens in Palawan. Though the exact relationships among these figures are not public, the men are known to be friends, and it is likely that all shared in the profits from cheap and poorly enforced timber concessions.[2]

Logging-related irregularities are on the rise in other parts of the world as well. In a textbook case of cowboy economics, as Asian companies exhaust timber supplies at home they are spreading to new countries throughout the tropics, bringing along their old ways of doing business. Allegations of bribery have dogged Indonesian and especially Malaysian companies as they have pressed for entry into timber-rich Brazil, Papua New Guinea, the Solomon Islands, and Suriname on terms that are favorable to themselves but potentially catastrophic for the forests' traditional owners. In Suriname, news of the government's intention to sell giant timber concessions far below value to Indonesian and Malaysian companies reached the press around the same time as rumors of rampant bribe-taking among parliamentarians.[3]

Though corruption can be found anywhere, it is legal influence-peddling that affects fiscal policy more in industrial democracies. The problem is particularly severe in the United States, as measured by the amount of money changing hands. There, candidates for

Congress and the presidency raised $2.4 billion in 1996—most from moneyed interests with their own agendas. Though this is a huge sum to spend on electing fewer than 500 people, it is trivial compared with the roughly $1.7 trillion at stake each year in federal spending and tax decisions. Donations of $10,000 or even $500,000 may make politicians' mouths water, but they are peanuts for large corporations, and excellent investments even if they influence legislators only occasionally. Carl Mayer, an elected official in Princeton, New Jersey, did not stretch the truth much when he told a reporter that "giving money to politicians is the best return on an investment...in the entire free world." This is what makes campaign contributions as stubborn an impediment to fiscal policy reform as corruption.[4]

It is politics, not sound policy, that best explains the remarkable resilience of outmoded resource regimes in the United States, for instance. In the 1995–96 election cycle, oil and gas companies gave $11.8 million to congressional candidates to protect tax breaks worth at least $3 billion over the period. Timber lobbies donated $3.6 million, mainly to members of committees that set the Forest Service's budget and logging quotas. Mining firms handed out $1.9 million in order to fend off royalty charges on public hardrock minerals, something they have succeeded in doing for more than 120 years. Ranching interests contributed $2.2 million in order to keep federal grazing fees low, as they have been since 1906.[5]

Illustrating the economics of campaign donations, the Cyprus Amax Minerals company gave $237,045 to members of Congress in 1995–96—a hefty sum, but only one twelve-thousandth the $3 billion in gross income it stood to gain from a pending mining claim in

Colorado as long as U.S. mining law remained unchanged. Yet that lone contribution equaled nearly one quarter of the $1.1 million that environmental groups donated during the period.[6]

The same conservative forces also materialize when politicians advocate environmental taxes. When President Bill Clinton proposed an energy tax in 1993, for example, its costs were clear to those who would pay it, but since it was intended to cut the budget deficit, its benefits were fuzzy even to the sharpest economists. Worse, the President did little to educate the public about the tax's environmental benefits. Support for the tax was thus weak. Major manufacturers and energy producers launched a multimillion-dollar lobbying and contribution campaign against it—until then, the largest such effort ever mounted to stop a bill in U.S. history. Many voters also disliked the Clinton bill. But, tellingly, the only bit of Clinton's proposal that survived the congressional battle was a small gasoline and diesel tax, coming largely out of the pockets of consumers, not the businesses that lobbied so effectively.[7]

It is hard to prove that checks buy legislators' votes. But people would not give the money, and in such strategic ways, if they did not think it worthwhile. In the case of American resource-based industries, lobbies have usually focused their efforts on the Senate, where it is easier for legislative minorities to obstruct progress, and where lightly populated, resource-rich states wield disproportionate clout. Candidates' dependence on such donations—and thus their vulnerability to industry pressure—is growing steadily, driven mainly by the competition to bombard the public with simplistic but expensive television spots during election campaigns.[8]

Completely removing money from politics would weaken the political advantage of those benefiting from the status quo—but it would not eliminate it. Tax hikes and subsidy cuts are usually asymmetric in their effects: there are a few big losers but a lot of small winners. With more at stake, individuals on the losing side are more apt to organize to lobby their representatives than are those who would save money or benefit from a healthier planet. Thus democracy at its best is still vulnerable to distortions by special interests.[9]

In Germany, hard-coal union locals now represent only 1 in 300 workers, yet they are influential enough within the Social Democratic Party to protect subsidies worth $86,000 per member, subsidies that would bankrupt the country if granted to all workers. In the United States, labor groups joined with the automobile and fossil fuel industries before the 1997 climate conference in Kyoto to mount a hard-hitting advertising and lobbying campaign against possible U.S. commitments to reducing greenhouse gas emissions—commitments that can probably only be met through policies that raise fossil fuel prices. These groups are likely to redouble their efforts when the Kyoto treaty comes to the U.S. Senate for ratification.[10]

*   *   *   *

Not surprisingly, corruption, campaign donation dependence, and special interest politics tend to hurt economies as well as the environment. As special interest groups strengthen their hold on policymaking, decisions on taxes, spending, and resource management tend increasingly to serve minority interests at the expense of society as a whole.

Of the various methods of influence, corruption perhaps costs societies the most. Nigeria provides one extreme example of what it can do. On the 1997 Corruption Perception Index, compiled by the Berlin-based watchdog group Transparency International (TI), Nigeria scored 1.8 on a 10-point scale, ranking it most corrupt among the 52 countries covered. As this statistic suggests, Nigeria's society and economy are in shambles. The wealth flowing in from oil production concentrates in the hands of a military elite while many Nigerians, including the Ogoni people, who live amidst Royal/Dutch Shell's pipelines and pollution, are losing out.[11]

In May 1997, Harvard economist Shang-Jin Wei released an international comparative study that suggested that corruption deters foreign investment in developing countries over the long run. Among the countries he studied, an increase in corruption from the level of the relatively bribe-free Singapore to that of Mexico, where illicit payments are more commonplace, had the same dampening effect on foreign investment as raising taxes on investment 21–24 percentage points would have. The paper made a minor splash in the financial papers as a fresh study on an issue most investors had thought little about—and probably soon forgot. But mere weeks later, in one of history's odd jokes, the Thai baht entered its free fall against the U.S. dollar, laying bare the prevalence of corruption in the region and triggering an international economic crisis. In a way no statistical tract could achieve, the crisis made graphically obvious the link between corruption and economic health. The political cultures that were ravaging the forests of the Pacific Rim were also ravaging its economies.[12]

The attempts by governments and the International

Monetary Fund (IMF) to wrestle with the Asian financial meltdown, as well as the struggles in many western legislatures to reform campaign finance, illustrate how difficult it is to straighten out a crooked system. President Suharto of Indonesia, for example, resisted IMF demands to break up the country's wealth-siphoning trade cartels, including Bob Hasan's plywood monopoly, even though his resistance pushed the country closer to economic and social meltdown. And the U.S. Congress has failed for two decades to reform the campaign finance system that so indebts it to the likes of Exxon and Cyprus Amax.[13]

Occasionally, it should be said, lack of accountability has made it easier for governments to pursue aggressive environmental fiscal reform. The iron hand of the autocrat can be effective when turned to the work of environmental protection. For example, one of the world's stiffest environmental taxes (on car ownership) and one of the only examples of tradable permit auctions (as opposed to giveaways) are both found in Singapore, a country not known for political pluralism.[14]

Another notable environmental tax regime—on water pollution in the Netherlands—also owes some of its effectiveness to a rather undemocratic institutional context, which in turn derives from the country's distinctive relationship with water. Dutch farmers had been managing waterways long before the modern national government appeared. In the early Middle Ages, peasants and landholders began claiming what is now a third of the country's area from the sea. The tools with which they staked this claim included dikes, raised canals, and windmill-driven pumps. But making so much water run uphill also required institutions. Farmers organized themselves into groups now called "water boards," which to this day exercise considerable control over the country's waters. Farmers have typically granted representatives of a new class of water users—factories looking for a place to dump chemical wastes—no more than a third of the seats on the boards.[15]

As a result, when the government mandated major reductions in water pollution starting in 1969, the responsibility fell largely to these institutions, dominated by people who had no interest in footing the bill. So farmers made the polluters pay for new treatment plants, in the process providing the world with one of its first and best examples of environmental taxation. (See Chapter 9.)[16]

Populism, meanwhile, sometimes slows reform. In the Philippines, Venezuela, and other developing countries, riots and street protests have greeted past attempts to cut gasoline subsidies, which are popular among the middle and upper classes. And like the government officials who profit from logging and therefore encourage it, members of the public tend to support extractive activities when they reap some of the windfalls themselves. In Alaska, residents have become accustomed to receiving $1,000 checks every October from the state government, their share of the royalties from oil production in Prudhoe Bay. Some recipients have argued that the state should pay lobbyists in Washington, D.C., to press for expansion of drilling in ecologically sensitive areas in order to boost future royalties. In the Netherlands, the very agricultural interests that have arranged for rapid progress against industrial water pollution have impeded legislation to reduce fertilizer and manure runoff from farms.[17]

Nevertheless, the balance of the evidence from this mixed picture says that democracy is a more reliable ally than authoritarianism in the campaign to protect the planet. Domestic pollution problems have rarely been allowed to become as severe in industrial democracies as they have in formerly communist countries, for example. How, then, are reformers within democracies to overcome, tame, or circumvent the political power of beneficiaries of the status quo? There are essentially two approaches. One is to fight fire with water—to reform the system to reduce the influence of special interests. The other is to fight fire with fire—to use the revenue money raised through taxes and subsidy cuts to buy political support. Since neither tack will succeed perfectly in a complex world, both need to be pursued.

In the area of corruption reduction, several guiding principles have emerged from recent academic work, particularly that of Susan Rose-Ackerman at Yale University Law School. One is that officials who formulate and implement policy should be paid well, in order to reduce the appeal of bribes. In the Philippines' Department of Environment and Natural Resources, as in many other governments, low pay is one factor that has contributed to corruption among timber concession administrators, which the department's own Secretary has called rampant.[18]

In addition, adoption and enforcement of strong anti-corruption laws, periodic auditing of officials, and an independent judiciary are also critical; enforcement will never stamp out corruption completely, but it will increase the risks for potential bribe takers. Finally, reducing the discretion of bureaucratic decisionmakers and making their actions public will further reduce the appeal of bribes. Competitive, public auctions for resource concessions, for example—like the ones

Honduras has used to sell logging rights—bear out the observation that sunlight is the best disinfectant. (See Chapter 7.)[19]

As Transparency International founder Peter Eigen is quick to point out, however, a bribe dirties the hands of both the giver and the receiver. Thus enforcement efforts need to be aimed at both parties. Working backward from TI's Corruption Perception Index and international trade data, TI scientist Johann Graf Lambsdorff pinpointed the major trading partners of the most corrupt countries, partners that are therefore probably home to major bribe givers. Topping the list were Belgium, France, Italy, the Netherlands, South Korea, and the United Kingdom. Their high rank is not surprising: in many industrial countries, bribes to foreign officials are tax-deductible.[20]

In a promising move, the world's industrial democracies signed a "soft law" treaty in 1997 to outlaw such bribes, much as the United States did unilaterally in the 1970s. The pact is viewed as less binding than most international accords, however, and enforcing it will be hard since companies often disguise bribes as consulting fees. But if enough governments implement the treaty aggressively, it could ultimately reduce corruption and its economic and environmental tolls.[21]

Lessening the influence of money in electoral politics while respecting people's right to freedom of expression is another knotty problem. During the last few decades, almost every industrial democracy has adopted its own mix of reform measures, including public campaign financing, bans on political television advertising, and limits on contributions and spending. None of these attempted solutions have come close to ridding politics of money, but some have worked better than others. In Canada, for instance, a 1974 package of reforms combined strong spending caps for political parties, disclosure requirements, tax credits for private donations, and direct public financing; as a result, campaign spending for the most recent federal elections was limited to 80¢ per capita, compared with $9 in the United States. And the reforms appear to have facilitated the rise of new political parties.[22]

*   *   *   *

Since curbing the power that special interests exercise through corruption and campaign donations is not easy, it is inevitably a long-term project. In the meantime, even as fiscal reformers work to change the rules of the system, they should also do their best to play by the rules, to fight fire with fire. They need to think strategically about how to spend the revenues generated by tax increases and subsidy cuts in order to forge political alliances. And they need to work hard to educate the public about issues such as climate change, and the value of fiscal reform in addressing them.

One of the most effective ways politicians have found to advance fiscal reform is to use environmentally protective taxes to pay for environmentally protective subsidies. In the same vein, earmarking such revenue to pay salaries at environmental protection agencies can be useful where these agencies are underfunded, which they often are, especially in developing countries. Earmarking of either sort can win over voters who do not trust policymakers to spend the money wisely otherwise. Indeed, A.C. Pigou had just this sort of tax-subsidy combination in mind when he first put forward the environmental tax idea in 1920, argues political scientist Mikael Skou Andersen at Århus University in

Denmark.[23]

The Canadian province of Ontario discovered the political merits of this approach when it adopted a tax on fuel-inefficient vehicles in 1991. Vehicle taxes can be particularly effective because they reach consumers just as they make one of the most important decisions affecting how much they pollute: what car to buy. But the Ontario tax, though modest, proved hugely unpopular, leading the government to scale it back and dedicate some of the remaining revenues to subsidizing the most efficient cars. The resulting tax-subsidy hybrid is the world's first "feebate" system. Under the system, for example, buyers of the fuel-efficient Chevrolet Sprint receive a subsidy of $100 (Canadian) while buyers of the Ford Explorer sport utility vehicle pay a tax of $400. Efficient cars did gain market share in Ontario in the early 1990s, though it is hard to prove that the feebates helped. But the experience demonstrated the political palatability of twinning environmentally friendly taxes and subsidies.[24]

A less virtuous strategy is to return the money to businesses without requiring them to invest it in pollution prevention. If tax revenues are refunded to companies in proportion to past emissions, for instance— an approach that has been called an "incremental tax"—firms end up paying a tax only on increases in their pollution above some baseline; if they emit below the baseline, they receive a net subsidy. Giving away tradable permits in proportion to past emissions has the same effect, which is why giveaways are much more common than auctions. In the effort to put the U.S. sulfur emissions trading plan into law (see Chapter 9), supporters made sophisticated use of free permits to buy votes. David Hawkins, who lobbied on behalf of the plan for the Natural Resources Defense Council in Washington, D.C., recounts how:

> As the legislation moved through Congress, there were various key votes. At each choke point, there were people in a position to say, "I'll go along with this bill only if you have an 'accommodation' for a utility in my district." What was done was to come up with "special rules" to give extra permits to these firms. Congress finds it distasteful to name specific companies. The job is to come up with criteria that only one set of companies fits. Other important features were a 20-percent bonus for the cleanest plants, and allocating permits based on 1985 emission rates. Some plants had cut emissions between 1985 and the time this was being legislated, in 1990. So some were being given more permits than their current emissions, permits they could sell. It turned them into at least quiet advocates for passage. It split the industry.[25]

This experience offers intriguing lessons in how to use tradable permits as political currency. Still, giving away permits subsidizes companies for past pollution, so it is bad for taxpayers and economies as a whole, just like giving away public minerals. Ideally, Hawkins agrees, they should be auctioned in order to generate revenues with which to cut taxes on work and investment. A compromise he suggests is to give away permits during the first years of a new trading system, but then gradually shift to auctions. For business executives focused on next quarter's bottom line, the costs of losing free permits would appear relatively distant, and thus modest. But in the long run, the public would benefit from tax cuts.[26]

Measures that do not recycle money directly back to polluters are not only better for taxpayers, they also have their own political merits since their revenues can buy support from other groups. When U.S.

Representative Pete Stark of California proposed in the late 1980s that the United States tax ozone-depleting chemicals such as chlorofluorocarbons (CFCs), he chose a tax rate sufficiently high to make less-damaging substitutes competitive. As Stark's proposal gathered steam, however, other members of Congress pressed successfully to raise the rate—to increase environmental protection—but for reasons having little to do with the environment. "Most members want to give away things through the tax code," explains Perry Plumart, Stark's environmental aide at the time. "One of the nice things about environmental taxes is that their benefit comes from raising money. So an environmental tax was always very welcome. It paid for tax cuts, such as for R&D, that helped other industries."[27]

Similar searches for revenue powered Europe's environmental tax shifts—explicit pairings of environmental taxes and across-the-board cuts in income taxes. (See Chapter 12.) The first of these came in Sweden, which in the postwar era had charted a middle course between capitalism and socialism, building a market-based economy that gave government a role in everything from child care to housing. By the early 1990s, structural flaws had appeared in the "Swedish model." Economic growth slowed and then stopped. Unemployment rose. Taxes captured 55 percent of economic output but were full of exemptions, which forced tax rates on nonexempt income as high as 85 percent, deterring work. Swedish politicians decided to eliminate some major exemptions, lower overall tax rates, and, more broadly, shift taxes from income to consumption (retail sales)—ambitious tasks made politically easier if they resulted in a net tax cut.[28]

One result of the ensuing hunt for revenue substitutes was Sweden's enactment of taxes on emissions of sulfur and carbon. (See Chapter 10.) But in a measure of how secondary environmental concerns were to this shift, Kjell-Olof Fält, the Minister of Finance at the time, now almost denies that any premeditated tax shift occurred. (Swedish environmentalists, however, point to government publications that detail the effects and scale—albeit modest—of the new taxes.)[29]

As Western Europe's unemployment crisis deepened during the 1990s, joblessness became the driving concern behind tax shifts in other countries, which focused more exclusively on cutting payroll taxes. (See Chapter 9.) This prism-like nature of environmental fiscal reform—what someone perceives as useful in it depends on where the person stands politically—can make it a political winner. There is something in it for nearly everyone.

As these stories show, one effective reform strategy is to inject ideas about environmental fiscal reform into seemingly unrelated tax and budget changes working their way through legislatures. Going the distance with environmental fiscal reform, however, will take more than opportunism. The economic stakes are too high to change hands without a major political fight. Since the vision of the transition to a sustainable society is ambitious, the political calculations it gives rise to must be ambitious too.

A 1994 tax proposal by Greenpeace Germany exemplifies the breadth of vision that is needed. It calls for a tax that would push energy prices up by roughly 7 percent a year over at least 15 years. The government would pool the tax receipts taken from consumers through their utility bills and then recycle it all by mailing "eco bonus" checks worth a flat amount per person—say, $100—to every home in the country. Poorer households, which spend less than average on energy, would gain from the redistribution. Rich households would lose—though very slightly compared with their incomes. As with the Institute for Public Policy Research proposal for a tax shift in the United Kingdom (see Chapter 12), industry would get its money back through across-the-board payroll tax cuts. As a result, according to modeling by the German Institute for Economic Research in Berlin, total energy use would fall and employment would increase.[30]

Though it has not affected German tax law yet, the Greenpeace proposal did divide industry, garner popular support, and help push tax shifting onto the public agenda. Under the plan, industries that use the most energy and the least labor, such as chemical manufacturers, steelmakers, and coal companies, would see their costs rise. They were responsible for 46 percent of value added in private industry in 1988, but only 42 percent of employment. Cleaner, more labor-intensive industries, from education to telecommunications to retail, would save money. As a result, their role in the German economy—already 50 percent of output in private industry and 54 of employment—would expand. The automobile industry, with 4 percent of output and employment, would break even. Thus a comfortable majority of the electorate in private industry would work for companies that would break even or gain. (See Table 14–1.)[31]

Impressively, the appliance maker AEG, the Tupperware company, and a dozen other big businesses have signed on with environmentalists in Germany to fight for tax reform. Even the head of BMW has endorsed the idea, perhaps because he believes, as U.S. automakers appear to, that energy taxes will encourage consumers to spend extra for more energy-efficient cars.[32]

The German metal workers' union, IG-Metall, the largest union in Europe, has also voiced strong support, in marked contrast with its U.S. counterparts. With employment already falling steadily in the German iron and steel industries, the status quo offers little security for union members. Payroll tax cuts and an accelerated transition to a sustainable, more labor-intensive steel-recycling industry would do them more good. The economic change would create more jobs—

Table 14–1. Selected Losers and Gainers under Greenpeace Germany Tax Shift

Industry	Share of Value Added[1] (percent)	Share of Employment[1] (percent)	Effect on Industry[2] (percent change in prices charged)
Industries That Lose	45.7	42.1	—
Coal[3]	0.6	0.8	+50.7
Chemicals	3.7	2.3	+12.5
Iron and steel	0.8	0.7	+5.0
Automobile Industry	4.1	4.1	0.0
Industries That Gain	50.1	53.8	—
Construction	3.9	4.8	–0.5
Electrical equipment	4.5	4.8	–1.4
Postal and telecommunications	2.6	2.2	–5.7

[1]Percentages are of private sector output and employment only, for 1988. Columns may not add to 100 percent because of rounding.   [2]After 15 years of tax shift phase-in, assuming all tax costs and savings are passed on to customers.   [3]For hard coal, subsidies would still exceed taxes unless phased out.
SOURCE: See endnote 31.

and jobs that would last. Yet major industry groups have opposed tax shifting, so far successfully, arguing that an energy tax increase would only deepen the unemployment crisis. They have the ear of Chancellor Kohl, who as a young man apprenticed at chemical giant BASF.[33]

One reason the Greenpeace proposal, Clinton's 1993 energy tax plan, and others like them have stalled is that those on the winning side of such major tax changes—as with subsidy cuts—have rarely lobbied as emphatically as those on the losing side. Polling data from the European Union and United States suggest that though many people support environmental fiscal reform in principle, the support is still broader than it is deep. On both sides of the Atlantic, 70 percent of those surveyed have favored tax shifting once they understood it. Many people's opinions swing quickly, however, when they discover what reform means for the price of gasoline or home heating oil. Evidently, a significant number people who worry about problems such as climate change are not yet convinced enough of the risks to endorse major fiscal changes.[34]

At base, then, the task of making tax and subsidy reform real is one of educating the public both about the risks we are taking with our children's future and about the promise of fiscal solutions to address these problems with minimal economic pain. Unfortunately, many environmental organizations shy away from this challenge. In the United States, for instance, not one of the million-member groups that have become household names—the National Wildlife Federation, the World Wildlife Fund, the Sierra Club—dedicates a single staffer to fiscal policy work, perhaps because they fear that calling for higher gasoline prices would cost them thousands of members. Yet fiscal reform is central to the creation of the sustainable world these groups are fighting for.[35]

Educating the public requires honesty about what fiscal reform can deliver and what it cannot. One of the quickest ways to lose the support of a public already grown cynical about self-styled tax reformers is to promise more than can be delivered. Under tax and subsidy reform, the biggest change most people will experience will not be in how much money they give to or get from the government, but in what they are taxed and subsidized for doing and not doing.

The questions the public must be asked run along these lines: Would you rather be subsidized for working in a dying industry or for buying electricity made from energy sources that do not raise the Earth's thermostat? Would you rather be taxed for the profits earned investing in companies that make new things or for taking a free ride as homeowners on local land value rises? Would you and your neighbor rather be taxed for working or for polluting each other's lungs on your way to work? Only when we can answer such questions in ways that make sense for society in the long run can fiscal reform fulfill its potential as a tool for environmental protection and economic strength.

It is a hopeful sign that public environmental concern has played, if not always the leading role, then a crucial supporting role in the passage of environmental taxes. In the decade leading up to the Swedish tax shift, for example, strange weather, the discovery of the ozone hole, and televised images of mass seal deaths along the coast of Sweden had heightened environmental concern within the country. When politicians needed new revenue in 1990, supporters of environmental taxation could present their proposal as a politically palatable option. Similarly, in the United States, public anxiety about the ozone hole helped the CFC tax sail through Congress in 1989 and win the signature of a President who had gained office on a "no new taxes" pledge.[36]

Looking ahead, the voices in support of change will only grow stronger. Environmental problems will increase in severity as population grows and throwaway consumerism spreads, prompting renewed calls for action. And the young but expanding companies on the winning side of reform, from wind turbine manufacturers to software makers, will likely organize themselves into increasingly effective coalitions. It is easy to lose sight of the long term in a world where commentators see the week as a relevant time unit in political analysis, and where articles written overnight seem stale by the time they reach newsstands. But from a historical perspective, the forces arrayed in defense of the status quo have never been weaker than they are in the modern era. For better and for worse, life has changed more profoundly for more people during the industrial age than during any other period in history.

★　★　★　★

The market system has scored amazing successes since Adam Smith's time. In the United Kingdom, wealth that once took 10 pairs of hands to produce in a day now takes only one. But because of its power, the market has also become a threat to its own survival. Nevertheless, the market can be used to save itself to a remarkable extent. The key is to change the way public institutions raise and spend money.[37]

Fiscal policies serve as translators between the natural world and the human economy. The translation they broadcast today is dangerously twisted. Subsidy policies channel hundreds of billions of dollars into activities that hurt the environment and cost consumers and taxpayers—even as they slow economic development, fail to protect jobs, and hardly help the poor. Tax codes, meanwhile, are designed as if to maximize reliance on levies that penalize work and entrepreneurship and minimize reliance on taxes that protect human health and national economies from environmental harm. As a result, fiscal policies say "raze your forests, grind down your mountains, siphon your rivers, pave your plains, modify your climate, pollute your air, and poison your blood." They tell us, in other words, to build a society that no one wants.

Joseph Schumpeter, an Austrian-born economist who died in 1950, wrote: "Public finances are one of the best starting points for an investigation of a society. The spirit of a people, its cultural level, its social structure, the deeds its policy may prepare—all this and more is written in its fiscal history, stripped of all phrases. He who knows how to listen to the message here discerns the thunder of world history more clearly than anywhere else."[38]

The turning of the new century brings a historic moment of truth for industrial society. Will we rescue what is good in the market system—the way it can encourage innovation and spread prosperity—while teaching it to cherish natural wealth and human health? Will we devise an economic system that can last for centuries? It is hard to see how we can do so without reforming the way governments raise and dispose of money. Our success—or our failure—will indeed thunder through the ages in the fiscal history of our times.

Notes

CHAPTER 1. Harnessing the Market

1. Adam Smith, *The Wealth of Nations* (New York: P.F. Collier and Son, 1902).
2. F.A. Hayek, "The Use of Knowledge in Society," *American Economic Review*, September 1945.
3. European Commission (EC), *ExternE: Externalities of Energy*, vol. 3, part I (Luxembourg: Office for Official Publications of the European Communities, 1995).
4. Environmental cost estimate is for a hypothetical new coal plant built in 1990 in Lauffen, 35 kilometers north of Stuttgart, and is from ibid. The figure here is based on a cost of 0.046 ECU per kilowatt-hour (including 0.018 ECU for global warming), and reflects an adjustment for estimated 8-percent transmission and distribution losses; current residential electricity price from Organisation for Economic Co-operation and

Some of the references in this book were obtained on-line from conferences of the Association for Progressive Communications (APC), which in the United States are maintained and archived by the Institute for Global Communications in San Francisco.

Development (OECD), *Energy Prices and Taxes, Second Quarter 1997* (Paris: 1997).

5. Ernst Ulrich von Weizsäcker, "Let Prices Tell the Ecological Truth," *Our Planet,* vol. 7, no. 1 (1995).

6. Toyota from Haig Simonian, "Staying in the Fast Lane of Innovation," *Financial Times,* 7 November 1997; surveys from Seth Dunn, "Power of Choice," *World Watch,* September/October 1997.

7. Factor of 10 assumes a global carbon emissions limit in 2100 of 2 billion tons, spread equitably among a global population of 10 billion. Emissions of more than 2 billion tons a year leading to atmospheric carbon dioxide concentrations above 400 parts per million from John T. Houghton et al., eds., *Stabilization of Atmospheric Greenhouse Gases: Physical, Biological and Socioeconomic Implications,* IPCC Technical Paper 3 (Geneva: Intergovernmental Panel on Climate Change, 1997). U.N. medium population projection from United Nations, *World Population Projections to 2150* (New York: 1998).

8. Ed Ayres, "Making Paper without Trees," *World Watch,* September/October 1993; Marcia Lowe, *Shaping Cities: The Environmental and Human Dimensions,* Worldwatch Paper 105 (Washington, DC: Worldwatch Institute, October 1991); Simonian, op. cit. note 6; David Malin Roodman and Nicholas Lenssen, *A Building Revolution: How Ecology and Health Concerns Are Transforming Construction,* Worldwatch Paper 124 (Washington, DC: Worldwatch Institute, March 1995).

9. Arthur Cecil Pigou, *The Economics of Welfare,* 4th ed. (London: Macmillan, 1932; first published 1920), cited in Mikael Skou Andersen, *Governance by Green Taxes: Making Pollution Prevention Pay* (Manchester, U.K.: Manchester University Press, 1994); William J. Baumol and Wallace E. Oates, *The Theory of Environmental Policy* (Cambridge, U.K.: Cambridge University Press, 1988).

10. David Malin Roodman, "The Obsolescent Incandescent," *World Watch,* May/June 1993.

11. William K. Stevens, "Meeting Reaches Accord to Reduce Greenhouse Gases," *New York Times,* 11 December 1997.

12. Revenue figures are Worldwatch estimates. See Chapter 9 for details. Typical tax rates from Lorenz Jarass and Gustav M. Obermair, *More Jobs, Less Tax Evasion, Cleaner Environment: Options for Compensating Reductions in the Taxation of Labour—Taxation of Other Factors of Production,* commissioned by the European Commission (Wiesbaden, Germany: College of Wiesbaden, August 1997).

13. European information from European Environment Agency,

Environmental Taxes: Implementation and Environmental Effectiveness (Copenhagen: 1996); U.S. January 1993 polling result from Greenberg-Lake/The Analysis Group, Washington, DC, and The Tarrance Group, Alexandria, VA, cited in Kate Stewart, Belden & Russonello, Washington, DC, letter to author, 10 March 1997.

14. OECD, *Environmental Taxes in OECD Countries* (Paris: 1995); Michel Potier, "China Charges for Pollution," *The OECD Observer*, February/March 1995; Hans Th. A. Bressers and Jeannette Schuddeboom, "A Survey of Effluent Charges and Other Economic Instruments in Dutch Environmental Policy," in OECD, *Applying Economic Instruments to Environmental Policies in OECD and Dynamic Non-member Economies* (Paris: 1994); Kees Baas, Central Bureau of Statistics, The Hague, e-mail to author, 24 September 1997; Rory McLeod, *Market Access Issues for the New Zealand Seafood Trade* (Wellington: New Zealand Fishing Industry Board, 1996); tax shifts from OECD, *Environmental Taxes and Green Tax Reform* (Paris: 1997).

15. Subsidy information from OECD, International Energy Agency, *Energy Policies of IEA Countries* (Paris: 1997), and from OECD, *Coal Information* (Paris: 1997). Subsidy value per kilowatt-hour is computed assuming coal plant efficiency of 37.6 percent (from EC, op. cit. note 3), and estimated transmission and distribution losses of 8 percent. Figure of $650 billion is a Worldwatch estimate, based on sources cited in Chapters 3–5 and 8.

16. Thomas J. Hilliard, *Golden Patents, Empty Pockets: A 19th Century Law Gives Miners Billions, the Public Pennies* (Washington, DC: Mineral Policy Center, 1994); Robert Repetto, *The Forest for the Trees? Government Policies and the Misuse of Forest Resources* (Washington, DC: World Resources Institute, 1988).

17. Worldwatch estimates; see Chapter 9 for details. Carolyn Webber and Aaron Wildavsky, *A History of Taxation and Expenditure in the Western World* (New York: Simon and Schuster, 1986).

18. Paul Krugman, "White Collars Turn Blue," *New York Times*, 29 September 1996.

CHAPTER 2. Subsidy Anatomy

1. Gross world product from Lester R. Brown, "World Economy Continues Rapid Expansion," in Lester R. Brown, Michael Renner, and Christopher Flavin, *Vital Signs 1998* (New York: W.W. Norton & Company, 1998); revenue figure is a

Worldwatch estimate, based on tax revenue figures for western industrial countries from Organisation for Economic Co-operation and Development (OECD), *Revenue Statistics of OECD Member Countries 1965–1995* (Paris: 1996), and on central government tax revenue as a share of gross domestic product (GDP) and GDP for other countries from World Bank, *World Development Indicators* (Washington, DC: 1997).

2. For a broad conservative attack on subsidies, see Stephen Moore and Dean Stansel, *Ending Corporate Welfare As We Know It*, Policy Analysis No. 225 (Washington, DC: Cato Institute, 1995); on the limitations of the economic viewpoint, see Mark Sagoff, *The Economy of the Earth: Philosophy, Law, and the Environment* (Cambridge, U.K.: University of Cambridge Press, 1988).

3. Charles F. Wilkinson, *Crossing the Next Meridian: Land, Water, and the Future of the West* (Washington, DC: Island Press, 1992); Edward C. Wolf, *Beyond the Green Revolution: New Approaches for Third World Agriculture*, Worldwatch Paper 73 (Washington, DC: Worldwatch Institute, October 1986); "Economic and Social Significance of Scientific and Engineering Research," in National Science Board, *Science & Engineering Indicators 1996* (Washington, DC: U.S. Government Printing Office, 1996).

4. Figure of $650 billion is a Worldwatch estimate, based on sources cited in Chapters 3–5 and 8; OECD, *Agricultural Policies, Markets and Trade in OECD Countries* (Paris: 1997).

5. Worldwatch estimate, based on Mark A. Delucchi, *The Annualized Social Cost of Motor-Vehicle Use in the U.S., 1990–1991: Summary of Theory, Data, Methods, and Results* (Davis, CA: University of California, Institute of Transportation Studies, 1997); formerly communist countries from Andrew Sunil Rajkumar, *Energy Subsidies*, Environment Department working paper (Washington, DC: World Bank, 1996); Shefali Rekhi, "Subsidies: Robbing Peter to Pay Paul," *India Today*, 30 April 1997.

6. "Quest for 'Green Gold' Fells One of Earth's Oldest Rain Forests," *Associated Press*, 7 May 1996.

7. Courtney Cuff and Gawain Kripke, eds., *Green Scissors: Cutting Wasteful and Environmentally Harmful Spending and Subsidies* (Washington, DC: Friends of the Earth, 1997).

8. Robert Repetto, *The Forest for the Trees? Government Policies and the Misuse of Forest Resources* (Washington, DC: World Resources Institute, 1988); U.S. Congress, Committee on Natural Resources, Subcommittee on Oversight and Investigations, *Taking from the Taxpayer: Public Subsidies for Natural Resource Development*, Majority Staff Report

(Washington, DC: 1994); Canada from Juri Peepre, Canadian Parks and Wilderness Society, White Horse, Yukon, discussion with author, 24 June 1996.

9. Marites Dañguilan Vitug, *Power from the Forest: The Politics of Logging* (Manila: Philippine Center for Investigative Journalism, 1993).

10. U.S. Congress, op. cit. note 8; Canada from A.P.G. de Moor, *Perverse Incentives* (The Hague: Institute for Research on Public Expenditure, 1997).

11. Tonnage from OECD, International Energy Agency, *Energy Policies of IEA Countries* (Paris: 1995); prices from Edmund L. Andrews, "Kohl Settles Mine Subsidy Issues, But More Worker Unrest Looms," *New York Times*, 14 March 1997; India from "Power Struggle," *The Economist*, 1–7 November 1997.

12. OECD, op. cit. note 4; Florida from Cuff and Kripke, op. cit. note 7.

13. Douglas Koplow, *Federal Energy Subsidies: Energy, Environmental, and Fiscal Impacts* (Washington, DC: Alliance to Save Energy, 1993).

14. Worldwatch estimates, based on Douglass B. Lee, *Full Cost Pricing of Highways*, presented at the annual meetings of the Transportation Research Board (Cambridge, MA: U.S. Department of Transportation (DOT), Volpe National Transportation Systems Center, 1995), on DOT, Federal Highway Administration, *Highway Statistics 1991* (Washington, DC: 1992), on Delucchi, op. cit. note 5, and on Michael Shelby et al., "Climate Change Implications of Eliminating U.S. Energy Subsidies," in OECD, *Reforming Energy and Transport Subsidies: Environmental and Economic Implications* (Paris: in press). See Chapter 5 for details.

CHAPTER 3. Resource Subsidies

1. John Murdock, retired economist, Dubois, WY, discussion with author, 23 September 1997.

2. Ibid.; Figure of $1.2 million is for 1986, excludes payments made by the federal government to counties in lieu of property taxes, and is from Cascade Holistic Environmental Consultants (now the Thoreau Institute), *Economic Database for the Greater Yellowstone Forests* (Eugene, OR: 1987).

3. Murdock, op. cit. note 1; Richard Manning, "Mountain Passages," *Wilderness*, fall 1992; Tom Bell, "Tourism Beats Logging in Wyoming," *High Country News*, 10 October 1988.

4. Murdock, op. cit. note 1.

5. Thomas Michael Power, *Lost Landscapes and Failed Economies:*

The Search for a Value of Place (Washington, DC: Island Press, 1996); Manning, op. cit. note 3.

6. Kenneth E. Boulding, *Environmental Quality in a Growing Economy* (Baltimore, MD: Johns Hopkins University Press, 1966), excerpted as Kenneth E. Boulding, "The Economics of the Coming Spaceship Earth," in Herman E. Daly and Kenneth N. Townsend, eds., *Valuing the Earth: Economics, Ecology, Ethics* (Cambridge, MA: The MIT Press, 1993).

7. Charles F. Wilkinson, *Crossing the Next Meridian: Land, Water, and the Future of the West* (Washington, DC: Island Press, 1992).

8. Ibid.; Canada from Juri Peepre, Canadian Parks and Wilderness Society, White Horse, Yukon, discussion with author, 24 June 1996.

9. History of heap leach mining from U.S. Congress, Committee on Natural Resources, Subcommittee on Oversight and Investigations, *Taking from the Taxpayer: Public Subsidies for Natural Resource Development*, Majority Staff Report (Washington, DC: 1994); South Dakota from Carlos D. Da Rosa and James S. Lyon, *Golden Dreams, Poisoned Streams: How Reckless Mining Pollutes America's Waters and How We Can Stop It* (Washington, DC: Mineral Policy Center (MPC), 1997); figure of 19,000 from MPC, "Environmental Impacts Packet," information packet (Washington, DC: undated); cleanup liability from Thomas J. Hilliard, *Golden Patents, Empty Pockets: A 19th Century Law Gives Miners Billions, the Public Pennies* (Washington, DC: MPC, 1994).

10. U.S. grazing subsidies from U.S. Congress, op. cit. note 9; Canadian grazing subsidies from Peepre, op. cit. note 8, and from John C. Ryan, *Hazardous Handouts: Taxpayer Subsidies to Environmental Degradation*, NEW Report No. 2 (Seattle, WA: Northwest Environment Watch (NEW), 1995); subleasing from Johanna H. Wald, "Beleaguered Rangelands Signify Policy Failure," *Forum for Applied Research and Public Policy*, winter 1996.

11. Charles Victor Barber, Nels C. Johnson, and Emmy Hafild, *Breaking the Logjam: Obstacles to Forest Policy Reform in Indonesia and the United States* (Washington, DC: World Resources Institute (WRI), 1994).

12. Randal O'Toole, "Timber Sale Subsidies, But Who Gets Them?" *Different Drummer* (Thoreau Institute, Oak Grove, OR), spring 1995; comparison to corporations from John Krist, "Managing the Woods for Loggers," *Journal of Commerce*, 25 June 1997; Andrew K. Dragun, "Equity and Sustainability in the Old Growth Forests of Victoria," *Journal of Income Distribution*, vol. 6, no. 2 (1997).

13. Total subsidy from U.S. Congress, op. cit. note 9; quote and other information from Kathie Durbin, "Sawdust Memories," *The Amicus Journal*, fall 1997.
14. Wilkinson, op. cit. note 7; Betty Ballantine and Ian Ballantine, eds., *The Native Americans: An Illustrated History* (Atlanta, GA: Turner Publishing, 1993); figure of 95 percent from Barber, Johnson, and Hafild, op. cit. note 11; Australia from Alan B. Durning and Holly B. Brough, *Taking Stock: Animal Farming and the Environment*, Worldwatch Paper 103 (Washington, DC: Worldwatch Institute, July 1991); American West from William E. Riebsame, "Ending the Range Wars?" *Environment*, May 1996; assessment from Wald, op. cit. note 10.
15. Power, op. cit. note 5; timber automation from Barber, Johnson, and Hafild, op. cit. note 11; "fastest growing" from Riebsame, op. cit. note 14.
16. Power, op. cit. note 5; John C. Ryan and Aaron M. Best, "NEW Indicator: Northwest Employment Depends Less on Timber and Mining," press release (Seattle, WA: NEW, 30 November 1994).
17. Polling data are based on a sample of 1,000 adults taken in September 1995 by Yankelovich Partners, Inc., Norwalk, CT, cited in Kate Stewart, Belden & Russonello, Washington, DC, letter to author, 10 September 1996; Timothy Egan, "Oregon, Foiling Forecasters, Thrives as It Protects Owls," *New York Times*, 11 October 1994.
18. Figure of 80 percent from Theodore Panayotou and Peter S. Ashton, *Not By Timber Alone: Economics and Ecology for Sustaining Tropical Forests* (Washington, DC: Island Press, 1992).
19. Figure 3–1 is based on U.N. Food and Agriculture Organization (FAO), *Forest Products Yearbook* (Rome: various years), on FAO, *Forest Products Electronic Database*, electronic database, Rome, updated 1995, on Crissis Vici, FAO, Rome, letter to author, 26 September 1997, on *ICSG Copper Bulletin* (International Copper Study Group, Lisbon), various issues, on United Nations, *World Energy Supplies* (New York: various years), on United Nations, *Yearbook of World Energy Statistics* (New York: 1983), on United Nations, *Energy Statistics Yearbook* (New York: various years), and on British Petroleum (BP), *BP Statistical Review of World Energy* (London: Group Media & Publications, 1997).
20. Asian Development Bank (ADB), *Emerging Asia: Changes and Challenges* (Manila: 1997); general pattern from A.H. Gelb, *Oil Windfalls: Blessing or Curse?* (New York: Oxford University Press, 1988).

21. Saudi windfall is a Worldwatch estimate based on oil prices and production from BP, op. cit. note 19; Saudi economic drop from National Bureau of Economic Research, *Penn World Tables (Mark 5.6)*, electronic database, Cambridge, MA, updated 1995, <http://www.nber.org/pwt56.html>, described in Robert Summers and Alan Heston, "The Penn World Table (Mark 5): An Expanded Set of International Comparisons, 1950–1988," *Quarterly Journal of Economics*, May 1991.

22. Gelb, op. cit. note 20.

23. Jane Jacobs, *The Economy of Cities* (New York: Vintage Books, 1969); ADB, op. cit. note 20.

24. Gelb, op. cit. note 20; Kyrgyzstan from "All that Glitters is Not Bre-X," *Business Week*, 19 May 1997.

25. World Bank study from Klaus Deininger and Lyn Squire, "Economic Growth and Income Inequality: Reexamining the Links," *Finance & Development*, March 1997; Fábio L.S. Petrarolpha, "Brazil: The Meek Want the Earth Now," *Bulletin of the Atomic Scientists*, November/December 1996; Jack Epstein, "Brazil Makes Land Grabs by Peasants Tougher," *Christian Science Monitor*, 10 July 1997.

26. Political clout of land-owning upper class from Rhys Jenkins, "The Political Economy of Industrialization: A Comparison of Latin American and East Asian Newly Industrializing Countries," *Development and Change*, vol. 22 (1991), pp. 197–231; Robin Broad, "The Political Economy of Natural Resources: Case Studies of the Indonesian and Philippine Forest Sectors," *Journal of Developing Areas*, April 1995; Marites Dañguilan Vitug, *Power from the Forest: The Politics of Logging* (Manila: Philippine Center for Investigative Journalism, 1993).

27. Ecuador and Nigeria from Aaron Sachs, *Eco-Justice: Linking Human Rights and the Environment*, Worldwatch Paper 127 (Washington, DC: Worldwatch Institute, December 1995); Guyana from Fred Pearce, "Caught in the Gold Rush," *New Scientist*, 11 May 1996; Helen Rosenbaum and Michael Krockenberger, *Report on the Impacts of the Ok Tedi Mine in Papua New Guinea* (Fitzroy, Victoria, Australia: Australian Conservation Foundation, 1993); Botswana from Durning and Brough, op. cit. note 14; Brazil and Côte d'Ivoire from Robert Repetto, *The Forest for the Trees? Government Policies and the Misuse of Forest Resources* (Washington, DC: WRI, 1988); Greenpeace International, "Logging In Solomon Islands Takes Its Toll," Greenpeace Briefing, Rome, undated, APC conference <rainfor.general>, posted 12 December 1995.

28. Barber, Johnson, and Hafild, op. cit. note 11.

CHAPTER 4. Cash Subsidies

1. Price drop from Campbell R. McConnell, *Economics*, 9th ed. (New York: Mcgraw-Hill, 1984); John Steinbeck, *The Grapes of Wrath* (New York: Penguin, 1967).
2. McConnell, op. cit. note 1.
3. Number of farms from U.S. Department of Commerce (DOC), Bureau of the Census, *Historical Statistics of the United States: Colonial Times to 1970* (Washington, DC: U.S. Government Printing Office (GPO), 1975), and from DOC, Bureau of the Census, *Statistical Abstract of the United States 1997* (Washington, DC: 1997).
4. International context from Ronald Steenblik, Organisation for Economic Co-operation and Development (OECD), Paris, e-mail to author, 4 February 1998; dollar costs from OECD, *Agricultural Policies, Markets and Trade in OECD Countries* (Paris: 1997); correlation between subsidies and environmental harm in the United States from Paul Faeth, *Growing Green: Enhancing the Economic and Environmental Performance of U.S. Agriculture* (Washington, DC: World Resources Institute (WRI), 1995), and in Western Europe from C. Ford Runge, "The Environmental Impacts of Agricultural and Forest Subsidies," in OECD, *Subsidies and Environment: Exploring the Linkages* (Paris: 1996); Pamela Wexler, "Iowa's 1987 Groundwater Protection Act," in Robert Gale and Stephan Barg, eds., *Green Budget Reform: An International Casebook of Leading Practices* (London: Earthscan, 1995).
5. China from Susan Cotts Watkins and Jane Menken, "Famines in Historical Perspective," *Population and Development Review*, December 1985.
6. Multinational strategy from Theodore H. Moran, "Mining Companies, Economic Nationalism, and Third World Development in the 1990s," in John E. Tilton, *Mineral Wealth and Economic Development* (Washington, DC: Resources For the Future, 1992); European Union subsidies from OECD, *Agricultural Policies*, op. cit. note 4.
7. Income doubling from National Bureau of Economic Research, *Penn World Tables (Mark 5.6)*, electronic database, Cambridge, MA, updated 1995, <http://www.nber.org/pwt56.html>, described in Robert Summers and Alan Heston, "The Penn World Table (Mark 5): An Expanded Set of International Comparisons, 1950–1988," *Quarterly Journal of Economics*, May 1991; divergence between income and reported happiness from David G. Myers and Ed Diener, "The Pursuit of

Happiness," *Scientific American*, May 1996.

8. Coal policies from OECD, International Energy Agency (IEA), *Energy Policies of IEA Countries* (Paris: various years); OECD, *Adjustment in OECD Agriculture: Issues and Policy Responses* (Paris: 1995).

9. Falling farm count from DOC, *Historical Statistics*, op. cit. note 3, and from DOC, *Statistical Abstract*, op. cit. note 3; subsidy distribution from U.S. Department of Agriculture, Economic Research Service, "Number of Farms and Net Cash Income by Size Class, 1996," <http://www.econ.ag.gov/briefing/fbe>, viewed 5 December 1997.

10. Surpluses from Réda Soufi and Mark Tuddenham, "The Reform of European Union Common Agricultural Policy," in Gale and Barg, op. cit. note 4; grain figures are for 1993–97, and are from U.S. Department of Agriculture, *Production, Supply, and Distribution*, electronic database, Washington, DC, updated January 1998. Export figure refers to net exports.

11. OECD, *Agricultural Policies*, op. cit. note 4. Figures include government spending on other assistance programs such as those relating to R&D, and are net of revenues raised through agricultural policies. Chemical subsidies from World Bank, Environment Department, *Expanding the Measure of Wealth: Indicators of Environmentally Sustainable Development* (Washington, DC: 1997).

12. Brian Chamberlin, *Farming and Subsidies: Debunking the Myths* (Pukekohe, New Zealand: Euroa Farms, 1996).

13. Effects in the United States from Faeth, op. cit. note 4; effects in Western Europe from Runge, op. cit. note 4; effects in the former Eastern bloc from Sergei Bobyliev and Bo Libert, "Prospects for Agricultural and Environmental Policy Integration in Russia," in OECD, *Agriculture and the Environment in the Transition to a Market Economy* (Paris: 1994).

14. Peter Weber, *Net Loss: Fish, Jobs, and the Marine Environment*, Worldwatch Paper 120 (Washington, DC: Worldwatch Institute, July 1994).

15. Subsidy estimate and China from Matteo J. Milazzo, *Subsidies in World Fisheries: A Reexamination*, World Bank Technical Paper No. 406, Fisheries Series (Washington, DC: World Bank, 1998); Viet Nam from Kim Anh, "Fishing Industries Surfing Toward the Year 2000," *Vietnam Economic News*, 13–19 June 1997, and from Achara Ashayagachat, "Vietnam: Offshore Fishing Industry," *Bangkok Post*, 10 June 1997; state of fisheries and figure of 86 million tons from Maurizio Perotti, Fishery Statistician, U.N. Food and Agriculture Organization (FAO), Rome, e-mail messages to Anne Platt McGinn, Research

Associate, Worldwatch Institute, 14 October and 11 November 1997; figure of 125 million tons from R.J.R. Grainger and S.M. Garcia, *Chronicles of Marine Fishery Landings (1950–1994): Trend Analysis and Fisheries Potential*, FAO Fisheries Technical Paper 359 (Rome: FAO, 1996).

16. Number of small fishers from Weber, op. cit. note 14; quotes from Stephen Buckley, "Senegalese Fish for a Living in Seas Teeming with Industrial Rivals," *International Herald Tribune*, 4 November 1997; EU agreement from Milazzo, op. cit. note 15.

17. Robert Greene, "President Signs Farm Legislation," *Philadelphia Inquirer*, 5 April 1996.

18. On the competitive advantages of large companies in many industries, see John Kenneth Galbraith, *Economics and the Public Purpose* (Boston: Houghton Mifflin, 1973).

19. Trawler length from David Helvarg, "Full Nets, Empty Seas," *The Progressive*, November 1997.

20. Douglas Koplow and Aaron Martin, *Federal Subsidies to Oil in the United States* (Washington, DC: Greenpeace USA, forthcoming); production and market share from U.S. Department of Energy, Energy Information Administration, *Annual Energy Review 1996* (Washington, DC: GPO, 1997); Canada from A.P.G. de Moor, *Perverse Incentives* (The Hague: Institute for Research on Public Expenditure, 1997).

21. Figure 4–1 and figures in text are based on OECD, IEA, *Coal Prospects and Policies in IEA Countries* (Paris: 1988), on OECD, IEA, *Energy Policies*, op. cit. note 8, and on OECD, IEA, *Coal Information* (Paris: various years), with costs converted to dollars using a 1996 exchange rate.

22. OECD, *Energy Policies*, op. cit. note 8, using a 1996 exchange rate; David Waddington and David Parry, "Coal Policy in Britain: Economic Reality or Political Vendetta?" in Chas Critcher, Klaus Schubert, and David Waddington, eds., *Regeneration of the Coalfield Areas: Anglo-German Perspectives* (London: Pinter, 1995); Soviet Union from World Bank, op. cit. note 11.

23. Runge, op. cit. note 4; German commitment from Christopher Flavin and Odil Tunali, *Climate of Hope: New Strategies for Stabilizing the World's Climate*, Worldwatch Paper 130 (Washington, DC: Worldwatch Institute, June 1996). For a full discussion of environment-security links, see Michael Renner, *Fighting for Survival* (New York: W.W. Norton & Company, 1996).

24. U.N. Development Programme, *Human Development Report 1997* (New York: Oxford University Press, 1997).

CHAPTER 5. Infrastructure Subsidies

1. Figure of 70 percent from World Bank, Environment Department, *Expanding the Measure of Wealth: Indicators of Environmentally Sustainable Development* (Washington, DC: 1997).

2. Relationship between income and expenditures on energy in Indonesia and other developing countries from Christine Kerr and Leslie Citroen, *Household Expenditures on Infrastructure Services*, background paper for *World Development Report 1994* (Washington, DC: World Bank, undated); relationship in United States from James Poterba, "Tax Policy to Combat Global Warming: On Designing a Carbon Tax," in Rudiger Dornbusch and James Poterba, eds., *Global Warming: Economic Policy Responses* (Cambridge, MA: The MIT Press, 1991); relationship in Western Europe from Mark Pearson, "Equity Issues and Carbon Taxes," in Organisation for Economic Co-operation and Development (OECD), *Climate Change: Designing a Practical Tax System* (Paris: 1993).

3. Fossil fuel subsidy figure, converted to dollars using market exchange rates, is a Worldwatch estimate based on Andrew Sunil Rajkumar, *Energy Subsidies*, Environment Department working paper (Washington, DC: World Bank, 1996), and includes $1 billion of the $10 billion the study estimates for countries not systematically analyzed (a Worldwatch estimate based on total carbon emissions of those countries); electricity subsidies from Bjorn Larsen and Anwar Shah, "Global Climate Change, Energy Subsidies and National Carbon Taxes," in Lans Bovenberg and Sijbren Cnossen, eds., *Public Economics and the Environment in an Imperfect World* (Boston: Kluwer Academic Press, 1995); energy waste from U.S. Congress, Office of Technology Assessment, *Energy Efficiency Technologies for Central and Eastern Europe* (Washington, DC: U.S. Government Printing Office (GPO), 1993).

4. Rajkumar, op. cit. note 3.

5. Fossil fuel subsidy figure, converted to dollars using market exchange rates, is a Worldwatch estimate based on ibid., and includes $1 billion of the $10 billion the study estimates for countries not systematically analyzed; power subsidy figure is a Worldwatch estimate.

6. Thomas T. Vogel, Jr., "Venezuela to Drive Up Gasoline Prices," *Wall Street Journal*, 15 April 1996.

7. China and India from World Bank, op. cit. note 1; fossil fuel totals are from Rajkumar, op. cit. note 3 and include $9 billion

of the $10 billion the study estimates for countries not system-
atically analyzed; pattern from David Malin Roodman, "Energy
Productivities Vary Widely," in Lester R. Brown, Hal Kane, and
David Malin Roodman, *Vital Signs 1994* (New York: W.W.
Norton & Company, 1994).

8. Electricity trend during the 1980s from World Bank, *Review of
Electricity Tariffs in Developing Countries during the 1980s*,
Industry and Energy Department Working Paper No. 32
(Washington, DC: 1990); recent electricity trend from World
Bank, op. cit. note 1; power subsidy figure is a Worldwatch esti-
mate; Shefali Rekhi, "Subsidies: Robbing Peter to Pay Paul,"
India Today, 30 April 1997.

9. Giancarlo Tosato, "Environmental Implications of Support to
the Electricity Sector in Italy," in OECD, *Reforming Energy and
Transport Subsidies: Environmental and Economic Implications*
(Paris: in press); Laurie Michaelis, "Electricity-Related
Supports in the United Kingdom," in ibid.; loss on power sales
from U.S. Department of Energy (DOE), Energy Information
Administration (EIA), *Federal Energy Subsidies: Direct and
Indirect Interventions in Energy Markets* (Washington, DC: GPO,
1992).

10. Michaelis, op. cit. note 9; Michael Shelby et al., "Climate
Change Implications of Eliminating U.S. Energy Subsidies," in
OECD, op. cit. note 9.

11. Tim Fisher, Natural Resources Campaign Coordinator,
Australian Conservation Foundation, Fitzroy, Victoria,
Australia, discussion with author, 8 July 1996; Sergei Bobyliev
and Bo Libert, "Prospects for Agricultural and Environmental
Policy Integration in Russia," in OECD, *Agriculture and the
Environment in the Transition to a Market Economy* (Paris: 1994);
historical U.S. losses are from U.S. Congress, Committee on
Natural Resources, Subcommittee on Oversight and
Investigations, *Taking from the Taxpayer: Public Subsidies for
Natural Resource Development*, Majority Staff Report
(Washington, DC: 1994), and are converted from the original
figures of $33.7–70.3 billion (from a 1988 source), assuming
they were expressed in 1987 dollars; current U.S. losses from
U.S. Department of Agriculture, Economic Research Service,
Agricultural Resources and Environmental Indicators, Agricultural
Handbook No. 705 (Washington, DC: 1994); China from
"Fees for Water Use Already Paid by Industry Added for
Residential Use, Government Says," *International Environment
Reporter*, 25 June 1997; figure of $23 billion from World Bank,
op. cit. note 1; figure of $14 billion from Gregory K. Ingraham
and Marianne Fay, *Valuing Infrastructure Stocks and Gains from*

Improved Performance, background paper for *World Development Report 1994* (Washington, DC: World Bank, 1994).

12. Marc Reisner, *Cadillac Desert: The American West and Its Disappearing Water*, rev. ed. (New York: Penguin Books, 1993); Patrick McCully, *The Ecology and Politics of Large Dams* (London: Zed Books, 1996).

13. McCully, op. cit. note 12; Sandra L. Postel, Gretchen Daily, and Paul R. Ehrlich, "Human Appropriation of Renewable Fresh Water," *Science*, 9 February 1996; Sandra Postel, "Where Have All the Rivers Gone?" *World Watch*, May/June 1995.

14. Ian G. Heggie, *Management and Financing of Roads: An Agenda for Reform*, World Bank Technical Paper No. 275, Africa Technical Series (Washington, DC: World Bank, 1995); Hisa Morisugi, "The Social Costs of Motor Vehicle Use in Japan," in OECD, op. cit. note 9; J-P. Orfeuil, "Evaluation of the External Costs of Road Transport in France and the Consequences of Cost Internalisation," in OECD, op. cit. note 9.

15. Douglass B. Lee, *Full Cost Pricing of Highways*, presented at the annual meetings of the Transportation Research Board (Cambridge, MA: U.S. Department of Transportation (DOT), Volpe National Transportation Systems Center, 1995).

16. Figure of $23 billion is a Worldwatch estimate, based on DOT, Federal Highway Administration (FHA), *Highway Statistics 1991* (Washington, DC: 1992); figure of $39 billion is a Worldwatch estimate, based on Mark A. Delucchi, *The Annualized Social Cost of Motor-Vehicle Use in the U.S., 1990–1991: Summary of Theory, Data, Methods, and Results* (Davis, CA: University of California, Institute of Transportation Studies, 1997). Figures here from Delucchi are based on taking the midpoints of revenue and expenditure ranges given in the report—a procedure Delucchi does not recommend.

17. Canada from Todd Litman, "Driving Out Subsidies," *Alternatives Journal*, winter 1998; Germany from A.P.G. de Moor, *Perverse Incentives* (The Hague: Institute for Research on Public Expenditure, 1997); U.K. from Transport 2000, *Company Cars*, briefing paper (London: 1995); U.S. free parking figure is a Worldwatch estimate, based on a market value of $123 billion (in 1997 dollars) a year for free employer-provided parking from Delucchi, op. cit. note 16, and an average marginal income tax rate of 36.5 percent, from Shelby et al., op. cit. note 10; mass transit coupons from Douglas Shoup, University of California at Los Angeles, Los Angeles, discussion with author, 6 September 1996. Value of general tax exemption is a Worldwatch estimate, based on Delucchi, op. cit. note 16, and

using the methodology of Lee, op. cit. note 15. Federal income and state sales tax losses are estimated at 1 and 3.9 percent of direct expenditures on roads and municipal parking, respectively, and local property taxes are estimated at 1.5 percent of value of land under roads, in this case estimated as half the annual direct road costs, divided by a discount rate of 7 percent.

18. Price rise is a Worldwatch estimate based on a motor fuel usage rate of 150 billion gallons per year from DOT, FHA, *Highway Statistics 1996* (Washington, DC: 1997); charge regime from Susan Haltmaier, "Transportation Subsidies: U.S. Case Study," in OECD, op. cit. note 9; New Zealand from "No Room, No Room," *The Economist*, 6 December 1997.

19. James E. Frank, *The Costs of Alternative Patterns of Development* (Washington, DC: Urban Land Institute, 1989).

20. James E. Frank and Paul B. Downing, "Patterns of Impact Fee Use," in Arthur C. Nelson, ed., *Development Impact Fees: Policy Rationale, Practice, Theory, and Issues* (Chicago: Planners Press, 1988).

21. Figure of 70 percent from World Bank, op. cit. note 1; Maria L. La Ganga, "Steelhead Trout Listed as Endangered in Region," *Los Angeles Times*, 12 August 1997; Sandra Postel, *Last Oasis*, rev. ed. (New York: W.W. Norton & Company, 1997).

22. E. Gurvich et al., "Greenhouse Gas Impacts of Russian Energy Subsidies," in OECD, op. cit. note 9; Doug Koplow, "Energy Subsidies and the Environment," in OECD, *Subsidies and Environment: Exploring the Linkages* (Paris: 1996).

23. Aluminum subsidies in the Northwest from Doug Koplow, "Federal Energy Subsidies and Recycling: A Case Study," *Resource Recycling*, November 1994; worldwide pattern from Jennifer S. Gitlitz, *The Relationship between Primary Aluminum Production and the Damming of World Rivers* (Berkeley, CA: International Rivers Network, 1993); effects of bauxite mining from John E. Young, *Mining the Earth*, Worldwatch Paper 109 (Washington, DC: Worldwatch Institute, July 1992).

24. DOE, EIA, *Monthly Energy Review—October 1997* (Washington, DC: GPO, 1997); Delucchi, op. cit. note 16; London from Martin Mogridge, *Travel in Towns* (London: Macmillan, 1990).

25. Ted Bardacke, "Bangkok May Ban New Cars until 2001," *Financial Times*, 8 July 1996; Christopher Elias, Senior Associate, The Population Council, Bangkok, discussion with author, 8 November 1997; Gordon Fairclough, "Motion Sickness: Little Relief in Sight for Bangkok's Traffic Ailments," *Far Eastern Economic Review*, 15 February 1996.

26. Marcia D. Lowe, *Back on Track: The Global Rail Revival*, Worldwatch Paper 118 (Washington, DC: Worldwatch Institute, April 1994); Richard Arnot and Kenneth Small, "The Economics of Traffic Congestion," *American Scientist*, September–October 1994.

27. World Bank, *World Development Report 1994* (Washington, DC: 1994).

28. Public water projects from Robert Repetto, *Skimming the Water: Rent-Seeking and the Performance of Public Irrigation Systems* (Washington, DC: World Resources Institute, 1986); figures on lack of access from World Bank, op. cit. note 27.

29. Jodi L. Jacobson, *Gender Bias: Roadblock to Sustainable Development*, Worldwatch Paper 110 (Washington, DC: Worldwatch Institute, September 1992); disease figure is computed in disability-adjusted life years, a unit that measures both disability and shortening of lives, and is from Christopher J.L. Murray and Alan D. Lopez, "Global Mortality, Disability, and the Contribution of Risk Factors: Global Burden of Disease Study," *The Lancet*, 17 May 1997.

30. Price disparities from Kerr and Citroen, op. cit. note 2; Bela Bhatia, *Lush Fields and Parched Throats: The Political Economy of Groundwater in Gujarat* (Helsinki: World Institute for Development Economics Research, 1992).

31. Bhatia, op. cit. note 30.

CHAPTER 6. Reforming Subsidies for the Polluter

1. Figure of 8 percent assumes 90-percent subsidy cuts and total revenue of $7.5 trillion a year, a Worldwatch estimate based on tax revenue figures for western industrial countries from Organisation for Economic Co-operation and Development (OECD), *Revenue Statistics of OECD Member Countries 1965–1995* (Paris: 1996), and on central government tax revenue as a share of gross domestic product (GDP) and GDP for other countries from World Bank, *World Development Indicators* (Washington, DC: 1997).

2. Michael B. Gordon, "Yeltsin Attacks Soviet-Era Housing Benefits," *New York Times*, 13 July 1997.

3. Ibid.; Caroline L. Freund and Christine I. Wallich, *Raising Household Energy Prices in Poland: Who Gains? Who Loses?* Policy Research Working Paper 1495 (Washington, DC: World Bank, 1995).

4. Douglas Koplow, *Federal Energy Subsidies: Energy, Environmental, and Fiscal Impacts* (Washington, DC: Alliance to Save Energy, 1993); reduced cost of living from Einar Hope

and Balbir Singh, *Energy Price Increases in Developing Countries: Case Studies of Colombia, Ghana, Indonesia, Malaysia, Turkey, and Zimbabwe,* Policy Research Working Paper 1442 (Washington, DC: World Bank, 1995); savings from targeting from Christine Kerr and Leslie Citroen, *Household Expenditures on Infrastructure Services,* background paper for *World Development Report 1994* (Washington, DC: World Bank, undated).

5. Targeting techniques from Margaret E. Grosh, "Toward Quantifying the Trade-off: Administrative Costs and Incidence in Targeted Programs in Latin America," in Dominique van de Walle and Kimberly Nead, eds., *Public Spending and the Poor: Theory and Evidence* (Baltimore, MD: Johns Hopkins University Press, for the World Bank, 1995); kerosene stamps from Rhamesh Bhatia, "Energy Pricing in Developing Countries: Role of Prices in Investment Allocation and Consumer Choices," in Corazón Morales Siddayao, ed., *Criteria for Energy Pricing Policy* (London: Graham & Trotman, 1985); "at least a dozen" from Jamshid Heidarian and Gary Wu, *Power Sector Statistics for Developing Countries, 1987–1991* (Washington, DC: World Bank, 1994); on the economics of lifeline pricing, see Freund and Wallich, op, cit. note 3.

6. Freund and Wallich, op. cit. note 3.

7. Réda Soufi and Mark Tuddenham, "The Reform of European Union Common Agricultural Policy," in Robert Gale and Stephan Barg, eds., *Green Budget Reform: An International Casebook of Leading Practices* (London: Earthscan, 1995); Robert Greene, "President Signs Farm Legislation," *Philadelphia Inquirer,* 5 April 1996.

8. "The Farmbelt Breaks Free," *Economist,* 12 July 1997; Edward Walsh, "It's Feast, Not Famine, So Far under New Law in Farm Belt," *Washington Post,* 28 August 1997.

9. Howard Schneider, "Booming Seal Pup Harvest in Canada Reopens Animal Rights Debate of the 1970s," *Washington Post,* 10 October 1997.

10. Brazil from Lester R. Brown, Christopher Flavin, and Sandra Postel, *Saving the Planet* (New York: W.W. Norton & Company, 1991); Susan Brackett, Communications Director, Mineral Policy Center, Washington, DC, discussion with author, 22 December 1997; Joby Warrick, "Clinton Plan to Halt New Roads in Wilderness Gets Icy Reviews," *Washington Post,* 23 January 1998.

11. Political case for rapid termination from Dani Rodrik, "Understanding Economic Policy Reform," *Journal of Economic Literature,* March 1996.

12. Paul E. Atkinson, "New Zealand's Radical Reforms," *OECD*

Observer, April/May 1997; Brian Chamberlin, *Farming and Subsidies: Debunking the Myths* (Pukekohe, New Zealand: Euroa Farms, 1996).

13. Production drop from OECD, International Energy Agency, *Energy Policies of IEA Countries* (Paris: various years); David Waddington and David Parry, "Coal Policy in Britain: Economic Reality or Political Vendetta?" in Chas Critcher, Klaus Schubert, and David Waddington, eds., *Regeneration of the Coalfield Areas: Anglo-German Perspectives* (London: Pinter, 1995).

14. OECD, op. cit. note 13; environmental effects of imported coal from Ronald P. Steenblik and Panos Coroyannikis, "Reform of Coal Policies in Western and Central Europe: Implications for the Environment," *Energy Policy*, June 1995; British Petroleum, *BP Statistical Review of World Energy* (London: Group Media & Publications, 1997).

15. OECD, *Agricultural Policies, Markets, and Trade in the Central and Eastern European Countries, the New Independent States, and China* (Paris: 1995); E. Gurvich et al., "Impacts of Russian Energy Subsidies on Greenhouse Gas Emissions," in OECD, *Reforming Energy and Transport Subsidies: Environmental and Economic Implications* (Paris: in press).

16. Courtney Cuff and Gawain Kripke, eds., *Green Scissors: Cutting Wasteful and Environmentally Harmful Spending and Subsidies* (Washington, DC: Friends of the Earth, 1997).

17. Andrew K. Dragun, "Equity and Sustainability in the Old Growth Forests of Victoria," *Journal of Income Distribution*, vol. 6, no. 2 (1997).

18. OECD, *Agricultural Policies, Markets and Trade in OECD Countries* (Paris: 1997); World Bank, Environment Department, *Expanding the Measure of Wealth: Indicators of Environmentally Sustainable Development* (Washington, DC: 1997); Andrew Sunil Rajkumar, *Energy Subsidies*, Environment Department working paper (Washington, DC: World Bank, 1996); killed study from Douglas Koplow, Industrial Economics, Cambridge, MA, e-mail to author, 10 December 1997.

19. Kevin Watkins and Michael Windfuhr, "Agriculture in the Uruguay Round: Implications for Sustainable Development in Developing Countries," WWF International Discussion Paper (Gland, Switzerland: World Wide Fund For Nature, 1995); role of OECD from Ronald Steenblik, OECD, Paris, discussion with author, 24 September 1996.

20. Structural adjustment from Robin Broad, "The Political Economy of Natural Resources: Case Studies of the Indonesian and Philippine Forest Sectors," *Journal of Developing Areas*,

April 1995; past problems from Hilary F. French, *Partnership for the Planet: An Environmental Agenda for the United Nations*, Worldwatch Paper 126 (Washington, DC: Worldwatch Institute, July 1996).

21. Abby Yadi, "World Bank Axes Loan," *The Independent* (Port Moresby, Papua New Guinea), 2 August 1996; Neville Togarewa, "World Bank Gets Its Way on Forests," *The National* (Port Moresby, Papua New Guinea), 9 October 1996; Indonesia from William B. Magrath, Agriculture and Forestry Systems Division, World Bank, Washington, DC, discussion with author, 23 July 1996.

22. Mexico from World Bank, *Five Years after Rio: Innovations in Environmental Policy*, Environmentally Sustainable Development Studies and Monograph Series No. 18 (Washington, DC: 1997).

23. World Bank, op. cit. note 18; China from Ved P. Gandhi, Dale Gray, and Ronald McMorran, "A Comprehensive Approach to Domestic Resource Mobilization for Sustainable Development," in U.N. Department for Policy Coordination and Sustainable Development, *Finance for Sustainable Development: The Road Ahead*, Proceedings of the Fourth Group Meeting on Financial Issues of Agenda 21, Santiago, Chile, 1997 (New York: 1997).

CHAPTER 7. Capturing Resource Windfalls

1. Historical reluctance to challenge moneyed interests from John Kenneth Galbraith, *Economics in Perspective: A Critical History* (Boston: Houghton Mifflin, 1987).

2. Information on American International Petroleum Corporation in this and following paragraphs from James Norman, "AIPC Stock Soars on News of a Billion Kazak Barrels," *Platt's Oilgram*, 15 July 1997, from James Norman, "US' AIPC Goes Offshore for Funding," *Platt's Oilgram*, 15 August 1997, from James Norman, "AIPC Signs Operating Deal on Kazak Tract," *Platt's Oilgram*, 25 November 1997, and from Sharon Behn and James Norman, "American Int'l Kazak Play May Be Even Bigger than Its 1-Bil BBL Estimate," *Platt's Oilgram*, 25 July 1997.

3. Alan Thein Durning and Yoram Bauman, *Tax Shift: How to Help the Economy, Improve the Environment, and Get the Tax Man off Our Backs*, NEW Report No. 7 (Seattle, WA: Northwest Environment Watch, 1998).

4. Marites Dañguilan Vitug, *Power from the Forest: The Politics of Logging* (Manila: Philippine Center for Investigative

Journalism, 1993); Kalaw from Robin Broad, "The Political Economy of Natural Resources: Case Studies of the Indonesian and Philippine Forest Sectors," *Journal of Developing Areas*, April 1995; Harvard study from Asian Development Bank, *Emerging Asia: Changes and Challenges* (Manila: 1997).

5. Charles Victor Barber, Nels C. Johnson, and Emmy Hafild, *Breaking the Logjam: Obstacles to Forest Policy Reform in Indonesia and the United States* (Washington, DC: World Resources Institute (WRI), 1994); Indonesian aid receipts from World Bank, *World Development Report 1993* (Washington, DC: 1993); other countries from Robert Repetto, *The Forest for the Trees? Government Policies and the Misuse of Forest Resources* (Washington, DC: WRI, 1988).

6. Ved P. Gandhi, Dale Gray, and Ronald McMorran, "A Comprehensive Approach to Domestic Resource Mobilization for Sustainable Development," in U.N. Department for Policy Coordination and Sustainable Development, *Finance for Sustainable Development: The Road Ahead*, Proceedings of the Fourth Group Meeting on Financial Issues of Agenda 21, Santiago, Chile, 1997 (New York: 1997).

7. Juri Peepre, Canadian Parks and Wilderness Society, White Horse, Yukon, discussion with author, 24 June 1996; Thomas J. Hilliard, *Golden Patents, Empty Pockets: A 19th Century Law Gives Miners Billions, the Public Pennies* (Washington, DC: Mineral Policy Center, 1994); federal debt from U.S. Office of Management and Budget, *Budget of the United States Government, Fiscal Year 1999* (Washington, DC: U.S. Government Printing Office (GPO), 1998).

8. Indonesia from David N. Smith and Louis T. Wells, Jr., *Negotiating Third-World Mineral Agreements: Promises as Prologue* (Cambridge, MA: Ballinger, 1975); Fred Barbash, "No Deficit, But No Joy, in Norway," *Washington Post*, 25 October 1996; Timothy Egan, "Fringe Benefits from Oil Give Alaska a Big Payday," *New York Times*, 9 October 1996.

9. "Nearly a quarter" based on a 15-million-acre-feet/year estimate of the river's average flow, from Marc Reisner, *Cadillac Desert: The American West and Its Disappearing Water*, rev. ed. (New York: Penguin Books, 1993), and on a figure of 3.3 million acre-feet/year for the Imperial Irrigation District's claim, from "CA: Imperial Irrigation District and San Diego Approve MOU for Long-Term Transfer," *Water Intelligence Monthly*, October 1995; canal from U.S. Department of Interior, Bureau of Reclamation, Lower Colorado Region, *Description and Assessment of Operations, Maintenance, and Sensitive Species of the Lower Colorado River* (Boulder City, NV: 1996); Central Valley

from U.S. Congress, Committee on Natural Resources, Subcommittee on Oversight and Investigations, *Taking from the Taxpayer: Public Subsidies for Natural Resource Development*, Majority Staff Report (Washington, DC: 1994); "few hundred square meters" is based on Peter H. Gleick, ed., *Water in Crisis: A Guide to the World's Fresh Water Resources* (New York: Oxford University Press, 1993); Norwegian Green Tax Commission, *Policies for a Better Environment and High Employment* (Oslo: 1996).

10. New Zealand from Rory McLeod, *Market Access Issues for the New Zealand Seafood Trade* (Wellington: New Zealand Fishing Industry Board, 1996); other information from Matteo J. Milazzo, *Subsidies in World Fisheries: A Reexamination*, World Bank Technical Paper No. 406, Fisheries Series (Washington, DC: World Bank, 1998).

11. Julie M. Feinsilver, "Biodiversity Prospecting: A New Panacea for Development?" *CEPAL Review*, December 1996; Nicolás Mateo, General Coordinator, Bioprospecting Program, Instituto Nacional de Biodiversidad, Santo Domingo, Costa Rica, letter to author, 9 March 1998; modest potential from Douglas Southgate, *Alternatives for Habitat Protection and Rural Income Generation* (Washington, DC: Inter-American Development Bank, Environment Division, 1997).

12. Executive Office of the President, *Economic Report of the President* (Washington, DC: GPO, 1997); "more than any other" from William Safire, "Sell That Spectrum," *New York Times*, 9 January 1997; problems with later auction from Seth Schiesel, "Juggling Goals, F.C.C. to Hold Wireless Sale," *New York Times*, 16 February 1998.

13. Mason Gaffney, "Soil Depletion and Land Rent," *Natural Resources Journal*, January 1961.

14. Calculation uses a 5-percent real discount rate, and assumes that the cost of a new building equals its value at completion.

15. Australia, Indonesia, and South Korea from Joan M. Youngman and Jane H. Malme, *An International Survey of Taxes on Land and Buildings* (Deventer, Netherlands: Kluwer Law and Taxation Publishers, 1994); Colombia from Fernando Rojas and Martim Smolka, "New Colombian Law Implements Value Capture," *Land Lines* (Lincoln Institute of Land Policy (LILP), Cambridge, MA), March 1998; other countries from Kenneth M. Lusht, *The Site Value Tax and Residential Development* (Cambridge, MA: LILP, 1992); economics of land taxes from Nicolaus Tideman, *Taxing Land is Better than Neutral: Land Taxation and the Timing of Development* (Cambridge, MA: LILP, 1995), and from Nicolaus Tideman, "The Economics of

Efficient Taxes on Land," in Nicolaus Tideman, ed., *Land and Taxation* (London: Shepheard-Walwyn, 1994).

16. Shift in perspective from Mason Gaffney, "Land as a Distinctive Factor of Production," in Tideman, *Land and Taxation*, op. cit. note 15; Adam Smith, *The Wealth of Nations*, Book V, Chapter II, Part II, Article 1 (New York: P.F. Collier and Son, 1902); David Ricardo, *The Principles of Political Economy and Taxation*, Chapter X (London: J.M. Dent & Sons, 1973); John Stuart Mill, *Principles of Political Economy*, 7th ed., Book V, Chapter II, Article 5, in Jonathan Riley, ed., *Principles of Political Economy and Chapters on Socialism* (Oxford: Oxford University Press, 1994).

17. Lusht, op. cit. note 15.

18. Wallace B. Oates and Robert M. Schwab, *The Impact of Urban Land Taxation: The Pittsburgh Experience* (Cambridge, MA: LILP, 1995); Philadelphia job losses from Ronald E. Grieson, "Theoretical Analysis and Empirical Measurements of the Effects of the Philadelphia Income Tax," *Journal of Urban Economics*, July 1980, and from Robert P. Inman, "Can Philadelphia Escape its Fiscal Crisis with Another Tax Increase?" *Business Review* (Federal Reserve Bank of Philadelphia), September-October 1992, both cited in ibid.

19. Rojas and Smolka, op. cit. note 15.

20. Dominance of urban land in total land values in United States from Alanna Hartzok, "Pennsylvania and the Split-Rate Tax," draft manuscript (Scotland, PA: International Union for Land Value Taxation, 1998), and in United Kingdom from James Robertson, *Benefits and Taxes* (London: New Economics Foundation, 1994); Andrew C. Revkin, "Land Sought for State Park is Up for Sale," *New York Times*, 10 January 1997; Raymond Hernandez, "Pataki Agrees to $17 Million Deal to Protect Swath of Adirondacks," *New York Times*, 23 December 1997.

21. Tax deferment from Clifford Cobb et al., *Fiscal Policy for a Sustainable California*, draft report prepared for Redefining Progress (San Francisco, CA: 1995); Timothy Egan, "Drawing a Hard Line against Urban Sprawl," *New York Times*, 30 December 1996; New Jersey from Dana Clark and David Downes, *What Price Biodiversity? Economic Incentives and Biodiversity Conservation in the United States* (Washington, DC: Center for International Environmental Law, 1995).

22. Justin R. Ward, F. Kaid Benfield, and Anne E. Kinsinger, *Reaping the Revenue Code: Why We Need Sensible Tax Reform For Sustainable Agriculture* (New York: Natural Resources Defense Council, 1989).

23. Gaffney, op. cit. note 13.
24. Robertson, op. cit. note 20.
25. Low land taxation in Western Europe from Lorenz Jarass, Professor, College of Wiesbaden, Wiesbaden, Germany, discussion with author, 31 January 1997; revenue shares from Organisation for Economic Co-operation and Development (OECD), *Revenue Statistics of OECD Member Countries 1965–1996* (Paris: 1997); low assessments from Cobb et al., op. cit. note 21; global tax revenue of $7.5 trillion is a Worldwatch estimate, based on revenue figures for western industrial countries from OECD, op. cit. this note, and on central government tax revenue as a share of gross domestic product (GDP) and on GDP for other countries from World Bank, *World Development Indicators* (Washington, DC: 1997).
26. Cobb et al., op. cit. note 21; federal tax revenues in California from *Treasury Bulletin* (U.S. Department of Treasury, Financial Management Service, Washington, DC), March 1995.
27. Durning and Bauman, op. cit. note 3.

Chapter 8. Paying the Non-Polluter

1. Frank Muller, "Tax Credits and the Development of Renewable Energy in California," in Robert Gale and Stephan Barg, eds., *Green Budget Reform: An International Casebook of Leading Practices* (London: Earthscan, 1995).
2. Douglas Koplow, *Federal Energy Subsidies: Energy, Environmental, and Fiscal Impacts* (Washington, DC: Alliance to Save Energy, 1993).
3. U.S. Department of Agriculture, *1996 Farm Bill Conservation Provisions* (Washington, DC: 1996); erosion reduction and targeting problems from Paul Faeth, *Growing Green: Enhancing the Economic and Environmental Performance of U.S. Agriculture* (Washington, DC: World Resources Institute (WRI), 1995); European information from Alison Maitland, "EU Agri-environment Programmes Cost £1bn," *Financial Times*, 22 May 1996.
4. Marcia D. Lowe, *Alternatives to the Automobile: Transport for Livable Cities*, Worldwatch Paper 98 (Washington, DC: Worldwatch Institute, October 1990); American Public Transit Association, *Transit Fact Book* (Washington, DC: 1997); Mark Lang, "Car Pool," *Adweek*, 3 November 1997; Jane's Information Group, *Jane's Urban Transport Systems 1997–98* (London: 1997).
5. "Economic and Social Significance of Scientific and Engineering Research," in National Science Board, *Science &*

Engineering Indicators—1996 (Washington, DC: U.S. Government Printing Office, 1996).

6. Edward C. Wolf, *Beyond the Green Revolution: New Approaches for Third World Agriculture*, Worldwatch Paper 73 (Washington, DC: Worldwatch Institute, October 1986).

7. Continuing subsidies from World Bank, Environment Department, *Expanding the Measure of Wealth: Indicators of Environmentally Sustainable Development* (Washington, DC: 1997); Robert Repetto, *Paying the Price: Pesticide Subsidies in Developing Countries* (Washington, DC: WRI, 1985).

8. World Bank, op. cit. note 7.

9. Howard Geller and Scott McGaraghan, *Successful Government-Industry Partnership: The U.S. Department of Energy's Role in Advancing Energy-Efficient Technologies* (Washington, DC: American Council for an Energy-Efficient Economy, 1996).

10. Ibid.

11. Ibid.; Figure 8–1 is based on British Petroleum, *BP Statistical Review of World Energy* (London: Group Media & Publications, 1997), and on Organisation for Economic Co-operation and Development (OECD), International Energy Agency, *Energy Policies of IEA Countries* (Paris: 1997), with wind growth statistics from Paul Gipe, Paul Gipe & Associates, Tehachapi, CA, discussion with author, 6 January 1998, and solar growth statistics from Bob Johnson, Director of Photovoltaics Group, Strategies Unlimited, Mountain View, CA, discussion with author, 6 January 1998. Growth figure for solar cells is based on domestic sales of solar cells, not electricity generated. Spending figures exclude support for transmission, storage, and other technologies from the denominator.

12. Nicholas Lenssen and Christopher Flavin, "Meltdown," *World Watch*, May/June 1996; U.S. subsidy total is based on Fred J. Sissine, *Energy Efficiency: A New National Commitment?* CRS Issue Brief (Washington, DC: Congressional Research Service (CRS), 1993), and on Fred J. Sissine, CRS, Washington, DC, discussion with author, 6 September 1996; "New Poll Finds Pessimism on Outlook for Nuclear," *Wind Energy Weekly* (American Wind Energy Association, Washington, DC), 26 February 1996.

13. Solar tower from Daniel B. Wood, "It Works, But Can Anyone Afford It?" *Christian Science Monitor*, 10 June 1996; Paul Gipe, *Wind Energy Comes of Age* (New York: John Wiley & Sons, 1995).

14. Andreas Wagner, *Feed-In Tariffs for Renewable Energies in Europe—An Overview* (Bonn: European Association for Solar Energy, 1997); Christina Olivecrona, "Wind Energy in

Denmark," in Gale and Barg, op. cit. note 1.

15. Keith Kozloff and Olatokumbo Shobowale, *Rethinking Development Assistance for Renewable Electricity* (Washington, DC: WRI, 1994); Neelam Mathews, "Dynamic Market Rapidly Unfolds," *Windpower Monthly*, September 1994; Neelam Mathews, "Tax Credits Just a Catalyst," *Windpower Monthly*, July 1995; Christopher Flavin, "Wind Power Sets Records," in Lester R. Brown, Michael Renner, and Christopher Flavin, *Vital Signs 1998* (New York: W.W. Norton & Company, 1998).

16. Kozloff and Shobowale, op. cit. note 15.

17. Ibid.; Christopher Flavin and Nicholas Lenssen, *Power Surge* (New York: W.W. Norton & Company, 1994).

18. Victoria P. Summers, "Tax Treatment of Pollution Control in the European and Central Asian Economies in Transition and Other Selected Countries," in Charles E. Walker, Mark A. Bloomfield, and Margot Thorning, eds., *Strategies for Improving Environmental Quality and Increasing Economic Growth* (Washington, DC: Center for Policy Research, 1995); Ronald T. McMorran and David C.L. Nellor, *Tax Policy and the Environment: Theory and Practice*, IMF Working Paper (Washington, DC: International Monetary Fund, 1994).

19. Ministry of Housing, Spatial Planning, and the Environment (VROM), *Accelerated Depreciation on Environmental Investment in the Netherlands* (The Hague: 1995); Peter J. Hamelink, paper presented at the Second European Roundtable on Cleaner Production and Cleaner Products (The Hague: VROM, November 1995).

20. Joseph J. Romm, *Lean and Clean Management: How to Boost Profits and Productivity by Reducing Pollution* (New York: Kodansha International, 1994).

21. Ibid.

CHAPTER 9. Taxing the Polluter

1. Denise Schmandt-Besserat, "The Earliest Precursors of Writing," *Scientific American*, June 1978; quote from "*Economic Tax Reform in Europe: Focusing the Market on Eco-efficiency and Employment*," Project Summary (London: WBMG Environmental Communications, May 1995).

2. Quote from "*Economic Tax Reform*," op. cit. note 1.

3. Carolyn Webber and Aaron Wildavsky, *A History of Taxation and Expenditure in the Western World* (New York: Simon and Schuster, 1986).

4. Ibid.; figures in Table 9–1 are Worldwatch estimates, based on Organisation for Economic Co-operation and Development

(OECD), *Revenue Statistics of OECD Member Countries 1965–1996* (Paris: 1997), on World Bank, *World Development Report 1996* (New York: Oxford University Press, 1996), on World Bank, *World Development Indicators* (Washington, DC: 1997), and, for Russia, on International Monetary Fund (IMF), *World Economic Outlook: October 1994* (Washington, DC: 1994), and on Richard Hemming, Adrienne Cheasty, and Ashok K. Lahiri, "The Revenue Decline," in Daniel A. Citrin and Ashok K. Lihiri, eds., *Policy Experiences and Issues in the Baltics, Russia, and Other Countries of the Former Soviet Union,* IMF Occasional Paper 133 (Washington, DC: IMF, 1995).

5. Effects of corruption from Anwar Shah and Bjorn Larsen, *Carbon Taxes, the Greenhouse Effect, and Developing Countries,* background paper for *World Development Report 1992* (Washington, DC: World Bank, 1992); shares of populations paying income tax from Michael P. Todaro, *Economic Development in the Third World,* 2nd ed. (New York: Longman, 1981).

6. Arthur Cecil Pigou, *The Economics of Welfare,* 4th ed. (London: Macmillan, 1932; first published 1920), cited in Mikael Skou Andersen, *Governance by Green Taxes: Making Pollution Prevention Pay* (Manchester, U.K.: Manchester University Press, 1994); conversion to 1997 dollars based on a price index relative to 1920, from U.K. Office for National Statistics, "International Purchasing Power of the Pound," <http://www.ons.gov.uk/ukinfigs/index.htm>, London, viewed 11 February 1997; technology effect from Michael Grubb, "Technologies, Energy Systems and the Timing of CO_2 Emissions Abatement," *Energy Policy,* February 1997.

7. Carol Kaesuk Yoon, "A 'Dead Zone' Grows in the Gulf of Mexico," *New York Times,* 20 January 1997; Gary Lee, "Hospitalizations Tied to Ozone Pollution," *Washington Post,* 21 June 1997; John Kellenberg and Herman Daly, *Counting User Cost in Evaluating Projects Involving Depletion of Natural Capital: World Bank Best Practice and Beyond,* Environment Working Paper No. 66 (Washington, DC: World Bank, Environment Department, 1994).

8. Pigou, op. cit. note 6. For the argument that the parties involved could solve environmental problems without government intervention, see R.H. Coase, "The Problem of Social Cost," *Journal of Law and Economics,* October 1960.

9. Sulfur emissions decline is a Worldwatch estimate, based on World Resources Institute (WRI) et al., *World Resources 1996–97* (New York: Oxford University Press, 1996); role of regulation from Hilary F. French, *Clearing the Air: A Global*

Agenda, Worldwatch Paper 94 (Washington, DC: Worldwatch Institute, January 1990); driving data and emissions standards from Stacy C. Davis and David N. McFarlin, *Transportation Energy Data Book: Edition 16* (Oak Ridge, TN: Oak Ridge National Laboratory, 1996); emissions data from U.S. Environmental Protection Agency, Office of Air Quality and Planning Standards, *National Air Pollutant Emission Estimates: 1900–1994* (Research Triangle Park, NC: 1995).

10. Keith Schneider, "Unbending Regulations Incite Move to Alter Pollution Laws," *New York Times,* 29 November 1993.

11. History from Andersen, op. cit. note 6; statistical analysis from Hans Th. A. Bressers and Jeannette Schuddeboom, "A Survey of Effluent Charges and Other Economic Instruments in Dutch Environmental Policy," in OECD, *Applying Economic Instruments to Environmental Policies in OECD and Dynamic Non-member Economies* (Paris: 1994); Figure 9–1 from Kees Baas, Central Bureau of Statistics, The Hague, e-mail to author, 24 September 1997.

12. Technology development from Jan Paul van Soest, Centre for Energy Conservation and Environmental Technology, Delft, Netherlands, letter to author, 11 October 1995.

13. Kenneth Boulding, *The Meaning of the Twentieth Century* (New York: Harper and Row, 1964), cited in Herman E. Daly, *Beyond Growth: The Economics of Sustainable Development* (Boston: Beacon Press, 1996); David O'Connor, "The Use of Economic Instruments in Environmental Management: The East Asian Experience," in OECD, op. cit. note 11.

14. U.S. General Accounting Office (GAO), *Air Pollution: Allowance Trading Offers an Opportunity to Reduce Emissions at Less Cost* (Washington, DC: 1994); trading activity from John J. Fialka, "Clear Skies are Goal as Pollution is Turned into a Commodity," *Wall Street Journal,* 31 October 1997.

15. Industry and government estimates from Martha Hamilton, "Selling Pollution Rights Cuts the Cost of Cleaner Air," 24 August 1994; environmentalist estimate from Jessica Mathews, "Environmental Success Story," *Washington Post,* 17 June 1996; current price from Executive Office of the President, *Economic Report of the President* (Washington, DC: U.S. Government Printing Office, 1998) (prices expressed per metric ton); quote from Hamilton, op. cit. this note; scrubber price and rail freight from Dallas Bertraw, "The SO_2 Emissions Trading Program: Cost Savings without Allowance Trades," *Contemporary Economic Policy,* April 1996; savings estimate from GAO, op. cit. note 14.

16. GAO, op. cit. note 14.

17. Peter T. Kilborn, "East's Coal Towns Wither in the Name of Cleaner Air," *New York Times*, 15 February 1996; Peter Galuszka, "Strip-Mining on Steroids," *Business Week*, 17 November; Penny Loeb, "Shear Madness," *U.S. News and World Report*, 11 August 1997.

18. Cartoon in James L. Johnston, "Pollution Trading in La La Land," *Regulation*, no. 3, 1994; Thomas Michael Power and Paul Rauber, "The Price of Everything," *Sierra*, November/December 1993. See also Michael J. Sandel, "It's Immoral to Buy the Right to Pollute," *New York Times*, 15 December 1997.

19. Christopher D. Stone, *Earth and Other Ethics: The Case for Moral Pluralism* (New York: Harper & Row, 1987); Peter Brimblecombe, *The Big Smoke: A History of Pollution in London since Medieval Times* (London: Methuen and Company, 1987); WRI et al., op. cit. note 9.

20. Mark Sagoff, *The Economy of the Earth: Philosophy, Law, and the Environment* (Cambridge, U.K.: University of Cambridge Press, 1988).

21. J. Andrew Hoerner, "Tax Tools for Protecting the Atmosphere: The U.S. Ozone-Depleting Chemicals Tax," in Robert Gale and Stephan Barg, eds., *Green Budget Reform: An International Casebook of Leading Practices* (London: Earthscan, 1995).

22. Relative merits from Thomas Sterner, *Environmental Tax Reform: The Swedish Experience* (Gothenburg, Sweden: Department of Economics, Gothenburg University, 1994); European Organization for Packaging and the Environment, *Economic Instruments in Environmental Policy* (Brussels: 1997).

23. History from Ernst Ulrich von Weizsäcker, *Earth Politics* (London: Zed Books, 1994); Agnar Sandmo, "Optimal Taxation in the Presence of Externalities," *Swedish Journal of Economics*, vol. 77, no. 1 (1975); Agnar Sandmo, Norwegian School of Economics and Business Administration, Bergen, Norway, discussion with author, 13 March 1998; for early discussion in German, see, for example, Hans Christophe Binswanger et al., *Arbeit ohne Umweltzerstörung* (Frankfurt: Fischer, 1983), cited in von Weizsäcker, op. cit. this note; Ernst U. von Weizsäcker and Jochen Jesinghaus, *Ecological Tax Reform: A Policy Proposal for Sustainable Development* (London: Zed Books, 1992).

24. Mikael Skou Andersen, Århus University, Department of Political Science, Århus, Denmark, discussion with author, 18 March 1998. Table 9–2 sources are as follows: Sweden description from P. Bohm, "Environment and Taxation: The Case of Sweden," in OECD, *Environment and Taxation: The Cases of the Netherlands, Sweden and the United States* (Paris: 1994); Sweden

quantity from Nordic Council of Ministers, *The Use of Economic Instruments in Nordic Environmental Policy* (Copenhagen: TemaNord, 1996); Denmark 1994 from Mikael Skou Andersen, "The Green Tax Reform in Denmark: Shifting the Focus of Tax Liability," *Journal of Environmental Liability*, vol. 2, no. 2 (1994); Spain description from Thomas Schröder, "Spain: Improve Competitiveness through an ETR," *Wuppertal Bulletin on Ecological Tax Reform* (Wuppertal, Germany: Wuppertal Institute for Climate, Environment, and Energy), summer 1995; Spain quantity from Juan-José Escobar, Ministry of Economy and Finance, Madrid, letter to author, 29 January 1997; Denmark 1996 from Ministry of Finance, *Energy Tax on Industry* (Copenhagen: 1995); Netherlands description from Ministry of Housing, Spatial Planning, and Environment, *The Netherlands' Regulatory Tax on Energy: Questions and Answers* (The Hague: 1996); Netherlands quantity from Koos van der Vaart, Ministry of Finance, The Hague, discussion with author, 18 December 1995; United Kingdom from "Landfill Tax Regime Takes Shape," *ENDS Report* (London: Environmental Data Services), November 1995; Finland from OECD, *Environmental Taxes and Green Tax Reform* (Paris: 1997); total tax revenues for all countries from OECD, op. cit. note 4.

25. Mark A. Delucchi, *The Annualized Social Cost of Motor-Vehicle Use in the U.S., 1990–1991: Summary of Theory, Data, Methods, and Results* (Davis, CA: University of California, Institute of Transportation Studies, 1997); price rise is a Worldwatch estimate based on a motor fuel usage rate of 150 billion gallons per year from U.S. Department of Transportation, Federal Highway Administration, *Highway Statistics 1996* (Washington, DC: 1997); European studies from European Environment Agency, *Environmental Taxes: Implementation and Environmental Effectiveness* (Copenhagen: 1996); comparisons to tax revenues based on OECD, op. cit. note 4. The U.S. payroll tax applies to roughly the first $65,000 in annual wages, so workers earning more would receive a smaller raise in percentage terms.

26. Australia from Department of the Environment, Sport and Territories, *Subsidies to the Use of Natural Resources* (Canberra: 1996); Japan from Jason C. Rylander, "Accounting for Nature: A Look at Attempts to Fashion a 'Green GDP'," *Renewable Resources Journal*, summer 1996; Vaclav Smil, "Environmental Change as a Source of Conflict and Economic Loss in China," in Project on Environmental Change and Acute Conflict, Occasional Paper Series, No. 2 (Washington, DC: American Academy of Arts and Sciences, 1992); Hans Diefenbacher, "The Index of Sustainable Economic Welfare: A Case Study of

the Federal Republic of Germany," in Clifford W. Cobb and John B. Cobb, Jr., *The Green National Product: A Proposed Index of Sustainable Economic Welfare* (Lanham, MD: University Press of America, 1994); Tim Jackson and Susanna Stymne, *Sustainable Economic Welfare in Sweden: A Pilot Index 1950–1992* (Stockholm: Stockholm Environment Institute, 1996), appendix; United States from Clifford Cobb, Ted Halstead, and Jonathan Rowe, *The Genuine Progress Indicator: Summary of Data and Methodology* (San Francisco, CA: Redefining Progress, 1995). In the studies on Germany, Sweden, and the United States, damage estimates for loss of wetlands, fertile soil, and old-growth forests, for ozone depletion, and for greenhouse gas buildup reflect current costs of past damage. The appropriate base for environmental taxes would be future costs of current damage, which are of at least comparable magnitude.

27. Current tax levels from OECD, op. cit. note 4.

28. William K. Stevens, "Meeting Reaches Accord to Reduce Greenhouse Gases," *New York Times,* 11 December 1997; U.N. Framework Convention on Climate Change (UNFCCC), "Kyoto Protocol to the United Nations Framework Convention on Climate Change," FCCC/CP/L.7/Add.1, 10 December 1997.

29. UNFCCC, op. cit. note 28.

30. Economic modeling results from John P. Weyant, Stanford University, Energy Modeling Forum, Stanford, CA, draft manuscript, June 1995, and from John P. Weyant, letter to author, 10 October 1995; carbon content of fuels from Gregg Marland, "Carbon Dioxide Emission Rates for Conventional and Synthetic Fuels," *Energy,* vol. 8, no. 12 (1983), and assumes a 90-percent efficiency in converting petroleum to gasoline; concentration stabilization based on T.M.L. Wigley, R. Richels, and J.A. Edmonds, "Economic and Environmental Choices in the Stabilization of Atmospheric CO_2 Concentrations," *Nature,* 18 January 1996.

31. Environmental revenue totals and shares in this and following paragraph are Worldwatch estimates, using European Union (EU) figures from European Commission (EC), Statistical Office of the European Communities (Eurostat), *Structures of the Taxation Systems in the European Union* (Luxembourg: Office for Official Publications of the European Communities, 1996), and non-EU figures from OECD, op. cit. note 4, and from OECD, *Environmental Taxes in OECD Countries* (Paris: 1995); evasion from Anton Steurer, EC, Eurostat, Luxembourg, discussion with author, 30 January 1997.

32. Figure of $7.5 trillion is a Worldwatch estimate, based on gross

domestic product (GDP) and tax revenue figures for western industrial countries from OECD, op. cit. note 4, on GDP figures for other countries from World Bank, *World Development Report 1996*, op. cit. note 4, and on central government tax revenue as a share of GDP for other countries from World Bank, *World Development Indicators*, op. cit. note 4.

33. Note that some of the subsidy cut would take the form of reduction in the effective taxes that arise from policies that raise food prices.

CHAPTER 10. Environmental Taxes: Practical Limits and Potential

1. J. Andrew Hoerner, "Harnessing the Tax Code for Environmental Protection: A Survey of State Initiatives," *State Tax Notes* (Tax Analysts, Arlington, VA) (forthcoming).

2. Swedish Environmental Protection Agency (SEPA), *Environmental Taxes in Sweden: Economic Instruments of Environmental Policy* (Stockholm: 1997); proposal for automobile emissions tax from Clifford Cobb et al., *Fiscal Policy for a Sustainable California* (draft) (San Francisco, CA: Redefining Progress, 1995).

3. SEPA, op. cit. note 2.

4. Gunnar S. Eskeland and Shantayanan Devarajan, *Taxing Bads by Taxing Goods: Pollution Control with Presumptive Charges*, Directions in Development Series (Washington, DC: World Bank, 1996).

5. Factors influencing driving from Marcia Lowe, *Shaping Cities: The Environmental and Human Dimensions*, Worldwatch Paper 105 (Washington, DC: Worldwatch Institute, October 1991). Figure 10–1 is based on T. Sterner, "The Price of Petroleum Products," in Thomas Sterner, ed., *Economic Policies for Sustainable Development* (Dordrecht, Netherlands: Kluwer Academic Publishers, 1994). Gasoline consumption figures from United Nations, *1994 Energy Statistics Yearbook* (New York: 1996). Prices are for premium unleaded (95 RON), converted to dollars based on purchasing-power parities, and are from Organisation for Economic Co-operation and Development (OECD), *Energy Prices and Taxes, Second Quarter 1997* (Paris: 1997); prices for Denmark, New Zealand, and Japan, where premium unleaded is not sold, are based on those for regular unleaded, however, and adjusted upward by 3¢ per liter—the average differential in OECD countries that sell both.

6. Alan H. Sanstad and Richard B. Howarth, "'Normal' Markets,

Market Imperfections, and Energy Efficiency," *Energy Policy*, October 1994; Steven Nadel and Miriam Pye, *Appliance and Equipment Efficiency Standards: Impacts by State* (Washington, DC: American Council for an Energy-Efficient Economy, 1996). Savings figures are net of the sometimes higher cost of more-efficient appliances.

7. Michael Renner, *Rethinking the Role of the Automobile*, Worldwatch Paper 84 (Washington, DC: Worldwatch Institute, June 1988).

8. Jodi L. Jacobson, *Gender Bias: Roadblock to Sustainable Development*, Worldwatch Paper 110 (Washington, DC: Worldwatch Institute, September 1992).

9. Table 10–1 is based on the following sources: Rory McLeod, *Market Access Issues for the New Zealand Seafood Trade* (Wellington: New Zealand Fishing Industry Board, 1996); Chile from Mateen Thobani, "Tradable Property Rights to Water," *FPD Note* (Washington, DC: World Bank, Vice Presidency for Finance and Private Sector Development), February 1995; Germany, Denmark, and Norway from European Environment Agency (EEA), *Environmental Taxes: Implementation and Environmental Effectiveness* (Copenhagen: 1996); Netherlands from Hans Th. A. Bressers and Jeannette Schuddeboom, "A Survey of Effluent Charges and Other Economic Instruments in Dutch Environmental Policy," in OECD, *Applying Economic Instruments to Environmental Policies in OECD and Dynamic Non-member Economies* (Paris: 1994), and from Kees Baas, Central Bureau of Statistics, The Hague, e-mail to author, 24 September 1997; Sweden from SEPA, op. cit. note 2; U.S. permit system from U.S. General Accounting Office, *Air Pollution: Allowance Trading Offers an Opportunity to Reduce Emissions at Less Cost* (Washington, DC: 1994); U.S. tax from J. Andrew Hoerner, "Tax Tools for Protecting the Atmosphere: The U.S. Ozone-Depleting Chemicals Tax," in Robert Gale and Stephan Barg, eds., *Green Budget Reform: An International Casebook of Leading Practices* (London: Earthscan, 1995); Singapore from David O'Connor, "The Use of Economic Instruments in Environmental Management: The East Asian Experience," in OECD, op. cit. this note; New Jersey from Dana Clark and David Downes, *What Price Biodiversity? Economic Incentives and Biodiversity Conservation in the United States* (Washington, DC: Center for International Environmental Law, 1995), and from John Ross, Pinelands Development Credit Bank, Trenton, discussion with author, 27 January 1998; J. Andrew Hoerner, "The Louisiana Environmental Tax Scorecard," in Gale and Barg, op. cit. this

note. For more complete surveys, see Gale and Barg, op. cit. this note; OECD, op. cit. this note; OECD, *Environmental Taxes in OECD Countries* (Paris: 1995); Janet E. Milne, *Environmental Taxes in New England: An Inventory of Environmental Tax and Fee Mechanisms Enacted by New England States and New York* (South Royalton, VT: Vermont Law School, Environmental Law Center, 1996); Victoria P. Summers, "Tax Treatment of Pollution Control in the European and Central Asian Economies in Transition and Other Selected Countries," in Charles E. Walker, Mark A. Bloomfield, and Margot Thorning, eds., *Strategies for Improving Environmental Quality and Increasing Economic Growth* (Washington, DC: Center for Policy Research, 1997); and Hoerner, op. cit. note 1.

10. Summers, op. cit. note 9; Michel Potier, "China Charges for Pollution," *The OECD Observer*, February/March 1995.

11. Summers, op. cit. note 9; Potier, op. cit. note 10.

12. Figure of 1 percent from Magda Lovei, *Financing Pollution Abatement: Theory and Practice*, Environment Department Paper No. 28 (Washington, DC: World Bank, 1995); China from "Government to Gradually Implement Program to Tax Polluters, Resource Users," *International Environment Reporter*, 15 October 1996, from "NEPA to Impose 'Pollution Tax' on Industry to Curb Dramatic Increase in SOx Emissions," *International Environment Reporter*, 6 March 1996, and from "Industry Facing New Tax to Fund Much-Needed Water Treatment Projects," *International Environment Reporter*, 15 May 1996.

13. Malaysia, Turkey, and Thailand from Earth Summit Watch, *Four in '94. Two Years After Rio: Assessing National Actions to Implement Agenda 21* (New York: Natural Resources Defense Council and Campaign for Action to Protect the Earth, 1994); David Tenenbaum, "The Greening of Costa Rica," *Technology Review*, October 1995; Philippines from World Bank, *Five Years after Rio: Innovations in Environmental Policy*, Environmentally Sustainable Development Studies and Monograph Series No. 18 (Washington, DC: 1997).

14. Rögnvaldur Hannesson, "The Political Economy of ITQs," prepared for Symposium on Fisheries Management, University of Washington, Seattle, 14–16 June 1994 (Bergen, Norway: Norwegian School of Economics and Business Administration, 1994); Larry D. Simpson, "Are Water Markets a Viable Option?" *Finance & Development*, June 1994.

15. OECD, *Environmental Taxes*, op. cit. note 9.

16. Australian and Danish ozone-depleter taxes and Danish sand and gravel tax from OECD, *Environmental Taxes*, op. cit. note 9;

revenue figure is for fiscal years, which begin one quarter before corresponding calendar years, and is from U.S. Office of Management and Budget, *Budget of the United States Government, Fiscal Year 1999*, Historical Tables (Washington, DC: U.S. Government Printing Office, 1998); environmental effects of U.S. tax from Hoerner, "Tax Tools for Protecting the Atmosphere," op. cit. note 9; Swedish tax from SEPA, op. cit. note 2.

17. Swedish tax from SEPA, op. cit. note 2; Danish waste charge from EEA, op. cit. note 9.

18. OECD, *Evaluating Economic Instruments for Environmental Protection* (Paris: 1997); California and Massachusetts from David P. Novello, "Capturing the Market's Power," *The Environmental Forum*, September/October 1994; use of fishing permit systems from Rögnvaldur Hannesson, Norwegian School of Economics and Business Administration, Bergen, Norway, discussion with author, 7 June 1995; Alicante from Arthur Maass and Raymond L. Anderson, *...and the Desert Shall Rejoice: Conflict, Growth, and Justice in Arid Environments* (Cambridge, MA: The MIT Press, 1978).

19. Sandra Postel, *Last Oasis*, rev. ed. (New York: W.W. Norton & Company, 1997); Clark and Downes, op. cit. note 9; Ross, op. cit. note 9.

20. Hoerner, "Louisiana Environmental Tax," op. cit. note 9.

21. Gregg Marland, "Carbon Dioxide Emission Rates for Conventional and Synthetic Fuels," *Energy*, vol. 8, no. 12 (1983).

22. Frank Muller, "Mitigating Climate Change: The Case for Energy Taxes," *Environment*, March 1996; Norway from EEA, op. cit. note 9; Sweden from SEPA, op. cit. note 2.

CHAPTER 11. Making Reform Fair

1. The author worked for the Institute for Human Development, a nonprofit organization based at the church, between September 1991 and August 1992. This account is based on transcripts of taped oral histories given in August 1992.

2. National Council of Senior Citizens (NCSC) and Villers Advocacy Associates (VAA), *Double Jeopardy: The Impact of Energy Taxes on Low-Income Households* (Washington, DC: 1988).

3. "Creating an Industrial Society..." image from Paul Hawken, speech given at First International Conference of CIB TG 16, Tampa, FL, 2 November 1993.

4. United States from James Poterba, "Tax Policy to Combat

Global Warming: On Designing a Carbon Tax," in Rudiger Dornbusch and James Poterba, eds., *Global Warming: Economic Policy Responses* (Cambridge, MA: The MIT Press, 1991); elderly from NCSC and VAA, op. cit. note 2; developing countries from Christine Kerr and Leslie Citroen, *Household Expenditures on Infrastructure Services*, background paper for *World Development Report 1994* (Washington, DC: World Bank, undated).

5. Stephen Tindale and Gerald Holtham, *Green Tax Reform: Pollution Payments and Labor Tax Cuts* (London: Institute for Public Policy Research, 1996).

6. Ibid.; Robert Greenstein and Frederick C. Hutchinson, *Offsetting the Effects of Regressive Tax Increases on Low- and Moderate-Income Households* (Washington, DC: Center on Budget and Policy Priorities, 1990); Southern Europe from Mark Pearson, "Equity Issues and Carbon Taxes," in Organisation for Economic Co-operation and Development (OECD), *Climate Change: Designing a Practical Tax System* (Paris: 1993).

7. Portugal from European Environment Agency, *Environmental Taxes: Implementation and Environmental Effectiveness* (Copenhagen: 1996); Netherlands from Ministry of Housing, Spatial Planning, and Environment (VROM), *The Netherlands' Regulatory Tax on Energy: Questions and Answers* (The Hague: 1996).

8. VROM, op. cit. note 7.

9. Keith Bradsher, "Gap in Wealth in U.S. Called Widest in West," *New York Times*, 17 April 1995; tax competition from Lorenz Jarass and Gustav M. Obermair, *More Jobs, Less Tax Evasion, Cleaner Environment: Options for Compensating Reductions in the Taxation of Labour—Taxation of Other Factors of Production*, commissioned by the European Commission (Wiesbaden, Germany: College of Wiesbaden, August 1997).

10. U.S. figure includes land indirectly owned through corporations and is from Clifford Cobb et al., "Fiscal Policy for a Sustainable California" (draft) (San Francisco, CA: Redefining Progress, 1995); Fábio L.S. Petrarolpha, "Brazil: The Meek Want the Earth Now," *Bulletin of the Atomic Scientists*, November/December 1996.

11. John Stuart Mill, *Principles of Political Economy*, 7th ed., in Jonathan Riley, ed., *Principles of Political Economy and Chapters on Socialism* (Oxford: Oxford University Press, 1994).

12. Ibid.

13. Cobb et al., op. cit. note 10.

14. Alanna Hartzok, "Pennsylvania's Success with Local Property

Tax Reform: The Split Tax Rate," *American Journal of Economics and Sociology*, April 1997.

15. Nikki Scarancke, Greenpeace, Auckland, and Maori former fisher, discussion with author, 8 October 1995.

16. Hal Bernton, "IFQ Reforms Create Fishing Elite," *Anchorage Daily News*, 6 May 1995; figure of $800 million from Paul Seaton, Alliance Against IFQs, testimony before U.S. Senate, Committee on Commerce, Science, and Transportation, Subcommittee on Oceans and Fisheries, Magnuson Act Field Hearing, Anchorage, AK, 25 March 1995; Neal D. Black, "Balancing the Advantages of Individual Transferable Quotas against Their Redistributive Effects: The Case of *Alliance Against IFQs v. Brown*," *Georgetown International Environmental Law Review*, spring 1997.

17. Black, op. cit. note 16; Seaton, op. cit. note 16; Timothy Egan, "Fringe Benefits from Oil Give Alaska a Big Payday," *New York Times*, 9 October 1996.

18. U.S. General Accounting Office, *Air Pollution: Allowance Trading Offers an Opportunity to Reduce Emissions at Less Cost* (Washington, DC: 1994); Matthew L. Wald, "Lilco's Emissions Sale Spurs Acid Rain Concerns," *New York Times*, 18 March 1993; Matthew L. Wald, "Suit Attacks Swap Plan on Pollution," *New York Times*, 14 March 1993; U.S. Environmental Agency (EPA), Acid Rain Program (ARP), "The Environmental Impacts of SO_2 Allowance Trading," <http://www.epa.gov/acidrain>, viewed 6 March 1998; dropping of suit from Dwight Alpern, EPA, ARP, Washington, DC, discussion with author, 6 March 1998.

19. U.N. Framework Convention on Climate Change, "Kyoto Protocol to the United Nations Framework Convention on Climate Change," FCCC/CP/L.7/Add.1, 10 December 1997.

20. William K. Stevens, "Meeting Reaches Accord to Reduce Greenhouse Gases," *New York Times*, 11 December 1997.

21. Figure of 20 percent is a Worldwatch estimate, based on Joel Darmstadter, Perry D. Teitelbaum, and Jaroslav G. Polach, *Energy in the World Economy: A Statistical Review of Trends in Output, Trade, and Consumption since 1925* (Baltimore, MD: Johns Hopkins University Press, for Resources For the Future, 1971), and on G. Marland, R. J. Andres, and T. A. Boden, *Global, Regional, and National CO_2 Emission Estimates from Fossil Fuel Burning, Cement Production, and Gas Flaring: 1950–1994*, electronic database, Oak Ridge National Laboratory, Oak Ridge, TN, revised February 1997, <http://cdiac.esd.ornl.gov>, viewed 3 March 1997; U.N. Development Programme, *Human Development Report 1994* (New York:

Oxford University Press, 1994).

22. Graciela Chichilnisky, Geoffrey Heal, and David Starrett, *International Markets with Emissions Rights: Equity and Efficiency*, Publication No. 81 (Stanford, CA: Stanford University, Center for Economic Policy Research, 1993).

23. Paul Craig Roberts, "Clinton's Energy Tax: Now That's a Scorched-Earth Policy," *Business Week*, 27 October 1997.

24. James Bennet, "Warm Globe, Hot Politics,"*New York Times*, 11 December 1997.

25. Robert Repetto, *Jobs, Competitiveness, and Environmental Regulation: What Are the Real Issues?* (Washington, DC: World Resources Institute, 1995).

26. Judith M. Dean, "Trade and the Environment: A Survey of the Literature," in Patrick Low, ed., *International Trade and the Environment*, World Bank Discussion Paper No. 159 (Washington, DC: 1992), quoted in OECD, *Implementation Strategies for Environmental Taxes* (Paris: 1996).

27. Frank Muller, "Mitigating Climate Change: The Case for Energy Taxes," *Environment*, March 1996; low energy taxes on industry from OECD, *Energy Prices and Taxes, Second Quarter 1997* (Paris: 1997), and from Ved P. Gandhi, Dale Gray, and Ronald McMorran, "A Comprehensive Approach to Domestic Resource Mobilization for Sustainable Development," in U.N. Department for Policy Coordination and Sustainable Development, *Finance for Sustainable Development: The Road Ahead*, Proceedings of the Fourth Group Meeting on Financial Issues of Agenda 21, Santiago, Chile, 1997 (New York: 1997).

28. Andrew Hoerner and Frank Muller, "The Impact of a Broad-based Energy Tax on the Competitiveness of U.S. Industry," *The Natural Resources Tax Review*, July/August 1993.

29. Paul Demaret and Raoul Stewardson, "Border Tax Adjustments under GATT and EC Law and General Implications for Environmental Taxes," *Journal of World Trade*, vol. 28, no. 4 (1994); Hilary Barnes, "Danish Emissions Tax Gets Go-ahead," *Financial Times*, 15–16 July 1995; Peter Behr, "Trade Panel Upholds U.S. Auto Fuel Law," *Washington Post*, 1 October 1994.

30. Conventional wisdom from Demaret and Stewardson, op. cit. note 29.

31. Barbara Bramble, "New Financial Mechanisms for Funding Sustainable Development," in Felix Dodds, ed., *The Way Forward: Beyond Agenda 21* (Washington, DC: Island Press, 1997).

CHAPTER 12. Tax Cuts

1. For the argument for a capital gains tax cut, see, for example, American Council for Capital Formation, *Update: Questions and Answers on Capital Gains*, Special Report (Washington, DC: September 1995).

2. Importance of human capital from World Bank, Environment Department, *Expanding the Measure of Wealth: Indicators of Environmentally Sustainable Development* (Washington, DC: 1997); possible effects of taxation from Christopher Farrell, "The Kindest Tax Cut: Social Security," *Business Week*, 16 June 1997.

3. Figure 12–1 is based on Kathryn Porter, *Poverty and Income Trends 1995* (Washington, DC: Center on Budget and Policy Priorities, 1997), and on European Commission (EC), Statistical Office of the European Communities (Eurostat), *European Economy* (Luxembourg: Office for Official Publications (OOP) of the European Communities), no. 64 (1997). European Union unemployment figures are for the 15 nations now members.

4. Apparent connection between European Union unemployment and U.S. wage declines from Rebecca M. Blank, "The Misdiagnosis of Eurosclerosis," *The American Prospect*, January–February 1997; European unemployment rates are from EC, op. cit. note 3, and number unemployed is from EC, Eurostat, "EU Unemployment Falls to 10.6% in November," press release (Luxembourg: January 1998).

5. Ray Marshall, "The Global Jobs Crisis," *Foreign Policy*, fall 1995.

6. "Why Wages Aren't Growing," interview with Gary Burtless, *Challenge*, November–December 1995; tax increases on lowest quintile from Organisation for Economic Co-operation and Development (OECD), *The OECD Jobs Study: Taxation, Employment and Unemployment* (Paris: 1995); 1970 figures from Lorenz Jarass and Gustav M. Obermair, "More Jobs, Less Pollution: Tax Incentives and Statutory Levies," *The Natural Resources Tax Review*, November 1994 (1970 Germany figure is for the former West Germany only); 1995 figures from Lorenz Jarass and Gustav M. Obermair, *More Jobs, Less Tax Evasion, Cleaner Environment: Options for Compensating Reductions in the Taxation of Labour—Taxation of Other Factors of Production*, commissioned by the European Commission (Wiesbaden, Germany: College of Wiesbaden, August 1997).

7. C.R. Bean, P.R.G. Layard, and S.J. Nickell, "The Rise in

Unemployment: A Multi-Country Study," *Economica* 53, S1–S22, cited in OECD, op. cit. note 6.

8. Effects of lowering wage tax and unemployment benefits of a progressive wage tax in Europe from OECD, op. cit. note 6.

9. Stephen Tindale and Gerald Holtham, *Green Tax Reform: Pollution Payments and Labor Tax Cuts* (London: Institute for Public Policy Research, 1996); figure of 6 percent based on OECD, *Revenue Statistics of OECD Member Countries 1965–1996* (Paris: 1997).

10. Table 12–1 from Tindale and Holtham, op. cit. note 9. Per-family costs in the table are converted to dollars based on purchasing power parity and use population projections from Charlie Hargreaves, Cambridge Econometrics, Cambridge, U.K., letter to author, 9 February 1998.

11. EC, *Growth, Competitiveness, Employment: The Challenges and Ways Forward into the 21st Century,* White Paper (Luxembourg: OOP, 1993); Jorgenson modeling reported in Bruce Schillo et al., "The Distributional Impacts of a Carbon Tax," draft report (Washington, DC: Environmental Protection Agency, Energy Policy Branch, August 1992). Figure of 1.5 million jobs is a Worldwatch estimate, based on unemployment rates and totals in EC, op. cit. note 4.

CHAPTER 13. An Eco-Industrial Revolution

1. Skeptics from Fred Pearce, "Greenhouse Wars," *New Scientist,* 19 July 1997; T.A. Boden, G. Marland, and R.J. Andres, *Estimates of Global, Regional and National Annual CO_2 Emissions from Fossil Fuel Burning, Hydraulic Cement Production, and Gas Flaring: 1950–92* (Oak Ridge, TN: Oak Ridge National Laboratory, Carbon Dioxide Information Analysis Center, 1995); emissions of more than 2 billion tons a year leading to atmospheric carbon dioxide concentrations above 400 parts per million from John T. Houghton et al., eds., *Stabilization of Atmospheric Greenhouse Gases: Physical, Biological and Socioeconomic Implications,* IPCC Technical Paper 3 (Geneva: Intergovernmental Panel on Climate Change, 1997).

2. Figure of 10 billion is the U.N. medium projection, from United Nations, *World Population Projections to 2150* (New York: 1998). Distance estimate based on U.S. Department of Energy, *Model Year 1998 Fuel Economy Guide* (Washington, DC: 1997), and on Gregg Marland, "Carbon Dioxide Emission Rates for Conventional and Synthetic Fuels," *Energy,* vol. 8, no. 12 (1983), and assumes 90-percent efficiency in converting petroleum to gasoline.

3. Worldwatch estimates, based on Boden, Marland, and Andres, op. cit. note 1, and on British Petroleum (BP), *BP Statistical Review of World Energy* (London: Group Media & Publications, 1997).

4. L.R. Oldeman et al., *World Map of the Status of Human-Induced Soil Degradation: An Explanatory Note*, 2nd ed. (Wageningen, Netherlands, and Nairobi: International Soil Reference and Information Centre and United Nations Environment Programme, 1991); Sandra L. Postel, Gretchen Daily, and Paul R. Ehrlich, "Human Appropriation of Renewable Fresh Water," *Science*, 9 February 1996; Alan Thein Durning, *Saving the Forests: What Will It Take?* Worldwatch Paper 117 (Washington, DC: December 1993); pollution from World Resources Institute (WRI) et al., *World Resources 1996–97* (New York: Oxford University Press, 1996).

5. Charles River Associates (CRA), *Economic Implications of the Adoption of Limits on Carbon Emissions from Industrialized Countries* (Washington, DC: 1997).

6. On the shortcomings of gross domestic product as an indicator of progress, see Herman E. Daly and John B. Cobb, Jr., *For the Common Good: Redirecting the Economy toward Community, the Environment, and a Sustainable Future* (Boston: Beacon Press, 1989).

7. Wolfgang Sachs, Reinhard Loske, and Manfred Linz, *Greening the North: A Post-Industrial Blueprint for Ecology and Equity* (London: Zed Books, 1998); Duncan McLaren, Simon Bullock, and Nusrat Yousuf, *Tomorrow's World: Britain's Share in a Sustainable Future* (London: Earthscan, 1998).

8. Sachs, Loske, and Linz, op. cit. note 7; McLaren, Bullock, and Yousuf, op. cit. note 7.

9. Robert Repetto et al., *Has Environmental Protection Really Reduced Productivity Growth?* (Washington, DC: WRI, 1996); Arthur Cecil Pigou, *The Economics of Welfare*, 4th ed. (London: Macmillan, 1932; first published 1920), cited in Mikael Skou Andersen, *Governance by Green Taxes: Making Pollution Prevention Pay* (Manchester, U.K.: Manchester University Press, 1994).

10. Employment figures are Worldwatch estimates, based on Organisation for Economic Co-operation and Development, *National Accounts 1983–1995*, Vol. II (Paris: 1997), and on International Labour Organization, *1996 Yearbook of Labour Statistics* (Geneva: 1996); commodities production from BP, op. cit. note 3, and from U.N. Food and Agriculture Organization, *FAOSTAT*, electronic database, Rome, <http://www.apps.fao.org>, viewed 15 February 1998.

11. Figure of $180 million and European Union from Gary Gardner, "Organic Farming Up Sharply," in Lester R. Brown, Christopher Flavin, and Hal Kane, *Vital Signs 1996* (New York: W.W. Norton & Company, 1996); figure of $3.5 billion from Carole Sugarman, "Organic? Industry Is Way Ahead of Government," *Washington Post*, 31 December 1997; on CFCs, see generally Elizabeth Cook, ed., *Ozone Protection in the United States: Elements of Success* (Washington, DC: WRI, 1996).

12. Christopher Flavin, "Wind Power Sets Records," in Lester R. Brown, Michael Renner, and Christopher Flavin, *Vital Signs 1998* (New York: W.W. Norton & Company, 1998); Marlise Simons, "In the New Europe, a Tilt to Using Wind's Power," *New York Times*, 7 December 1997; Molly O'Meara, "Solar Cell Shipments Hit New High," in Brown, Renner, and Flavin, op. cit. this note; comparison to aerospace industry from Stephen Tindale and Gerald Holtham, *Green Tax Reform: Pollution Payments and Labor Tax Cuts* (London: Institute for Public Policy Research, 1996); Table 13–1 is based on Environmental Business International, *The Global Environmental Market and United States Industry Competitiveness* (San Diego, CA: 1996).

13. U.S. preference for trading from "International Trading Should Allow Emission Trading between Companies, U.S. Says," *International Environment Reporter*, 21 January 1998; Robert Repetto and Duncan Austin, *The Costs of Climate Protection: A Guide for the Perplexed* (Washington, DC: WRI, 1997).

14. Hart Hodges, *Falling Prices: Cost of Complying with Environmental Regulations Almost Always Less than Advertised*, Briefing Paper (Washington, DC: Economic Policy Institute, 1997).

15. Elizabeth Cook, "Overview," in Cook, op. cit. note 11.

16. Pamela Wexler, "Saying Yes to 'No Clean'," in Cook, op. cit. note 11.

17. Michael E. Porter and Claas van der Linde, "Toward a New Conception of the Environment-Competitiveness Relationship," *Journal of Economic Perspectives*, fall 1995.

18. Paul A. David, "Clio and the Economics of QWERTY," *American Economic Review*, vol. 75, no. 2 (1985).

19. Herbert Simon, *The Sciences of the Artificial*, 3rd ed. (Cambridge, MA: The MIT Press, 1996); Stephen J. DeCanio, "Barriers within Firms to Energy-Efficient Investments," *Energy Policy*, September 1993; Alan H. Sanstad, "'Normal' Markets, Market Imperfections and Energy Efficiency," *Energy Policy*, October 1994; Wexler, op. cit. note 16.

20. W. Brian Arthur, *Increasing Returns and Path Dependence in the Economy* (Ann Arbor, MI: University of Michigan Press, 1994);

Kenneth Arrow, "The Economic Implications of Learning by Doing," *Review of Economic Studies*, June 1962; Ford from Joseph J. Romm, *Lean and Clean Management: How to Boost Profits and Productivity by Reducing Pollution* (New York: Kodansha International, 1994); Figure 13–1 from William J. Abernathy and Kenneth Wayne, "Limits of the Learning Curve," *Harvard Business Review*, September-October 1974.

21. Figure 13–2 and 30 percent based on price and cumulative sales data, from *PV News* (Photovoltaic Energy Systems, Warrenton, VA), various issues; solar savings is net present value of future savings, and is from Dennis Anderson and Robert Williams, *The Cost-Effectiveness of GEF Projects*, Working Paper no. 6 (Washington, DC: Global Environment Facility, 1993).

22. Michael Grubb, "Technologies, Energy Systems and the Timing of CO_2 Emissions Abatement," *Energy Policy*, February 1997.

23. Ibid.

24. Notebook computer from Steven Levy, *Insanely Great: The Life and Times of Macintosh, the Computer That Changed Everything* (New York: Penguin Books, 1994); quote from Alan Kay's office, Apple Computer, Los Angeles, CA, discussion with Harvey Sachs, Center for Global Change, College Park, MD, 6 July 1992.

CHAPTER 14. The Political Marketplace

1. Robin Broad, "The Political Economy of Natural Resources: Case Studies of the Indonesian and Philippine Forest Sectors," *Journal of Developing Areas*, April 1995; John McBeth and Jay Solomon, "First Friend," *Far Eastern Economic Review*, 20 February 1997; Sander Thoenes, "Indonesian Wood Cartel Resists IMF Reforms," *Financial Times*, 13 February 1998.

2. Daniel Stiles, "Power and Patronage in the Philippines," *Cultural Survival Quarterly*, summer 1991.

3. Indianist Missionary Council, "Another Scandal in the Extraction of Brazilian Mahogany," Brasilia, 5 August 1996, APC conference <rainfor.general>, posted 7 August 1996; David Robie, "Papua New Guinea: Government Gets Drilled by Australian Oil Man," *InterPress Service*, 24 May 1996; Greenpeace International, "Logging in Solomon Islands Takes Its Toll," Greenpeace Briefing, Rome, undated, APC conference <rainfor.general>, posted 12 December 1995; Marcus Colchester, "Asia Logs Suriname," *Multinational Monitor*,

November 1995.

4. Center for Responsive Politics (CRP), *The Big Picture: Where the Money Came from in the 1996 Elections* (Washington, DC: 1997); U.S. Office of Management and Budget, *Budget of the United States Government, Fiscal Year 1999* (Washington, DC: U.S. Government Printing Office, 1998); quote from CRP, "Back Talk, Vol. 3, No. 4," Washington, DC, APC conference <crp.pol.news>, posted 26 June 1996.

5. Value of oil and gas tax breaks is based on low estimate for oil tax breaks only, from Douglas Koplow and Aaron Martin, *Federal Subsidies to Oil in the United States* (Washington, DC: Greenpeace USA, forthcoming); contributions exclude "party" and "soft" money, and are from CRP, *The Big Picture*, op. cit. note 4, except for grazing contribution, which is from Douglas Weber, CRP, Washington, DC, e-mail to author, 17 December 1997; history of subsidizing legislation from Charles F. Wilkinson, *Crossing the Next Meridian: Land, Water, and the Future of the West* (Washington, DC: Island Press, 1992).

6. CRP, *The Big Picture*, op. cit. note 4.

7. Dawn Erlandson, "The Btu Tax Experience: What Happened and Why It Happened," *Pace Environmental Law Review*, fall 1994; Dawn Erlandson, Friends of the Earth, Washington, DC, discussion with author, 11 May 1995.

8. Senate preference from Ned Daly, "PAC Dollars and the Mining Reform Conferees," Taxpayer Assets Project, Washington, DC, APC conference <list.tap-resources>, posted 23 September 1994.

9. Mancur Olson, *The Logic of Collective Action: Public Goods and the Theory of Groups* (Cambridge, MA: Harvard University Press, 1971).

10. Organisation for Economic Co-operation and Development (OECD), International Energy Agency, *Energy Policies of IEA Countries* (Paris: various years); share of workforce based on OECD, *Coal Information* (Paris: 1997), and on OECD, *Employment Outlook—July 1996* (Paris: 1996); Judy Dempsey, "Decision Time Looms for German Energy," *Financial Times*, 9 February 1995; John H. Cushman, Jr., "Intense Lobbying against Global Warming Treaty," *New York Times*, 7 December 1997.

11. Philip R. Lane and Aaron Tornell, *Power Concentration and Growth*, Discussion Paper No. 1720 (Cambridge, MA: Harvard University, Harvard Institute of Economic Research, 1995); Paolo Mauro, "Corruption and Growth," *Quarterly Journal of Economics*, August 1995; Transparency International, Berlin, "1997 Corruption Perception Index," <http://www.

transparency.de>, viewed 16 February 1998; Aaron Sachs, "Dying for Oil," *World Watch*, May/June 1996.

12. Shang-Jin Wei, *How Taxing is Corruption on International Investors?* Working Paper 6030 (Cambridge, MA: National Bureau of Economic Research, 1997).

13. Thoenes, op. cit. note 1; Michael Duffy and Nancy Gibbs, "The Money Mess," *Time*, 11 November 1996.

14. David O'Connor, "The Use of Economic Instruments in Environmental Management: The East Asian Experience," in OECD, *Applying Economic Instruments to Environmental Policies in OECD and Dynamic Non-member Economies* (Paris: 1994).

15. Mikael Skou Andersen, *Governance by Green Taxes: Making Pollution Prevention Pay* (Manchester, U.K.: Manchester University Press, 1994).

16. Ibid.

17. Philippines from Anne Counsell, "Deregulation Hurts As It Kicks In," *Financial Times*, 18 September 1996; Thomas T. Vogel, Jr., "Venezuela to Drive Up Gasoline Prices," *Wall Street Journal*, 15 April 1996; Timothy Egan, "Fringe Benefits from Oil Give Alaska a Big Payday," *New York Times*, 9 October 1996; Andersen, op. cit. note 15.

18. Susan Rose-Ackerman, *Redesigning the State to Fight Corruption: Transparency, Competition, and Privatization*, Viewpoint Note No. 75 (Washington, DC: World Bank, 1996); Robin Broad, with John Cavanagh, *Plundering Paradise: The Struggle for the Environment in the Philippines* (Berkeley: University of California Press, 1993).

19. Rose-Ackerman, op. cit. note 18; Honduras from Ved P. Gandhi, Dale Gray, and Ronald McMorran, "A Comprehensive Approach to Domestic Resource Mobilization for Sustainable Development," in U.N. Department for Policy Coordination and Sustainable Development, *Finance for Sustainable Development: The Road Ahead*, Proceedings of the Fourth Group Meeting on Financial Issues of Agenda 21, Santiago, Chile, 1997 (New York: 1997).

20. "Who Will Listen to Mr Clean?" *Economist*, 2 August 1997; Johann Graf Lambsdorff, "An Empirical Investigation of Bribery in International Trade," *European Journal of Development Research*, June 1998.

21. OECD, "Convention on Combating Bribery of Foreign Officials in International Business Transactions," Paris, 1997.

22. F. Leslie Seidle, "Regulating Canadian Political Finance: Established Rules in a Dynamic Political System," prepared for the Round Table on Political Reform in the Mature Democracies, Tokyo, 25–27 August 1996; figure of $9 based on

$2.4 billion total spending figure from CRP, *The Big Picture*, op. cit. note 4.

23. Underfunding of environmental agencies in developing countries from Michel Potier, "China Charges for Pollution," *The OECD Observer*, February/March 1995, and from Sergio Margulis, "The Use of Economic Instruments in Environmental Policies: The Experiences of Brazil, Mexico, Chile and Argentina," in OECD, op. cit. note 14; Andersen, op. cit. note 15.

24. François Bregha and John Moffet, "The Tax for Fuel Conservation in Ontario," in Robert Gale and Stephan Barg, eds., *Green Budget Reform: An International Casebook of Leading Practices* (London: Earthscan, 1995).

25. On incremental taxes, see J. Andrew Hoerner and Frank Muller, "The Impact of a Broad-based Energy Tax on the Competitiveness of U.S. Industry," *The Natural Resources Tax Review*, July/August 1993; David Hawkins, Natural Resource Defense Council, Washington, DC, discussions with author, 23 January 1998. Quote condensed with permission from original interview.

26. Hawkins, op. cit. note 25.

27. Perry Plumart, National Audubon Society, Washington, DC, discussion with author, 12 February 1998. Quote condensed with permission from original interview.

28. European Commission, Statistical Office of the European Communities (Eurostat), *European Economy* (Luxembourg: Office for Official Publications of the European Communities), no. 64 (1997); OECD, *Revenue Statistics of OECD Member Countries 1965–1996* (Paris: 1997).

29. Kjell-Olof Fält, Chairman, Central Bank of Sweden, Stockholm, discussion with author, 27 February 1998; Svante Axelsson, Swedish Nature Protection Society, Stockholm, discussion with author, 29 January 1998; Swedish Environmental Protection Agency, *Environmental Taxes in Sweden: Economic Instruments of Environmental Policy* (Stockholm: 1997).

30. Stefan Bach, Michael Kohlhaas, and Barbara Praetorius, "Ecological Tax Reform Even If Germany Has to Go It Alone," *Economic Bulletin* (Berlin: German Institute for Economic Research (DIW)), July 1994.

31. Table 14–1 contains Worldwatch estimates, based on Statistisches Bundesamt, *Volkswirtschaftliche Gesamtrechnungen* (Stuttgart: Metzler-Poeschel, 1990), on Michael Kohlhaas, DIW, Berlin, letter to author, 20 June 1995, and on Hans Wessels, DIW, Berlin, letter to author, 10 August 1995.

32. Kristina Steenbock, consultant to Greenpeace Germany, New

York, discussion with author, 16 June 1995; "Group Gets Support for CO$_2$ Tax from 16 German Producers, Service Industries," *International Environment Reporter*, 21 September 1994; "Big 3 Carmakers Back Higher Gasoline Taxes," *Journal of Commerce*, 21 December 1992.

33. Steenbock, op. cit. note 32; "Eco-tax Possibility Dwindling in Face of Industry Opposition, Unemployment," *International Environment Reporter*, 1 May 1996; Kohl from Kai Schlegelmilch, Wuppertal Institute for Climate, Environment, and Energy, Wuppertal, Germany, discussion with author, 10 February 1997.

34. European information from European Environment Agency, *Environmental Taxes: Implementation and Environmental Effectiveness* (Copenhagen: 1996); U.S. polling result is based on a sample of 1,000 adults taken in January 1993 by Greenberg-Lake/The Analysis Group, Washington, DC, and The Tarrance Group, Alexandria, VA, cited in Kate Stewart, Belden & Russonello, Washington, DC, letter to author, 10 March 1997.

35. Lack of staffers from Dawn Erlandson, Center for a Sustainable Economy, Washington, DC, discussion with author, 4 March 1998.

36. Thomas Sterner, *Environmental Tax Reform: The Swedish Experience* (Gothenburg, Sweden: Department of Economics, Gothenburg University, 1994); Axelsson, op. cit. note 29; Plumart, op. cit. note 27.

37. Angus Maddison, *The World Economy in the Twentieth Century* (Paris: OECD, 1989).

38. Quote from Geoff Mulgan and Robin Murray, *Reconnecting Taxation* (London: Demos, 1993).

Index

ABOUT THE AUTHOR

DAVID MALIN ROODMAN is a Senior Researcher at the Worldwatch Institute, where he investigates and writes about the economics and political economy of environmental problems. He has also studied energy policy and the human and ecological impacts of buildings. He contributes regularly to the Institute's two annuals, *State of the World* and *Vital Signs*, and to its magazine, *World Watch*. He has written three Worldwatch papers. Mr. Roodman graduated from Harvard College in 1990 with a Bachelor's degree in theoretical mathematics. He then spent a year at the University of Cambridge, U.K., where his interests shifted to the relationships between economy and environment. During academic year 1998–99, he is taking temporary leave from the Worldwatch Institute in order to spend time on a Fulbright Scholarship in Viet Nam, where he will study firsthand the connections between economic change and environmental stresses in a developing country.